Econometric Society Monographs in Pure Theory

Game theoretic analysis of
voting in committees

T0339883

Econometric Society Publication No. 7

Books in both the Econometric Society Monographs in Pure Theory
and the Econometric Society Monographs in Quantitative Economics
are numbered in a single sequence for the purposes of the
Econometric Society. A listing of books in the Econometric Society
Monographs in Pure Theory is given on the following page.

Econometric Society Monographs in Pure Theory

Edited by
Frank Hahn, *Cambridge University*
Editorial adviser: Hugo Sonnenschein, *Princeton University*

The Econometric Society is an international society for the
advancement of economic theory in relation to statistics and
mathematics. The Econometric Society Monograph Series in Pure
Theory is designed to promote the publication of original research
contributions of high quality in mathematical economics.

Other titles in the series

Gerard Debreu *Mathematical economics: twenty papers of Gerard
Debreu*
J.-M. Grandmont *Money and value: a reconsideration of classical
and neoclassical monetary economics*
Franklin M. Fisher *Disequilibrium foundations of equilibrium
economics*

Game theoretic analysis of voting in committees

BEZALEL PELEG
The Hebrew University of Jerusalem

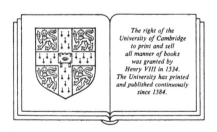

The right of the
University of Cambridge
to print and sell
all manner of books
was granted by
Henry VIII in 1534.
The University has printed
and published continuously
since 1584.

CAMBRIDGE UNIVERSITY PRESS

Cambridge
London   New York   New Rochelle
Melbourne   Sydney

CAMBRIDGE UNIVERSITY PRESS
Cambridge, New York, Melbourne, Madrid, Cape Town, Singapore, São Paulo

Cambridge University Press
The Edinburgh Building, Cambridge CB2 8RU, UK

Published in the United States of America by Cambridge University Press, New York

www.cambridge.org
Information on this title: www.cambridge.org/9780521259644

First published 1984
This digitally printed version 2008

A catalogue record for this publication is available from the British Library

Library of Congress Cataloguing in Publication data
Peleg, Bezalel.
Game theoretic analysis of voting in committees.
(Econometric Society monographs in pure theory;
no. 7)
Includes index.
1. Social choice – Mathematical models.   2. Voting –
Mathematical models.   3. Committees – Mathematical models.
4. Game theory.   I. Title.   II. Series.
HB846.8.P44   1984   302.3′4   83–20854

ISBN 978-0-521-25964-4 hardback
ISBN 978-0-521-07465-0 paperback

To Zmira, Gad, Avner, and Orith

Contents

Preface

The main part of this book (namely, Chapters 3-6) consists of a systematic investigation of strategic voting in committees. We start in Section 3.1 with an analysis of the power distribution among coalitions of voters, induced by a given voting rule. We proceed in Sections 3.2 and 3.3 to study representations of committees. Roughly, a voting rule is a representation of a given committee if it induces the same power distribution as that prescribed by the committee itself. We are interested primarily in "nice" representations, that is, representations that are Paretian, monotonic, and symmetry-preserving (or "faithful"). The existence of neutral representations is also investigated; dynamic representations are considered in Section 4.4. In Section 4.1 we discuss the manipulability of representations. We note that, by the Gibbard–Satterthwaite Theorem, practically all "interesting" representations are manipulable. Then we introduce the class of strong representations, namely, those representations that are not distorted by manipulation of preferences by *coalitions*. Section 4.2 contains an existence theorem for strong representations of committees with vetoers. Chapter 5 is devoted to a detailed investigation of strong representations of symmetric committees. Section 4.3 contains a game theoretic interpretation of Arrow's condition of independence of irrelevant alternatives, which is closely related to our study of strong representations. The investigation of strong representations relies on a study of effectivity functions. Chapter 6 is therefore devoted to exploring effectivity functions and their cores. As a by-product, we obtain also some new results on implementation of social choice correspondences (see Sections 6.4 and 6.5).

As for the remaining chapters, Chapter 2 contains proofs of some well-known basic results, Chapter 7 contains some remarks on the relationship between our study and previous work on voting rules, and Chapter 1 provides an almost self-contained verbal presentation of our theory.

It is the author's hope that this book may serve as a solid foundation for the theory of representations of committees. However, it should be emphasized that many important problems remain unresolved. In particular, the problem of determining all the strong representations of a given committee in the general case is still open.

I am grateful to B. Dutta and P. K. Pattanaik for their very helpful remarks on an early version of my first paper on consistent voting (Peleg [1978*a*]). Further helpful remarks on that paper were received from D. Schmeidler, A. K. Sen, and M. Sengupta. Also, the writing of this book has benefited from my collaboration with H. Moulin. Indeed, Sections 6.2–6.5 are based almost entirely on our joint paper (Moulin and Peleg [1982]).

I am greatly indebted to three of my students: I. Oren, I. Polishchuk, and R. Holzman. The works of Oren [1981] and Polishchuk [1978] are presented in full detail in Chapter 5. In that chapter we also quote some of the recent results of Holzman [1982]. R. Holzman has also read the entire manuscript and suggested many improvements.

I am grateful to R. J. Aumann, M. Maschler, and S. Zamir for many helpful discussions, and I am also indebted to A. Mann, M. Perles, and E. Rips for their helpful remarks. The support, criticism, and advice of M. Yaari throughout the writing merit special thanks.

The editors of this series, F. Hahn and H. Sonnenschein, have been most supportive. The constant encouragement and advice of H. Sonnenschein have been very helpful, and it was F. Hahn who suggested the writing of the introductory section, "Background and Motivation," which greatly improves the entire presentation.

Finally, I am very grateful to Mrs. Yolanda Benusiglio for her very devoted and highly skillful typing of the manuscript.

It is also a pleasure to acknowledge the support of The Institute for Advanced Studies of the Hebrew University, which offered me its hospitality during the academic years 1979–80 and 1982–83, and that of The Center for Research in Mathematical Economics and Game Theory, which made the typing and distribution of the first version of the typescript possible.

B. Peleg

February 1984

Background and motivation

The theory of voting in committees began with the basic contributions of Borda [1781] and Condorcet [1785]. Borda had been concerned about the inadequacy of choice by plurality voting, and he suggested a different method of assigning marks to alternatives, a method now known as Borda's rule (see Black [1958], pp. 156-9). It is interesting that Borda's method is still a subject of active research (see, e.g., Young [1974] and Gardner [1977]). Indeed, Borda's rule also serves as an important example in this book (see Example 3.1.18).

Condorcet developed an extensive formal theory of voting (see Black [1958], pp. 159-80). One of his profound discoveries was the "paradox of voting," which is known also as Condorcet's paradox. His most important contribution was the formulation of the *Condorcet condition* (i.e., the alternative that receives a majority, against each of the other alternatives, should be chosen). This condition plays an important role in so many works in modern social choice theory that it is impossible to give a full record of its use. We, also, apply the Condorcet condition to the theory of committees (see, e.g., Theorem 3.2.5).

Nanson [1882] examined several systems of voting and suggested a modification of Borda's rule that is compatible with the Condorcet condition. (Borda's rule itself does not satisfy the Condorcet condition.) Further details on Nanson's work may be found in Black [1958].

Dodgson, in his three pamphlets, also examined several methods of voting and investigated the occurrence and possible ways of resolution of cyclical majorities (see Black [1958], pp. 189-238). Of particular interest to us is his remark that, according to the known voting procedures, the choice of an alternative, or the election of a candidate, is actually a *game of skill* (see Black [1958], pp. 232-3). It is interesting that Dodgson's observation was made approximately 70 years before the appearance of the book *Theory of Games and Economic Behavior* by von Neumann and Morgenstern. However, the fact that elections may involve strategic behavior had already been known to Borda (see Black [1958], p. 182).

Arrow, in the introduction to his treatise on social choice, reconfirmed Dodgson's observation that, usually, voting situations are games in the sense of von Neumann and Morgenstern (Arrow [1963], p. 7). Arrow, however, decided to ignore the game aspects of the problem of social choice. But, quite surprisingly, it has turned out that Arrow's Impossibility Theorem is a very powerful tool in the analysis of strategic voting. This is apparent from the work of Gibbard [1973], Satterthwaite [1975], Schmeidler and Sonnenschein [1978], and others. Indeed, we also make strong use of Arrow's Impossibility Theorem (see the proof of Theorem 2.4.11). For a very illuminating discussion of the relationship between Arrow's Impossibility Theorem and manipulation of voting schemes, the reader is referred to Blin and Satterthwaite [1978].

The comprehensive essay by Black on the theory of committees (Black [1958]) does not include an investigation of strategic voting. The first study that considered voting situations as games (in normal form) was that of Farquharson [1969]. Farquharson's book contains a fairly extensive game theoretic analysis of voting procedures. His discussions of straightforward strategies and sophisticated voting have strongly influenced the works of many writers (see, e.g., Gibbard [1973] and Moulin [1979]). It is also interesting that Farquharson has given a complete, self-contained generalization of cooperative game theory to games with ordinal utilities (Farquharson [1969], pp. 73-5). His model, with various modifications, is used in this book.

One of the outstanding applications of game theory to the theory of social choice is the Gibbard–Satterthwaite Manipulability Theorem. We shall now formulate this theorem. Consider a group $N = \{1, \ldots, n\}$ of voters and a set $A = \{a_1, \ldots, a_m\}$ of alternatives. A (linear) order on A is, simply, a permutation of A. A profile is an n-tuple of linear orders, $R^N = (R^1, \ldots, R^n)$, where R^i is the preference relation of voter i on A (for $i = 1, \ldots, n$). A social choice function (SCF) is a function that maps profiles into alternatives. An SCF F is manipulable if for some profile of (true) preferences there is a voter who can improve the outcome for himself by reporting a false preference order. Formally, F is manipulable if there exist profiles R^N and R_*^N and voter i such that

(a) if $x = F(R^N)$ and $y = F(R_*^N)$, then $x \neq y$ and yR^ix; and
(b) $R^j = R_*^j$ for all $j \neq i$.

Arrow [1963], Vickrey [1960], and Dummett and Farquharson [1961] all conjectured that manipulability is a universal property of SCFs. The works of Gibbard [1973], Pattanaik [1973], Satterthwaite [1975], and others have essentially confirmed this conjecture. More precisely, the following theorem is true. Let F be an SCF, and let $R(F)$ be the range of F. A voter $d \in N$ is a dictator for F, if for every profile R^N, $F(R^N)$ is the best alternative in $R(F)$ according to R^d. F is dictatorial if there exists a dictator (for F). The Gibbard–Satterthwaite Theorem is as follows.

Theorem. *If F is a nondictatorial SCF and $R(F)$ contains at least three alternatives, then F is manipulable.*

(We should mention at this point that Gibbard [1973] actually derives the foregoing theorem from a more general result on game forms.)

The Gibbard–Satterthwaite Theorem may be viewed as a starting point of our investigation. We are interested in the analysis and construction of SCFs for nondictatorial committees. By the preceding, such SCFs are necessarily manipulable. Thus, we mostly study manipulable voting schemes, and one of our main problems is how to minimize the effect of possible manipulation. We shall now describe our study.

A committee is a set $N = \{1, \ldots, n\}$, $n \geq 2$, of voters, together with a set W of winning coalitions of voters. A coalition S is winning (i.e., $S \in W$) if S fully controls the decisions of (the committee) $G = (N, W)$. For example, the Knesset (the Israeli parliament) is a committee. It has 120 members, and every set of 61 members or more is a winning coalition. Also, under party discipline (i.e., when all the members of the same party should vote in the same way), the current Knesset is a weighted majority committee of 10 parties.

Let $G = (N, W)$ be a committee, and let $A = \{a_1, \ldots, a_m\}$, $m \geq 2$, be a set of alternatives. We are interested in the construction of voting procedures (i.e., SCFs) that enable the members of G to choose one alternative out of A. Let F be an SCF that maps profiles of preferences (of the members of N) into alternatives. The following conditions are (intuitively) necessary in order to render F acceptable:

(1) The distribution of power (among voters) induced by F should be equal to the distribution of power specified by W.

(2) F should satisfy some well-known conditions like Pareto optimality, monotonicity, and neutrality. (The reader who would like to refresh his memory may look at Section 2.3.)

(3) F should not be distorted by manipulation of preferences by the members of N.

Consideration of (1) leads to the following problem. Let N be a set of voters, let A be a (finite) set of alternatives, and let F be an SCF. Then we ask: What is the distribution of power induced by F among the (coalitions of) members of N?

In order to resolve this problem, we associate with every SCF three simple games (i.e., committees). These simple games are derived from three different notions of effectiveness (in game theory; see Aumann [1961] and Aumann and Peleg [1960]), and they specify the winning (or "decisive") coalitions with respect to F. We remark that these games appear also in the work of Hurwicz and Schmeidler [1978] and Peleg [1980]. (It is interesting that the idea of associating a simple game with a social *welfare* function (SWF) is inherent in Arrow's original proof; see, e.g., Luce and Raiffa [1957]. Wilson [1972], Bloomfield [1971], and others also investigated simple games that correspond to SWFs.)

We can now describe our solution of (1). Let $G = (N, W)$ be a committee, and let A be a set of alternatives. An SCF F is a *representation* of G if the first simple game that corresponds to F equals G. F is a *tight representation* (of G) if (a) the three simple games of F coincide and (b) F is a representation of G. From a game theoretic point of view, tight representations are very desirable, because they lead to voting games for which all the effectivity concepts coincide. Chapters 3–5 of this book are devoted to an investigation of the existence of tight representations of committees, which meet also the requirements specified by (2) and (3).

Let, again, $G = (N, W)$ be a committee, and let A be a set of alternatives. An SCF F is a *faithful* representation of G if (a) F is a representation of G and (b) F and G have the same symmetry group (i.e., F and G are invariant under exactly the same permutations of the players). All our constructions of representations of committees yield faithful representations.

Let N be a set of voters, let A be a set of alternatives, and let F be an SCF. The three simple games that are associated with F give record only of the winning (or "decisive") coalitions of voters with respect to F (and the three different notions of effectiveness). Now, a winning coalition is a coalition that is effective for *every* subset of the set of alternatives. Thus, a coalition that is *not* winning may still be effective for *some* subsets of A. Hence, a complete list of an effectiveness relation, which we call an *effectivity function* (EF), conveys more information than the corresponding simple game. Moreover, EFs have proved to be very powerful tools in the analysis of voting schemes (see Moulin and Peleg [1982]). Sections 4.1, 5.1, and 5.2 and Chapter 6 of this book contain an extensive investigation of EFs.

We now turn to examine (2). In view of our solution of (1), we have to reformulate the *conjunction* of (2) and (1) as follows:

(2*)   Let $G = (N, W)$ be a committee, and let A be a (finite) set of alternatives. Is it possible to construct a tight and faithful representation of G that is also Paretian, monotonic, and neutral?

In Chapter 3 we prove the existence of tight, faithful, Paretian, and monotonic representations of committees. However, a committee may have no faithful, Paretian, and neutral representation. Essentially, the two kinds of symmetry that we deal with – faithfulness and neutrality – may be incompatible. (Moulin [1980] has investigated a similar phenomenon.) We also remark that all our constructions (of representations) satisfy the Condorcet condition. Moreover, they are intimately related to the core of a voting game (see, e.g., Nakamura [1975]).

Let $N = \{1, \ldots, n\}$ be a set of voters, let A be a set of alternatives, and let F be an SCF. When the members of N choose a member of A according to the rule F, they actually play the following n-person game (in normal form). Let L be the set of all (linear) orders on A. Then L is the set of *strategies* for every $i \in N$ (i.e., each voter may, legally, declare every member of L). The *outcome function* is, clearly, F. Finally, each voter $i \in N$ values the outcome according to his *true* preference order R^i. We shall denote the foregoing game by $g(F, R^N)$. Also, for a coalition S, we denote by L^S the set of all profiles of preferences of the members of S. Q^N is a *strong equilibrium point* (e.p.) of $g(F, R^N)$ if no coalition can profit by deviation from Q^N (formally, for every coalition S and for every $P^S \in L^S$ there exists a voter $i \in S$ such that $F(Q^N) R^i F(Q^{N-S}, P^S)$).

We consider now the following situation:

(4) $g(F, R^N)$ has at least one strong e.p.
(5) For every strong e.p. Q^N of $g(F, R^N)$, $F(Q^N) \neq F(R^N)$.

Assume further that coordination of strategies by coalitions is unrestricted (as is usually the case in voting in committees). Then, (normative) game theory recommends the selection of a strong e.p. [see (4)]. Hence, by (5), it precludes the choice of $F(R^N)$. Thus, in the foregoing situation, the result of voting will be distorted (as a consequence of strategic considerations).

Complete elimination of distortion would be obtained by the following requirement:

(6) For every strong e.p. Q^N of $g(F, R^N)$, $F(Q^N) = F(R^N)$.

However, if we insist that (6) hold for *every* profile R^N, then F must be dictatorial (provided that $R(F)$ contains at least three alternatives; see, e.g., Sengupta [1982]). Hence, we should be content with partial elimination of distortion. Thus, we are led to the following definition.

Definition. An SCF is *exactly and strongly consistent* if for every profile R^N there exists a strong e.p. Q^N of $g(F, R^N)$ such that $F(Q^N) = F(R^N)$.

Let F be an exactly and strongly consistent SCF, and let R^N be a profile of true preferences. Then the game $g(F, R^N)$ has a strong e.p. Q^N

such that $F(Q^N) = F(R^N)$. Hence, the outcome of the voting game $g(F, R^N)$ is *not necessarily* distorted.

We remark that an exactly and strongly consistent SCF F is *strongly tight*, i.e., the three *effectivity functions* of F coincide. Hence, F is tight.

Let $G = (N, W)$ be a committee, and let A be a (finite) set of alternatives. An SCF F is a *strong* representation (SR) of G if (a) F is exactly and strongly consistent and (b) F is a representation of G. We remark that an SR is Paretian (provided that G is non-null, i.e., $N \in W$).

In view of the foregoing discussion, we have to reformulate the *conjunction* of (2*) and (3) as follows:

(3*)   Let $G = (N, W)$ be a committee, and let A be a (finite) set of alternatives. Is it possible to find a faithful and monotonic SR of G?

A complete solution of (3*) would consist of a solution to our problem of construction of voting procedures for committees. In this book we shall prove the following:

(7)   If G is *weak* (i.e., G has a vetoer), then G has a (faithful and monotonic) SR for every finite A (with at least two alternatives).

(8)   If G is *symmetric* (i.e., G is a special majority (n, k) game, with special majority $n/2 < k < n$), then G has a (faithful and monotonic) SR for a set A of m alternatives, $m \geq 2$, if

$$m \leq [(n+1)/(n-k+1)] \tag{I}$$

Holzman [1982] has shown that (I) is a sharp bound.

The results on SRs for general committees are, presently, far from being complete (see, however, Addendum, p. 162).

We conclude with the following remarks. First, we emphasize that the theory of committees is just one facet of the general theory of social choice. Thus, our results apply only to the (limited) model of voting in committees in this study, *not* to social choice in general. For a very illuminating discussion of classification of the various aggregation problems of social choice theory, the reader is referred to Sen [1977]. Two recent comprehensive surveys of social choice theory are those of Plott [1976] and Sen [1982].

Second, our theory may also be considered as part of the general "theory of incentives" (see Laffont and Maskin [1981]). However, this inclusion is rather formal (and not substantial). The theory of incentive schemes is concerned primarily with solution concepts that fit into very restrictive assumptions on the information available to the players (ibidem, Section 1.2), whereas we allow unrestricted *coordination* of strategies, which is possible only if the members of each coalition (of voters) may communicate (and thereby get partial information on one another's preferences) (see also Moulin [1982b] for a discussion of the problem of information in the theory of committees).

Finally, we comment on the relationship between game theory in general and our study. A game theoretic analysis of a real-life phenomenon usually consists of two steps: (i) a choice of a (mathematical) model that represents the real-life situation and (ii) application of various solution concepts to the model. Now, voting schemes are usually given by precise arithmetical rules. Hence, in the (descriptive) theory of voting, step (i) is straightforward. Also, in step (ii) we encounter a pleasant surprise: Most voting games possess Nash e.p.'s in *pure* strategies. Hence, we need not consider mixed strategies, and, furthermore, we may investigate the existence of special kinds of Nash e.p.'s (e.g., perfect or strong e.p.'s). However, the analysis of existing voting systems occupies only a small part of our study. Most of our work is devoted to the construction of *new* voting schemes that have certain desirable properties. In particular, we have shown the existence of voting systems that have strong e.p.'s (in pure strategies), and for which all the (game theoretic) notions of effectiveness coincide. Consequently, the game theoretic analysis of our new constructions is free of some of the common weaknesses of the general approach of game theory. Thus, this new application of (normative) game theory (i.e., the devising of (voting) games) looks, indeed, promising. We add that the foregoing remarks hold also for the solution of the more general problem of implementation by strong e.p.'s of social choice correspondences (see Maskin [1979] and Moulin and Peleg [1982]).

CHAPTER 1

Introduction and summary of the main results

This chapter is mainly devoted to a survey of Chapters 2–6. Section 1.1 consists of an almost self-contained presentation of our theory. In particular, it contains a detailed formulation of the central problems that we try to solve in this book and the definitions of the main solution concepts. The reader will get a fairly good picture of the qualitative side of our theory by reading the survey. We conclude in Section 1.2 with brief remarks on possible uses of our results.

1.1   Survey

This section presents a summary of the most important results of our study. The main problems that we try to solve and the key solution concepts are presented independent of the following chapters. This should enable the reader to get a fairly good idea of the nature of this book. However, it should be mentioned that only the most important theorems are mentioned in this chapter. Moreover, in order to keep this section as readable as possible, we refrain from discussing proofs. Thus, in order to become familiar with our techniques, one has to look at the proofs of the main theorems. Finally, it should be remembered that we have written the survey as an almost self-contained description of our theory. Hence, for the sake of clarity and briefness, the order in which the various topics are discussed in the book has been slightly changed; however, this has not diminished the usefulness of the survey.

1.1.1   *Committees*

A *simple game* is a pair (N, W), where $N = \{1, \ldots, n\}$ is a set of *players* (or *voters*) and W is the set of *winning coalitions* (a coalition is a non-empty subset of N). We always assume

8

$[S \in W$ and $T \supset S] \Rightarrow T \in W$ (*monotonicity*)

Throughout this monograph, by a "committee" we mean a simple game. We remark that "committee" may have (somewhat) different meanings in other essays on simple games (see, e.g., Shapley [1967]).

Let $G = (N, W)$ be a committee. G is *proper* if

$$S \in W \Rightarrow N - S \notin W$$

We shall mostly deal with proper committees. We observe that every parliament is a (proper) committee; every town council is a committee; the UN Security Council is a committee, and so forth.

1.1.2 Choice problems

Let $G = (N, W)$ be a committee. A *choice problem* is, simply, a finite set A of m alternatives, $m \geq 2$. In order to resolve a choice problem A, the members of N have to choose one alternative out of A. Usually, one may observe several stages in the process of selection of an element of A. First, the committee members have to learn to know the various alternatives. At the end of the first stage the players are (tentatively) partitioned according to their rankings of the alternatives. Then each group of the preceding partition is given time to explain and defend its position. Also, each voter may persuade other voters to adopt his point of view. A third stage may be devoted to coalition formation and coordination of strategies. However, the final stage (at least in our model) is always devoted to actual voting; that is, each voter writes down his ranking on, say, a piece of paper, and an alternative is chosen by means of a *social choice function* (SCF) that maps profiles of preferences into alternatives.

Our investigation focuses on the final stage: We seek to find and characterize those SCFs that satisfy certain desirable criteria. However, we allow coordination of strategies, as is explained later.

1.1.3 Cores of committees

Let $G = (N, W)$ be a committee, and let A be a finite set of m alternatives, $m \geq 2$. We denote by L the set of all *linear orderings* of A (a linear ordering is a complete, transitive, and antisymmetric binary relation on A). If S is a coalition, then L^S is the set of all profiles of preferences of the members of S. Let $R^N \in L^N$, and let $x, y \in A$, $x \neq y$; x *dominates* y (with respect to R^N), written $x \, \mathrm{Dom}(R^N) \, y$, if $\{i \mid xR^iy\} \in W$. The *core* is the set of undominated alternatives in A and is denoted by $C(N, W, A, R^N) = C(R^N)$. If $a \in C(R^N)$, then a is "coalitionally stable"; that is, no winning coalition can improve upon a. Thus, for example, if the status quo s is an alternative (i.e., $s \in A$), and $s \in C(R^N)$, then s will prevail as long as R^N is the profile of (true) preferences of the voters. $\text{Dom}(R^N)$ may be cyclic, and, consequently, $C(R^N)$ may be empty. Indeed, consider the following example.

Example 1.1.1. Let $N = \{1, 2, 3\}$, and let $W = \{S \mid S \subset N$ and $|S| \geqslant 2\}$ (if B is a finite set, then $|B|$ denotes the number of members of B). Then (N, W) is the simple majority three-person game. Let $A = \{a, b, c\}$, and let $R^N \in L^N$ be given by

R^1	R^2	R^3
a	c	b
b	a	c
c	b	a

Then $a \, \text{Dom}(R^N) b$, $b \, \text{Dom}(R^N) c$, and $c \, \text{Dom}(R^N) a$. Thus, $C(R^N) = \varnothing$. (The reader may notice that Example 1.1.1 is the familiar "paradox of voting.")

In Section 2.6 we investigate cores of committees. First we observe that if a committee (N, W) has a *vetoer*, then $C(N, W, A, R^N) \neq \varnothing$ for every (finite) A and every $R^N \in L^N$ ($= L^N(A)$) (v is a vetoer in (N, W) if $v \in S$ for all $S \in W$). Then we find a necessary and sufficient condition for the nonemptiness of all cores of a committee without vetoers (see Theorem 2.6.14). Furthermore, in Section 7.1, we observe that under the usual restrictions on preferences (e.g., value restriction), cores of committees are always nonempty.

1.1.4   *Strategic aspects of a voting situation*

Let N be a set of voters (or players), let A be a set of alternatives, let $F: L^N \to A$ be an SCF, and let $R^N \in L^N$ be the profile of true preferences of the voters. When the voters choose one alternative out of A according to the rule F, they actually play the following n-person game in normal form. Each $i \in N$ chooses a member $P^i \in L$ (i.e., every $R \in L$ is a *legal* strategy for all $i \in N$). Then the outcome is determined by F (i.e., it is $F(P^N)$). Finally, R^i is the preference relation of player $i \in N$ on the outcome space A. The foregoing game will be called *the game associated with F and R^N*, and it will be denoted by $g(F, R^N)$.

The following remarks apply to the game $g(F, R^N)$.

Remark 1.1.2. There are no (exogenous) restrictions on communication between the members of N. Hence, *coordination of strategies is possible*.

Remark 1.1.3. The members of N are free to choose between open voting and voting by secret ballot. (In both cases, all the voters vote simultaneously.) Also, certain coalitions may have the prerogative of enforcing a secret ballot.

Remark 1.1.4. Binding agreements between the players (i.e., agreements whose violation entails high monetary penalties) are excluded. Notice that (a) if the outcome of $g(F, R^N)$ is determined by secret ballot, then binding agreements are impossible, and (b) binding agreements are, usually, not permitted in (political) voting games.

1.1.5 *Strategic effects*

Let N be a set of voters (or players), let A be a set of alternatives, and let $F: L^N \to A$ be an SCF. We denote by M the set of all coalitions that may coordinate strategies (see Remark 1.1.2). Clearly, $M \supset M_1$, where $M_1 = \{\{i\} \mid i \in N\}$. Let $R^N \in L^N$. $Q^N \in L^N$ is an *M-equilibrium point* (*M*-e.p.) of the game $g(F, R^N)$ if for every $S \in M$ and for every $P^S \in L^S$ there exists a voter $i \in S$ such that $F(Q^N) R^i F(Q^{N-S}, P^S)$.

Remark 1.1.5. An M_1-e.p. is a *Nash* e.p. A 2^N-e.p. is a *strong* e.p. Also, if $M^* \supset M$, then every M^*-e.p. is an M-e.p.

Let e.p.(M, F, R^N) be the set of all M-e.p.'s of $g(F, R^N)$. F is *manipulable at* R^N if $R^N \notin$ e.p.(M, F, R^N). Thus, if F is manipulable at R^N, then (normative) game theory precludes sincere voting (we recall that every $P \in L$ is a *legal* strategy for every $i \in N$). Manipulability will be considered as *a strategic effect of the first kind*. By the Gibbard–Satterthwaite Theorem, if F is nonmanipulable and $|R(F)| \geqslant 3$ (where $R(F)$ is the range of F), then F is dictatorial (see Theorem 2.5.5). Thus, manipulability is unavoidable when we seek SCFs for nondictatorial committees (see also Lemma 4.1.1).

We now proceed to analyze another, worse, aspect of strategic voting. Let, again, $R^N \in L^N$. F is *distorted at* R^N if there exists no $Q^N \in$ e.p.(M, F, R^N) such that $F(Q^N) = F(R^N)$. Thus, if F is distorted at R^N, then, according to (normative) game theory, $F(R^N)$ will *not* be the outcome of $g(F, R^N)$. Clearly, if F is distorted, then F is manipulable.

Remark 1.1.6. Let $R^N \in L^N$. F is *totally inconsistent* at R^N if e.p.$(M, F, R^N) = \varnothing$. Clearly, if F is totally inconsistent, then F is distorted. As our subsequent theory resolves the problem of distortion, it also, a fortiori, resolves the inconsistency problem. Thus, there is no need for further discussion of totally inconsistent SCFs.

Distortion is considered as *a strategic effect of the second kind*. Clearly, distortion is a very undesirable property. Indeed, if an SCF is distorted, then it does not consist of a reliable predictor of the voting procedure that it represents. Moreover, if we want to adopt a distorted SCF F as, say, part of a constitution, then we should be able to tell what will be the (distorted) outcome according to F in every possible situation. This last requirement is, in many cases, an impossible task. Thus, we conclude that the investigation of undistorted SCFs is very important from the theoretical as well as the practical point of view.

Let, again, N be a set of voters, let A be a set of alternatives, and let $F: L^N \to A$ be an SCF. Denote, again, by M the set of all coalitions that may coordinate strategies. Then F is *exactly M-consistent* if for every $R^N \in L^N$ there exists $Q^N \in \text{e.p.}(M, F, R^N)$ such that $F(Q^N) = F(R^N)$. Thus, F is exactly M-consistent if it is not (necessarily) distorted by manipulation. We say that F is *exactly and strongly consistent* if it is 2^N-consistent. Clearly, an exactly and strongly consistent SCF is exactly M-consistent for every $M \subset 2^N$. Sections 4.1–4.3 and Chapter 5 are devoted to an investigation of exactly and strongly consistent SCFs.

The following remark is in order.

Remark 1.1.7. Let N be a set of voters, let A be a set of alternatives, let $M \subset 2^N$, $M \supset M_1$, and let $F: L^N \to A$ be exactly M-consistent. Then there may exist $Q^N, R^N \in L^N$ such that $Q^N \in \text{e.p.}(M, F, R^N)$ and, still, $F(Q^N) \neq F(R^N)$. Thus, exact M-consistency may not be a sufficient condition for complete elimination of distortion. Unfortunately, complete elimination of distortion is impossible. Indeed, call an exactly M-consistent SCF $F_*: L^N \to A$ *undistorted* if for every $R^N \in L^N$ and every $Q^N \in \text{e.p.}(M, F_*, R^N)$, $F_*(R^N) = F_*(Q^N)$. By Corollary 6.5.3, if F_* is undistorted and $|R(F_*)| \geqslant 3$, then F_* is dictatorial (see also Definition 5.1.8).

1.1.6   *Power distributions induced by voting procedures*

Let N be a set of voters (or players), and let A be a set of alternatives. A *social choice correspondence* (SCC) is a function $H: L^N \to 2^A$. (We remark that, in our notation, $\varnothing \notin 2^A$.) SCCs are very helpful in the study of SCFs. Also, almost all practical voting systems are given as SCCs (because tie-breaking rules usually are disregarded or not specified). Moreover, an SCF is, simply, a single-valued SCC. Thus, the study of SCCs has immediate corollaries for SCFs.

Let $H: L^N \to 2^A$ be an SCC. We associate with H three measures of power distribution in the following way. Let $S \in 2^N$, $S \neq \varnothing$, and let $B \in 2^A$. S is *winning for B* if

$[R^N \in L^N$ and xR^iy for all $x \in B$, $y \notin B$, and $i \in S] \Rightarrow H(R^N) \subset B$

The *first effectivity function* (associated with H) is the function $E^* = E^*(H): 2^N \rightarrow P(2^A)$ defined by

$$E^*(S) = \{B \mid B \in 2^A \text{ and } S \text{ is winning for } B\}$$

for every $S \in 2^N$, $S \neq \varnothing$ (here, $P(2^A)$ is the set of all *nonempty* subsets of 2^A). It is convenient to define $E^*(\varnothing) = \varnothing$. Also, we observe that $A \in E^*(S)$ for every $S \in 2^N$, $S \neq \varnothing$. E^* is the first measure of the power distribution induced by H. We now proceed to define the second and third effectivity functions.

Let $S \in 2^N$, $S \neq \varnothing$, and let $B \in 2^A$. S is α-*effective for B* if there exists $R^S \in L^S$ such that for all $Q^{N-S} \in L^{N-S}$, $H(R^S, Q^{N-S}) \subset B$. The α-*effectivity function* (associated with H), $E_\alpha = E_\alpha(H): 2^N \rightarrow P(2^A)$, is defined by

$$E_\alpha(S) = \{B \mid B \in 2^A \text{ and } S \text{ is } \alpha\text{-effective for } B\}$$

for every $S \in 2^N$, $S \neq \varnothing$. Again, we define $E_\alpha(\varnothing) = \varnothing$. Also, $A \in E_\alpha(S)$ for every $S \in 2^N$, $S \neq \varnothing$. Let, again, $S \in 2^N$, $S \neq \varnothing$, and let $B \in 2^A$. S is β-*effective for B* if for every $Q^{N-S} \in L^{N-S}$ there exists $R^S \in L^S$ such that $H(R^S, Q^{N-S}) \subset B$. The β-*effectivity function* (associated with H), $E_\beta = E_\beta(H): 2^N \rightarrow P(2^A)$, is defined by

$$E_\beta(S) = \{B \mid B \in 2^A \text{ and } S \text{ is } \beta\text{-effective for } B\}$$

for every $S \in 2^N$, $S \neq \varnothing$. Again, we define $E_\beta(\varnothing) = \varnothing$ and observe that $A \in E_\beta(S)$ for every $S \in 2^N$, $S \neq \varnothing$.

Let $H: L^N \rightarrow 2^A$ be an SCC. Clearly, $E^*(S) \subset E_\alpha(S) \subset E_\beta(S)$ for every $S \in 2^N$. We say that H is *strongly tight* if $E^* = E_\beta$. A function $E: 2^N \rightarrow P(2^A)$ is a *well-behaved function* (w.b.f.) if (a) $E(\varnothing) = \varnothing$, (b) $\varnothing \notin E(S)$ for every $S \in 2^N$, and (c) $A \in E(S)$ for every $S \in 2^N$, $S \neq \varnothing$. If H is an SCC, then $E^*(H)$, $E_\alpha(H)$, and $E_\beta(H)$ are w.b.f.'s. Let $E: 2^N \rightarrow P(2^A)$ be a w.b.f., let $R^N \in L^N$, let $B \in 2^A$, and let $x \in A - B$. B *dominates x* if there exists a coalition $S \in 2^N$ such that (a) $B \in E(S)$ and (b) bR^ix for all $b \in B$ and all $i \in S$. The *core* $C(E, R^N)$ is the set of all undominated alternatives. An SCC $H: L^N \rightarrow 2^A$ is *stable* if $H(R^N) \subset C(E^*, R^N)$ for every $R^N \in L^N$. In Sections 4.1, 5.1, 5.2, and 6.1 we investigate the three functions $E^*(\cdot)$, $E_\alpha(\cdot)$, and $E_\beta(\cdot)$. We are particularly interested in the tightness and stability of SCCs.

Let $H: L^N \rightarrow 2^A$ be an SCC. We associate with H three simple games, $G^* = (N, W^*)$, $G_\alpha = (N, W_\alpha)$, and $G_\beta = (N, W_\beta)$, in the following way:

$$W^* = \{S \mid S \in 2^N \text{ and } \{x\} \in E^*(S) \text{ for every } x \in A\}$$

$$W_\alpha = \{S \mid S \in 2^N \text{ and } E_\alpha(S) = 2^A\}$$

and

$$W_\beta = \{ S \mid S \in 2^N \text{ and } E_\beta(S) = 2^A \}$$

The three games characterize, in three possible (different) ways, the "fully decisive" coalitions with respect to H. In Section 3.1 we investigate the simple games associated with an SCC. In particular, we compute the games that correspond to Borda's rule.

1.1.7   Classical properties of SCCs

We are interested in the following well-known properties of SCCs: Pareto optimality (see Definition 2.3.4), anonymity (see Definition 2.3.6), neutrality (see Definition 2.3.8), and monotonicity. We investigate (mainly) two kinds of monotonicity (see Definitions 2.3.11 and 2.3.15; see also Definition 3.2.17). In particular, we prove that (a) strong monotonicity is equivalent to strong positive association (SPA) (see Lemma 2.3.25), (b) if F is a strongly monotonic SCF and $|R(F)| \geqslant 3$, then F is dictatorial (see Theorem 2.4.11), and (c) a strongly monotonic SCC is stable (see Lemma 6.5.6).

1.1.8   Representations of committees

Let $G = (N, W)$ be a (proper) committee, and let A be a set of m alternatives, $m \geqslant 2$. An SCC $H: L^N \to 2^A$ is a *representation* of G (of order m) if $G^*(H) = G$. Intuitively, a representation of G is a feasible choice procedure (for the choice problem A) that reflects "faithfully" the distribution of power in G. An SCC $H: L^N \to 2^A$ is a *core extension* if $H(R^N) = C(N, W, A, R^N)$ whenever $C(N, W, A, R^N) \neq \varnothing$. Every core extension is a representation of G (see Remark 3.2.6). A representation H of G is *faithful* if it has the same symmetry group as G (see Definition 3.2.7). We point out the existence of Paretian, faithful, neutral, and monotonic core extensions (see Example 3.2.20). Also, we show that G has a strongly monotonic representation if and only if $C(N, W, A, R^N) \neq \varnothing$ for every $R^N \in L^N$ (see Theorem 3.2.13). A representation of G is "nice" if it has as many classical properties as possible. Nice representations of G *by SCFs* are obtained as selections from nice representations by SCCs (see Lemma 3.3.9). However, if $m \geqslant 3$, then G may have no Paretian, faithful, and neutral representations (of order m) by SCFs (see Remark 3.3.14). Some results on the existence of Paretian, faithful, and neutral SCFs that represent a given committee are contained in Section 3.3 (see Theorems 3.3.19 and 3.3.35 and Corollary 3.3.30; see also Section 7.3).

1.1.9 *Strong representations of committees*

Let $G = (N, W)$ be a (proper) committee, and let A be a set of m alternatives, $m \geqslant 2$. An SCF $F: L^N \to A$ is a *strong representation* (SR) *of G of order m* if (a) F is a representation of G and (b) F is exactly and strongly consistent. Thus, an SR of G is a choice procedure that (a) reflects correctly the distribution of power in G and (b) is not distorted by manipulation of preferences by coalitions. We observe that every proper simple game has a monotonic and faithful SR of order 2 (see Lemma 4.1.32). Also, every SR of G is strongly tight and stable (see Lemma 4.1.25 and Corollary 4.1.29). Hence, if G has an SR, then the core $C(N, W, A, R^N) \neq \emptyset$ for every $R^N \in L^N$ (see Corollary 4.1.26). This leads to the following result. We say that G is *strong* if $S \notin W$ implies that $N - S \in W$. Now, if G is strong (and nondictatorial), then G has no SRs of order greater than 2 (see Theorem 4.1.35). We proceed now to describe the main results on the existence of SRs.

First, let $G = (N, W)$ contain at least one vetoer. Then G has a faithful and monotonic SR of every order $m \geqslant 2$ (see Theorem 4.2.1). Next, let G be a *symmetric* simple game. Then G can be completely specified by a pair (n, k) of natural numbers, where n is the number of players and k is the size of a minimal winning coalition. In what follows, we assume that $n/2 < k < n$. Let $F: L^N \to A$ be a faithful SR of G. Then, clearly, F is anonymous. For $x \in A$, let $\beta(F; x)$ be the size of a minimal blocking coalition for x (see Definition 5.2.8). Since F is a representation of G, we must have

$$\min\{\beta(F; x) \mid x \in A\} = b$$

where $b = n - k + 1$ is the size of a minimal blocking coalition (in G). Also, from Holzman [1982],

$$\sum_{x \in A} \beta(F; x) = n + 1$$

A w.b.f. $E: 2^N \to P(2^A)$ is an *effectivity function* (EF) if every $B \in 2^A$ is a member of $E(N)$. We define an EF E_* by the following rule:

$$B \in E_*(S) \Leftrightarrow |S| \geqslant \sum_{x \in A - B} \beta(F; x)$$

Then, by Lemma 5.3.3, $E^*(F) = E_*$. Because F is stable, F is a selection from the core $C(E_*, \cdot)$.

Conversely, let $\beta_*: A \to \{1, \dots, n\}$ satisfy $\sum_{x \in A} \beta_*(x) = n + 1$ and $\min_{x \in A} \beta_*(x) = b$, and let E_* be the EF that is defined by

$$B \in E_*(S) \Leftrightarrow |S| \geqslant \sum_{x \in A - B} \beta_*(x)$$

Then, by Theorem 5.3.7, every anonymous selection from $C(E_*, \cdot)$ is a (faithful) SR of (n, k). Furthermore, $C(E_*, R^N) \neq \emptyset$ for every $R^N \in L^N$. Also, since every nonempty core correspondence is (strongly) monotonic, $C(E_*, \cdot)$ admits monotonic selections (see Corollary 5.3.13).

1.1.10 *Dynamic representations*

Let $G = (N, W)$ be a proper simple game without vetoers. If $m \geqslant \nu(G)$ (see (2.6.7)), then G has no SR of order m (see Theorem 4.1.34). Hence, the following problem arises naturally: Is it possible to find *dynamic* representations (i.e., representations by means of dynamic voting procedures) of G of orders $m \geqslant \nu(G)$? In particular, in view of Theorem 4.1.35 we are interested in binary procedures. In Section 4.3 we provide the following negative answer to the foregoing problem. Let A be a finite set of m alternatives, $m \geqslant 3$, and let $G = (N, W)$ be a (proper) committee. A *voting procedure* (VP) is a function $K : 2^A \times L^N \to A$ that satisfies $K(B, R^N) \in B$ for all $B \in 2^A$ and $R^N \in L^N$. K is *binary* if there exists a *social welfare function* (SWF) $\varphi : L^N \to L$ such that for every $B \in 2^A$ and every $R^N \in L^N$

$$K(B, R^N) \varphi(R^N) x \quad \text{for all } x \in B$$

(see Remark 4.3.5). If K is binary, then K is *dictatorial* if φ is dictatorial (in the sense of Arrow). K is *exactly and strongly consistent in the limited sense* if for each $B \in 2^A$ such that $|B| = 2$, the SCF $K(B, \cdot)$ is exactly and strongly consistent. K is a *dynamic representation of G in the limited sense* if for every $B \in 2^A$ such that $|B| = 2$, $K(B, \cdot)$ is a representation of G in an appropriate sense (see Definitions 4.3.15 and 4.3.16). The existence of strong and dynamic binary representations (in the limited sense) would consist of a complete solution to the representation problem. Unfortunately, by Corollary 4.3.17, if G is essential (i.e., $N \in W$, and G is nondictatorial), then G has no strong and dynamic representation (in the limited sense) by means of a binary VP (recall that we are assuming that $|A| \geqslant 3$).

Section 4.3 contains also a game theoretic analysis of Arrow's Impossibility Theorem. In particular, we determine the game theoretic equivalent of Arrow's Independence of Irrelevant Alternatives (see Theorem 4.3.13).

Finally, we remark that Section 4.4 contains an axiomatic characterization of the core of a simple game. Roughly, the core of a simple game G is the unique dynamic representation of G that satisfies (a) *binariness* and (b) neutrality, independence of irrelevant alternatives, and monotonicity (NIM). (The reader is referred to Theorem 4.4.14 for details.)

1.1.11 *Implementation of SCCs*

In all our constructions of representations of committees we have assumed that the set of available strategies (for every voter) is the set of (linear) preferences. Some authors (e.g., Dasgupta, Hammond, and Maskin [1979]) take the point of view that the sets of available strategies may be arbitrary. Clearly, it is easier to prove the existence of "desirable" voting procedures with unrestricted sets of strategies than with restricted sets of strategies. However, there is a price to pay for the preceding generalization. First, since the notion of "sincere outcome" no longer exists, one has to specify, *in advance,* the set of "desirable outcomes" by means of an SCC. Second, the very fact that strategy sets are not a priori restricted has led to constructions of (generalized) voting procedures that have no "intrinsic consistency" or elegance. We shall now review briefly the construction of "generalized" voting schemes.

Let A be a (finite) set of m alternatives, $m \geq 2$, and let $N = \{1, \ldots, n\}$ be a set of n voters. A *game form* (GF) is an $(n+1)$-tuple $\Gamma = (\Sigma^1, \ldots, \Sigma^n; \pi)$, where Σ^i is a nonempty set (of *strategies*) for $i = 1, \ldots, n$, and π is a function from $\Sigma^N = \times_{i \in N} \Sigma^i$ to A (the *outcome function*). Intuitively, Γ is a "generalized voting scheme" that enables the members of N to choose one alternative out of A. Let $\Gamma = (\Sigma^1, \ldots, \Sigma^n; \pi)$ be a GF, and let $R^N \in L^N$; $x^N \in \Sigma^N$ is a *strong* e.p. if for every $S \in 2^N$ and for every $y^S \in \Sigma^S$ (where $\Sigma^S = \times_{i \in S} \Sigma^i$) there exists $i \in S$ such that $\pi(x^N) R^i \pi(x^{N-S}, y^S)$. We denote by s.e.p.$(\Gamma, R^N)$ the set of all strong e.p.'s of the pair (Γ, R^N). Now let $H: L^N \to 2^A$ be an SCC. Intuitively, for each $R^N \in L^N$, $H(R^N)$ is the set of "desirable" states (for the society N), or the set of "welfare optima" (see, again, Dasgupta, Hammond, and Maskin [1979]). H is (*partially*) *implemented* by Γ if for every $R^N \in L^N$

$$H(R^N) = \pi(\text{s.e.p.}(\Gamma, R^N)) \qquad (H(R^N) \subset \pi(\text{s.e.p.}(\Gamma, R^N)))$$

(see Section 5.1 for a more general approach).

Remark 1.1.8. Let $H: L^N \to 2^A$ be an SCC, and let $\Gamma = (\Sigma^1, \ldots, \Sigma^n; \pi)$ be a GF. Assume that the choice from A is performed by a play of Γ and that coordination of strategies is unrestricted. Then H is partially implementable if and only if for every $R^N \in L^N$ every member of $H(R^N)$ is a strong equilibrium outcome (of the pair (Γ, R^N)). Thus, a *necessary* condition for H to be "acceptable" is that it be partially implementable by Γ. Indeed, one may insist, in addition, that Γ itself has to be "acceptable" in the first place (i.e., Γ has to be a "reasonable" (generalized) voting scheme).

The relationship between exact and strong consistency and partial implementability is clarified by the following remark.

Remark 1.1.9. Let $F: L^N \to A$ be an SCF. Then F is exactly and strongly consistent if and only if the GF $(L, \dots, L; F)$ partially implements F (i.e., F partially implements itself, or F is partially *self-implementable*).

We show that a partially implementable SCC is strongly tight (see Corollary 5.1.15). Furthermore, we supply the following characterization of partial implementation: Let H be a (Paretian) SCC, and let $E = E^*(H)$. Then *H is partially implementable if and only if E is maximal and H is stable* (see Theorem 6.4.4). Section 6.5 contains some remarks on the more difficult problem of full implementation.

1.2   Possible uses of the theory

In this section we discuss very briefly possible applications of our theory in the analysis of power distributions induced by existing choice rules, in constructing voting procedures for committees, and in the design of committees.

Analysis of power distributions induced by social choice rules

Let A be a finite set of m alternatives, $m \geqslant 2$, and let N be a society. A social choice rule for the pair (A, N) is simply an SCC $H: L^N \to 2^A$. Using the three effectivity functions associated with an SCC H, we can determine in a precise and detailed manner the power distribution induced by H. (Sometimes the three simple games associated with H are sufficient for that purpose.) This may help in comparing voting rules in current use. For example, the α-effectivity function of Borda's rule is different from the α-effectivity function of choice by plurality voting (see Section 3.1). Thus, we know precisely how the power distribution changes when we replace one procedure by the other. It would be very interesting to compute the simple games (or the effectivity functions) associated with other SCCs in current use.

Voting procedures and design of committees

It is quite obvious that our results provide "nice" and "stable" voting procedures for weak and symmetric committees. For example, by Theorem 4.2.1, for every (finite) set A of alternatives, the UN Security Council has a faithful, monotonic, and exactly and strongly consistent procedure for choosing one alternative out of A. We shall now point out that our results may also be used in the design of ad hoc committees. In order to be both concrete and brief we shall consider only the following two examples.

Example 1.2.1. A department of economics contains n^* professors. There is one vacant position in the department, and there are m applicants. The head of the department has to appoint a committee that will choose one candidate. What is an "optimal" committee for that task? In order to try to solve this problem, we shall list several desirable properties of a possible committee.

   (a)   Symmetry: The committee should be an (n, k) game (see Definition 2.6.4).
   (b)   No vetoer condition: $k < n$.
   (c)   Consistency: The committee has a (monotonic and faithful) strong representation of order m (see Definition 4.1.31).

By Theorem 5.6.7 there exists an (n, k) game that satisfies (b) and (c) if $(n+1)/(n-k+1) \geqslant m$. Thus, for example, if $n^* = 11$ and $m = 4$, then $(7, 6)$, $(8, 7)$, $(9, 8)$, $(10, 9)$, $(11, 9)$, and $(11, 10)$ are possible committees. We may add a fourth condition:

   (d)   Efficiency: n is the smallest integer that satisfies (a), (b), and (c).

The unique solution to (a)-(d) is, by Theorem 5.6.7 and Holzman [1982], $n_0 = 2m - 1$. Thus, the inequality $n^* \geqslant 2m - 1$ is a necessary and sufficient condition for the existence of a committee with the foregoing properties.

Example 1.2.2. A family consists of three members: 1, the mother; 2, the father; 3, a child. The family has to rent one of three available apartments. Our problem is, What are the power distributions among the members of the family that allow for consistent choice? Clearly, we want all the members of the family to take part in the decision. Now, there are exactly four 3-person simple games (*without* dummies) that have strong representations of order 3. These are (a) $[3; 2, 1, 1]$, (b) $[3; 1, 2, 1]$, (c) $[3; 1, 1, 2]$, and (d) $[3; 1, 1, 1]$ (see Definition 3.3.25). Clearly, (a) is the "matriarchal" solution, (b) is the "patriarchal" solution, (c) is the "spoiled child" domination, and (d) is the symmetric solution (notice, however, that games (a)-(c) are also *nondictatorial*).

Remark 1.2.3. The reader may notice that by excluding the committee $[2; 1, 1, 1]$ we have avoided the "voting paradox" in Example 1.2.2.

CHAPTER 2

Preliminary concepts and basic results

In this chapter we introduce three families of choice rules that play important roles in social choice theory, namely, social welfare functions, social choice correspondences, and social choice functions, and we investigate their basic properties, such as Pareto optimality, anonymity, neutrality, and monotonicity. The study of social welfare functions culminates in Section 2.2 with Arrow's Impossibility Theorem. The study of social choice correspondences and functions focuses on monotonicity properties and leads to the conclusion that every strongly monotonic social choice function whose range contains at least three alternatives is dictatorial (see Theorem 2.4.11). The Gibbard–Satterthwaite Theorem is shown, in Section 2.5, to be a corollary of the preceding theorem. Simple games and their basic properties are defined in Section 2.6. We conclude with a proof of Nakamura's theorem on cores of simple games (see Theorem 2.6.14).

2.1 Binary relations

We shall be interested in the following properties of binary relations. Let A be a set, and let R be a binary relation on A.

Definition 2.1.1. R is *complete* if for all $x, y \in A$, xRy or yRx. R is *transitive* if for all $x, y, z \in A$, if xRy and yRz, then xRz. R is *antisymmetric* if for all $x, y \in A$, xRy and yRx imply that $y = x$. R is *irreflexive* if for all $x \in A$, xRx does not hold. R is *asymmetric* if for all $x, y \in A$, xRy implies that yRx does not hold. R is *acyclic* if it satisfies the following condition: If $x_1, \ldots, x_k \in A$, $k \geq 2$, and $x_i R x_{i+1}$ for $i = 1, \ldots, k-1$, then $x_k R x_1$ does not hold.

Remark 2.1.2. We note that a binary relation is asymmetric if and only if it is irreflexive and antisymmetric. Also, an acyclic relation is asymmetric.

Throughout this essay we shall deal mainly with linear order relations. The formal definition is as follows.

Definition 2.1.3. R is a *linear order* if it is complete, transitive, and anti-symmetric. We denote by $L = L(A)$ the set of all linear orders on A.

Remark 2.1.4. If R is complete, then it is *reflexive* (i.e., xRx for all $x \in A$). Hence, a linear order is reflexive.

The following notation is useful.

Notation 2.1.5. Let $R \in L$ (see Definition 2.1.3), and let $B \subset A$. We denote by $R \mid B$ the restriction of R to B. (Thus, $R \mid B \in L(B)$, and for $x, y \in B$, $x(R \mid B)y$ if and only if xRy.)

Notation 2.1.6. Let $R_1, R_2 \in L$, and let $B \subset A$. We denote by $R = \rho(R_1, R_2; B)$ the following linear order on A: $R \mid B = R_1 \mid B$ (see Notation 2.1.5), $R \mid (A - B) = R_2 \mid (A - B)$, and if $x \in B$ and $y \in A - B$, then xRy. If $R_* \in L$ and $B \subset A$, then we denote $R_*(B) = \rho(R_*, R_*; B)$.

Notation 2.1.7. If S is a finite set, then we denote by $|S|$ the number of members of S.

Notation 2.1.8. Assume that A is finite, with $|A| = m$ (see Notation 2.1.7), and let $R \in L$. We denote by $t_i(R)$, for $i = 1, \ldots, m$, the ith alternative in the order R. Thus, $t_1(R)$ is the best alternative according to R, $t_2(R)$ is the second alternative, and so on. We also write $R = (t_1(R), t_2(R), \ldots, t_m(R))$.

2.2   Social welfare functions and Arrow's Impossibility Theorem

Let N be a finite set with n members. N is called a *society*, members of N are called *voters* or *players*, and nonempty subsets of N are called *coalitions*. Now let A be a set of *alternatives*. We recall that L denotes the set of all linear orders on A (see Definition 2.1.3). Intuitively, a member R of L represents a possible preference relation of a voter i in N over the set of alternatives A. The following notation will be used in the sequel.

Notation 2.2.1. Let S be a coalition. We denote by L^S the set of all functions from S to L.

Intuitively, if S is a coalition and $R^S \in L^S$, then R^S consists of a possible combination of preference relations of the members of S.

Definition 2.2.2. A *social welfare function* (SWF) is a function F from L^N to L.

Thus, an SWF is a method of associating with every n-tuple of individual orderings a social preference relation. (For a detailed discussion of SWFs, see Sen [1970, Chapters 3 and 3*].)

In order to formulate Arrow's Impossibility Theorem, we have to define the following properties of SWFs.

Definition 2.2.3. Let F be an SWF. F is *Paretian* if it satisfies the following condition: For all $R^N \in L^N$ and for all $x, y \in A$,

$$[xR^i y \text{ for all } i \in N] \Rightarrow xF(R^N)y$$

Clearly, Definition 2.2.3 is simply the unanimity principle for SWFs. (See Sen [1970, Chapters 2 and 2*] for a discussion of the Pareto principle.)

In order to define the second property of SWFs we need the following notation.

Notation 2.2.4. Let S be a coalition, and let $B \subset A$. For $R^S \in L^S$ (see Notation 2.2.1) we denote by $R^S | B$ the member of $L^S(B)$ (see Definition 2.1.3) whose ith component is $R^i | B$ (see Notation 2.1.5), for $i \in S$.

Definition 2.2.5. An SWF F satisfies the condition of *independence of irrelevant alternatives* if for all $R^N, Q^N \in L^N$ and for all $x, y \in A$,

$$[R^N | \{x, y\} = Q^N | \{x, y\}] \Rightarrow F(R^N) | \{x, y\} = F(Q^N) | \{x, y\}$$

(see Notation 2.2.4).

For a discussion of Definition 2.2.5, see Sen [1970, Chapter 3]. Later we shall supply a "technical" game theoretic interpretation for the condition of independence of irrelevant alternatives (see Section 4.3).

Finally, the notion of a dictatorial SWF is formalized by the following definition.

Definition 2.2.6. An SWF F is *dictatorial* if there exists a player $j \in N$ (a *dictator*) such that $F(R^N) = R^j$ for all $R^N \in L^N$.

We are now able to state the following.

Theorem 2.2.7 (Arrow's Impossibility Theorem). *Let* $F: L^N \to L$ *be an SWF. If F is Paretian (see Definition 2.2.3) and satisfies the condition of independence of irrelevant alternatives (see Definition 2.2.5), and if A (the set of alternatives) contains at least three members, then F is dictatorial (see Definition 2.2.6).*

Sen [1970] contains a discussion of Theorem 2.2.7. Reading the original book, Arrow [1963], is, of course, highly instructive. For the sake of completeness, a proof of Theorem 2.2.7 is given in the Appendix to this chapter.

2.3 Social choice correspondences

Let A be a set of alternatives. Henceforth we shall assume that

$$A \text{ is finite and } |A| = m \geqslant 2 \tag{2.3.1}$$

(see Notation 2.1.7). We shall use the following customary notation.

Notation 2.3.1. We denote by 2^A the set of all *nonempty* subsets of A.
Let N be a society.

Definition 2.3.2. A *social choice correspondence* (SCC) is a function H from L^N (see Notation 2.2.1) to 2^A.
Intuitively, if H is an SCC and $R^N \in L^N$, then $H(R^N)$ is the set of alternatives chosen by the society, according to the rule H. In order for an SCC to be reasonable, it has to satisfy certain requirements. We shall now discuss several basic properties of SCCs.

Definition 2.3.3. Let $R^N \in L^N$, and let $x \in A$; x is *Pareto-optimal* (with respect to R^N) if there exists no $y \in A$, $y \neq x$, such that yR^ix for all $i \in N$. The set of all Pareto-optimal alternatives is denoted by $\text{PAR}(R^N)$.
Clearly, because A is finite (see (2.3.1)), $\text{PAR}(R^N) \neq \varnothing$ for all $R^N \in L^N$. Hence, $\text{PAR}(\cdot)$ is an SCC (see Definition 2.3.2). The unanimity principle for SCCs has the following form.

Definition 2.3.4. An SCC H is *Paretian* if for all $R^N \in L^N$, $H(R^N) \subset \text{PAR}(R^N)$.
Symmetries of an SCC are defined as follows.

Definition 2.3.5. Let H be an SCC. A permutation π of N is a *symmetry* of H if for all $R^N = (R^1, \ldots, R^n)$ in L^N, $H(R^N) = H(R^{\pi(1)}, \ldots, R^{\pi(n)})$. The group of all symmetries of H will be denoted by $\text{SYM}(H)$.
Using Definition 2.3.5, we now introduce the following important class of SCCs.

Definition 2.3.6. An SCC H is *anonymous* if $\text{SYM}(H) = S_n$, the group of all permutations of N.

Remark 2.3.7. $PAR(\cdot)$ (see Definition 2.3.3) is anonymous.

Relative invariance of SCCs with respect to permutations of A is defined as follows. Let σ be a permutation of A, and let $R \in L$ (see Definition 2.1.3). We denote by $\sigma(R)$ the linear order defined by the following condition: For all $x, y \in A$, $\sigma(x)\sigma(R)\sigma(y)$ if and only if xRy. Note that $t_i(\sigma(R)) = \sigma(t_i(R))$ for $i = 1, \ldots, m$ (see Notation 2.1.8).

Definition 2.3.8. An SCC H is *neutral* if for every permutation σ of A, and for every $R^N = (R^1, \ldots, R^n)$ in L^N (see Notation 2.2.1), $H(\sigma(R^1), \ldots, \sigma(R^N)) = \sigma(H(R^N))$. (Here, $\sigma(H(R^N))$ is the image of $H(R^N)$ under σ.)

Remark 2.3.9. $PAR(\cdot)$ is neutral.

We now discuss the very important property of monotonicity of SCCs. Roughly, an SCC is monotonic if it "responds positively" to improvements in the position of a *single* alternative. However, the formal analysis of monotonicity is somewhat elaborate.

Definition 2.3.10. Let $R^N \in L^N$ (see Notation 2.2.1), and let $x \in A$. $R_1^N \in L^N$ is obtained from R^N by an improvement of the position of x if

$$\text{for all } a, b \in A - \{x\} \text{ and for all } i \in N, \ aR^i b \Leftrightarrow aR_1^i b \qquad (2.3.2)$$

and

$$\text{for all } a \in A \text{ and for all } i \in N, \ xR^i a \Rightarrow xR_1^i a \qquad (2.3.3)$$

Definition 2.3.11. An SCC H is *monotonic* if it satisfies the following:

$$\begin{aligned} &\text{If } R^N \in L^N, \ x \in H(R^N), \text{ and } R_1^N \text{ is obtained from } R^N \text{ by} \\ &\text{an improvement of the position of } x \text{ (see Definition 2.3.10),} \\ &\text{then } x \in H(R_1^N) \text{ and } H(R_1^N) \subset H(R^N). \end{aligned} \qquad (2.3.4)$$

Thus, an SCC is monotonic if whenever the position of an alternative *in the choice set* is improved, then (a) that alternative remains in the choice set and (b) the choice set does not expand.

Almost all the voting rules that are used in practice are monotonic. In particular, "rank-order" methods, which we shall now describe, are monotonic.

Example 2.3.12. Let $u = (u_1, \ldots, u_m)$ be an m-tuple of real numbers (where $m = |A|$ (see (2.3.1))), such that $u_i - u_{i+1} \geqslant 0$ for $i = 1, \ldots, m-1$, and there exists $1 \leqslant j \leqslant m-1$ such that $u_j - u_{j+1} > 0$. For $R \in L$ (see Definition 2.1.3) and $x \in A$, we define $w(R, x) = u_i$ if $t_i(R) = x$ (see Notation 2.1.8). Thus, if R is a linear preference ordering and x is an alternative, x

gets u_i "points" if it is the ith alternative in the order R. Now, for $R^N \in L^N$ (see Notation 2.2.1) and $x \in A$, we define

$$w(R^N, x) = \sum_{i=1}^{n} w(R^i, x) \qquad (\text{where } N = \{1, \dots, n\}) \qquad (2.3.5)$$

Finally, the *rank-order method* for N, which is specified by u, is the SCC $\text{RAN} = \text{RAN}(u, n)$ defined by $\text{RAN}(R^N; u, n) = \text{RAN}(R^N) = \{x \mid x \in A \text{ and } w(R^N, x) \geqslant w(R^N, y) \text{ for all } y \in A\}$ (see (2.3.5)), for all $R^N \in L^N$.

Remark 2.3.13. If $u = (1, 0, \dots, 0)$, then $\text{RAN}(u, n)$ is the familiar rule of choice by plurality voting, and if $u = (m-1, m-2, \dots, 0)$, then $\text{RAN}(u, n)$ is the well-known Borda rule.

Remark 2.3.14. Every rank-order method is anonymous, neutral, and monotonic (see Definitions 2.3.6, 2.3.8, and 2.3.11, respectively). Notice, however, that a rank-order method may *not* be Paretian (see Definition 2.3.4). For example, if $m = 3$ and $u = (1, 1, 0)$, then $\text{RAN}(u, n)$ is not Paretian.

The following stronger notion of monotonicity is sometimes useful.

Definition 2.3.15. An SCC H is *strongly monotonic* if it satisfies the following:

> If $R^N \in L^N$ (see Notation 2.2.1), $x \in A$, and R_1^N is obtained from R^N by an improvement of the position of x (see Definition 2.3.10), then $H(R_1^N) \subset \{x\} \cup H(R^N)$. $\qquad (2.3.6)$

Our first task is to prove the following lemma.

Lemma 2.3.16. *A strongly monotonic SCC is monotonic.*

Before proving the lemma, it is convenient to introduce the following definition.

Definition 2.3.17. Let $R^N \in L^N$, and let $x \in A$. $R_1^N \in L^N$ is obtained from R^N by an *elementary* improvement of the position of x, if there exist $i \in N$, $y \in A$, $y \neq x$, and $1 < h \leqslant m$ such that

$$\text{if } j \in N, j \neq i, \text{ then } R_1^j = R^j \qquad (2.3.7)$$

$$x = t_h(R^i) = t_{h-1}(R_1^i), \quad y = t_{h-1}(R^i) = t_h(R_1^i), \quad \text{and}$$
$$t_k(R^i) = t_k(R_1^i) \quad \text{for } k \neq h, h-1 \qquad (2.3.8)$$

(see Notation 2.1.8).

The following remark is obvious.

Remark 2.3.18. Let $R^N \in L^N$, and let $x \in A$. If R_1^N is obtained from R^N by an improvement of the position of x, then there exist $Q_1^N, \ldots, Q_k^N \in L^N$, $k \geq 1$, such that $Q_1^N = R^N$, $Q_k^N = R_1^N$, and Q_{j+1}^N is obtained from Q_j^N by an elementary improvement of the position of x for $1 \leq j \leq k-1$. (If $k=1$, then $R^N = R_1^N$.)

We now return to the proof of Lemma 2.3.16.

Proof of Lemma 2.3.16. Let $H: L^N \to 2^A$ be an SCC. Further, let $R^N \in L^N$ and $x \in H(R^N)$. If R_1^N is obtained from R^N by an improvement of the position of x, we have to show that $x \in H(R_1^N)$ (compare (2.3.4) and (2.3.6)). Assume, on the contrary, that $x \notin H(R_1^N)$. Then, clearly, $R_1^N \neq R^N$. Hence, there exist $Q_1^N, \ldots, Q_k^N \in L^N$, $k \geq 2$, such that $Q_1^N = R^N$, $Q_k^N = R_1^N$, and Q_{j+1}^N is obtained from Q_j^N by an elementary improvement of the position of x, for $j = 1, \ldots, k-1$ (see Remark 2.3.18). There exists j, $1 \leq j \leq k-1$, such that $x \in H(Q_j^N)$ and $x \notin H(Q_{j+1}^N)$. By Definition 2.3.17, there exist $h \in N$ and $y \in A$, $y \neq x$, such that $Q_{j+1}^i = Q_j^i$ for $i \neq h$, and Q_{j+1}^h is obtained from Q_j^h by moving x one place up and lowering y one place (to the place that was occupied by x). Now, it is clear that Q_j^N is obtained from Q_{j+1}^N by an elementary improvement of the position of y. Hence, by (2.3.6), $H(Q_j^N) \subset \{y\} \cup H(Q_{j+1}^N)$, contradicting the fact that $x \in H(Q_j^N)$.

Remark 2.3.19. Condition (2.3.6) has a simple and clear meaning: If the position of an alternative is improved, then only that alternative and the alternatives that were chosen in the initial situation are candidates for choice in the new situation.

Remark 2.3.20. PAR$(\cdot)$ is strongly monotonic (see Definition 2.3.3).

Remark 2.3.21. If $m=2$ (see (2.3.1)), then every monotonic SCC is strongly monotonic.

In contrast, the following result is true.

Theorem 2.3.22. Let $RAN(u, n)$, where $u = (u_1, \ldots, u_m)$, be a rank-order method (see Example 2.3.12). If $m=3$ and $n=3$, or $m=3$ and $n \geq 5$, or $m \geq 4$ and $n \geq m$, then $RAN(u, n)$ is not strongly monotonic.

Proof: Without loss of generality we may assume that $u_1 = 1$ and $u_m = 0$. We first prove the following:

> If $u = (1, \ldots, 1, 0)$ and $n \geq m \geq 3$, then
> RAN(u, n) is not strongly monotonic.   (2.3.9)

Indeed, let $N = \{1, \ldots, n\}$, and let $A = \{x_1, \ldots, x_m\}$. Let $R^N \in L^N$ satisfy $t_{m-1}(R^1) = x_1$, $t_m(R^1) = x_m$, $t_m(R^i) = x_i$ if $i = 2, \ldots, m-1$, and $t_m(R^i) = x_m$ if $i \geq m$ (see Notation 2.1.8). Then $w(R^N, x_1) = n$, $w(R^N, x_j) = n-1$ if $j = 2, \ldots, m-1$, and $w(R^N, x_m) = m-2$ (see (2.3.5)). Hence, $\mathrm{RAN}(R^N) = \{x_1\}$. Now define $R_1^N \in L^N$ by $R_1^i = R^i$ if $i \neq 1$, $t_m(R_1^1) = x_1$, $t_{m-1}(R_1^1) = x_m$, and $R_1^1 \mid \{x_2, \ldots, x_{m-1}\} = R^1 \mid \{x_2, \ldots, x_{m-1}\}$ (see Notation 2.1.5). Then R_1^N is obtained from R^N by an improvement of the position of x_m (see Definition 2.3.10). Now, $w(R_1^N, x_j) = n-1$ if $j \neq m$, and $w(R_1^N, x_m) = m-1 \leq n-1$. Hence, $x_2 \in \mathrm{RAN}(R_1^N)$, which implies that $\mathrm{RAN}(u, n)$ is not strongly monotonic (see (2.3.6)).

Our second claim is as follows:

> If $m = 3$ and $n = 3$ or $n \geq 5$, then $\mathrm{RAN}(u, n)$ is
> not strongly monotonic. (2.3.10)

By (2.3.9) we may assume that $u_2 < 1$. Let $N = \{1, \ldots, n\}$, and let $A = \{x, y, z\}$. We distinguish the following subcases:

> n is even (2.3.10.1)

Thus, $n = 2k$, where $k \geq 3$. Define $R^N \in L^N$ by $R^i = (x, y, z)$ for $i = 1, \ldots, k-1$, $R^i = (y, x, z)$ for $i = k, \ldots, n-2$, $R^{n-1} = (x, z, y)$, and $R^n = (z, y, x)$. Then $w(R^N, x) = k + (k-1)u_2$, $w(R^N, y) = k-1+ku_2$, and $w(R^N, z) = 1 + u_2$ (see (2.3.5)). Since $k \geq 3$ and $u_2 < 1$, $\mathrm{RAN}(R^N) = \{x\}$. Now, if R_1^N is defined by $R_1^i = R^i$ if $i \neq n-1$, and $R_1^{n-1} = (z, x, y)$, then, clearly, R_1^N is obtained from R^N by an improvement of the position of z (see Definition 2.3.10). Now, $w(R_1^N, x) = w(R_1^N, y) = k-1+ku_2$, and $w(R_1^N, z) = 2$. Hence, as $k \geq 3$, $w(R_1^N, y) \geq w(R_1^N, z)$. Thus, $y \in \mathrm{RAN}(R_1^N)$, which implies that $\mathrm{RAN}(u, n)$ is not strongly monotonic (see (2.3.6)).

> n is odd (2.3.10.2)

Then, $n = 3 + 2k$, where $k \geq 0$. Define $R^N \in L^N$ by $R^i = (x, y, z)$ for $i = 1, 3, \ldots, n$, and $R^i = (y, x, z)$ for $i = 2, 4, \ldots, n-1$. Then, $w(R^N, x) = k+2+(k+1)u_2$, $w(R^N, y) = k+1+(k+2)u_2$, and $w(R^N, z) = 0$. Hence, $\mathrm{RAN}(R^N) = \{x\}$. Now define R_1^N by $R_1^i = R^i$ if $i \neq 2, 3$, $R_1^2 = (y, z, x)$, and $R_1^3 = (z, x, y)$. Then R_1^N is obtained from R^N by an improvement of the position of z. Furthermore, $w(R_1^N x) = w(R_1^N, y) = (k+1)(1+u_2)$, and $w(R_1^N, z) = 1 + u_2$. Thus, $y \in \mathrm{RAN}(R_1^N)$. Hence, $\mathrm{RAN}(u, n)$ is not strongly monotonic.

We now remark that

if $m = n = 4$, then $\mathrm{RAN}(u, n)$ is not strongly monotonic (2.3.11)

The proof of (2.3.11) is similar to the proof for the case $m = n = 3$ (see the proof of (2.3.10.2)); hence, it will be omitted.

We now complete the proof by induction on m. Let $m > 3$, and assume that if $3 \leqslant m^* < m$ and $n \geqslant \max(m^*, 5)$, then $\text{RAN}(u, n)$ is not strongly monotonic (where $u = (u_1, \ldots, u_{m^*})$). Now let $\text{RAN}(u, n)$, where $u = (u_1, \ldots, u_m)$ and $n \geqslant \max(m, 5)$, be a rank-order method. We have to show that $\text{RAN}(u, n)$ is not strongly monotonic. If $u_{m-1} = 1$, then the proof follows from (2.3.9). If $u_{m-1} < 1$, let $u^* = (u_1, \ldots, u_{m-1})$. By the induction hypothesis, $\text{RAN}(u^*, n)$ is not strongly monotonic. (Note that since $u_{m-1} < 1$, $\text{RAN}(u^*, n)$ is, indeed, a rank-order method (see Example 2.3.12).) Now, the fact that $\text{RAN}(u^*, n)$ is not strongly monotonic implies that $\text{RAN}(u, n)$ is not strongly monotonic. (Indeed, let A be a set of alternatives for $\text{RAN}(u, n)$, and let $x \in A$. Denote by L_* the set of all linear orders of A (see Definition 2.1.3) in which x is the last alternative. Then the restriction of $\text{RAN}(u, n)$ to L_*^N is, essentially, identical with $\text{RAN}(u^*, n)$ applied to $A - \{x\}$.)

Remark 2.3.23. We note that if $n < m$ and $u = (u_1, \ldots, u_m) = (1, \ldots, 1, 0)$, then $\text{RAN}(u, n)$ *is* strongly monotonic. Also, $\text{RAN}((1, 0, 0), 4)$ *is* strongly monotonic. Hence, Theorem 2.3.22 cannot be strengthened.

The following property of SCCs, which has been investigated in Muller and Satterthwaite [1977], is equivalent to strong monotonicity.

Definition 2.3.24. An SCC H has the *strong positive association* (SPA) property if it satisfies the following:

Let $R^N \in L^N$ and $x \in H(R^N)$. If $R_1^N \in L^N$ and for all $i \in N$
and $y \in A$, xR^iy implies $xR_1^i y$, then $x \in H(R_1^N)$.   (2.3.12)

Lemma 2.3.25. *An SCC is strongly monotonic if and only if it has the SPA property.*

Proof: Sufficiency. Let H be an SCC with the SPA property, $R^N \in L^N$, and $x \in A$. If $R_1^N \in L^N$ is obtained from R^N by an improvement of the position of x, then we have to show that $H(R_1^N) \subset \{x\} \cup H(R^N)$ (see (2.3.6)). So let $y \in H(R_1^N)$, $y \neq x$. By (2.3.12), $y \in H(R^N)$.

Necessity. Let H be a strongly monotonic SCC, $R^N \in L^N$, and $x \in H(R^N)$. If $R_1^N \in L^N$ and for all $i \in N$ and $y \in A$, xR^iy implies $xR_1^i y$, then we have to show that $x \in H(R_1^N)$. Now, as the reader can easily verify, there exist $Q_1^N, \ldots, Q_k^N \in L^N$, $k \geqslant 2$, such that $Q_1^N = R_1^N$, $Q_k^N = R^N$, and Q_{j+1}^N is obtained from Q_j^N by an improvement of the position of some x_j for $j = 1, \ldots, k-1$, where $x_j \neq x$ for $j = 1, \ldots, k-1$. Because H is strongly monotonic,

$$H(R^N) \subset H(R_1^N) \cup \{x_1, \ldots, x_{k-1}\}$$

Hence, $x \in H(R^N)$ implies that $x \in H(R_1^N)$.

2.4   Social choice functions

In many practical choice problems the choice of a *single* alternative is required. Thus, the class of single-valued SCCs deserves a special investigation. This section consists of the beginning of such an investigation.

Definition 2.4.1. A *social choice function* (SCF) is an SCC (see Definition 2.3.2) whose values are singletons (i.e., one-element sets).

Remark 2.4.2. An SCF is, essentially, a function from L^N to A (see Notation 2.2.1).

Notation 2.4.3. Let H be an SCC, and let $R^N \in L^N$. If $H(R^N) = \{x\}$, then we shall also write $H(R^N) = x$. In particular, if F is an SCF and $R^N \in L^N$, then we shall write $x = F(R^N)$ instead of $\{x\} = F(R^N)$.

Definition 2.4.4. Let H be an SCC. An SCF F is a *selection* from H if for every $R^N \in L^N$, $F(R^N) \in H(R^N)$.

Remark 2.4.5. A selection from a Paretian SCC (see Definition 2.3.4) is Paretian.

A selection from an anonymous (respectively monotonic, strongly monotonic) SCC (see Definitions 2.3.6, 2.3.11, and 2.3.15) may not be anonymous (respectively monotonic, strongly monotonic). Hence, we should restrict our attention to "regular" selections. One way to obtain "nice" selections is the following.

Definition 2.4.6. Let H be an SCC (see Definition 2.3.2), and let $R \in L$ (see Definition 2.1.3). The *selection from H according to the order R* is the following SCF $F = F(H, R)$. For each $R^N \in L^N$ (see Notation 2.2.1), $F(R^N) = F(R^N; H, R)$ is the first alternative according to the order R in the set $H(R^N)$. (Thus, if $R^N \in L^N$, then $x = F(R^N)$ if and only if $x \in H(R^N)$ and xRy for all $y \in H(R^N)$.)

Remark 2.4.7. If H is an SCC, $R \in L$, and $F = F(H, R)$, then SYM(H) $\subset$ SYM(F) (see Definition 2.3.5). In particular, if H is anonymous (see Definition 2.3.6), then F is anonymous.

Lemma 2.4.8. *Let H be an SCC, and let $R \in L$. If H is monotonic (see Definition 2.3.11), then $F(H, R)$ is monotonic.*

Proof: Let $R^N \in L^N$, and let $x = F(R^N) = F(R^N; H, R)$. We have to show that if R_1^N is obtained from R^N by an improvement of the position of x (see Definition 2.3.10), then $F(R_1^N) = x$. By Definition 2.4.6, $x \in H(R^N)$. Hence, by (2.3.4), $x \in H(R_1^N)$ and $H(R_1^N) \subset H(R^N)$. Therefore, x is the first alternative according to R in $H(R_1^N)$ (i.e., $x = F(R_1^N)$).

We shall now prove that every strongly monotonic SCF whose range contains at least three alternatives is dictatorial. We start with the following notation and definition.

Notation 2.4.9. Let F be an SCF. The range of F is denoted by

$$R(F) = \{x \mid x = F(R^N) \text{ for some } R^N \in L^N\} \tag{2.4.1}$$

Definition 2.4.10. Let F be an SCF, and let $A^* = R(F)$ (see (2.4.1)). F is *dictatorial* if there exists a player $j \in N$ (a *dictator*) such that for every $R^N \in L^N$ and for every $x \in A^*$, $F(R^N) R^j x$.

We are now able to state the following theorem.

Theorem 2.4.11. *Let F be a strongly monotonic SCF, and let $A^* = R(F)$. If $|A^*| \geqslant 3$ (see Notation 2.1.7), then F is dictatorial. (See Definition 2.4.10.)*

The following notation is useful for the proof of Theorem 2.4.11.

Notation 2.4.12. Let $R_1^N, R_2^N \in L^N$, and let $B \subset A$. We denote by $R^N = \rho^N(R_1^N, R_2^N; B)$ the member of L^N whose ith component is $R^i = \rho(R_1^i, R_2^i; B)$ (see Notation 2.1.6), for $i \in N$. Also, if $R_*^N \in L^N$ and $B \subset A$, then we denote $R_*^N(B) = \rho^N(R_*^N, R_*^N; B)$.

The main tool in the proof of Theorem 2.4.11 is the following lemma.

Lemma 2.4.13. *Let $H: L^N \to 2^A$ be a strongly monotonic SCC (see Definition 2.3.15), and let $B \subset A$. If $R_1^N, R_2^N \in L^N$, $R^N = \rho^N(R_1^N, R_2^N; B)$ (see Notation 2.4.12), $x \in B$, and $x \notin H(R^N)$, then $x \notin H(R_1^N)$.*

Proof: If $B = A$, then $R^N = R_1^N$. Hence, we may assume that $A - B \neq \varnothing$. Let $A - B = \{a_1, \ldots, a_k\}$, and let $B_j = B \cup \{a_h \mid 1 \leqslant h \leqslant j\}$, $j = 0, 1, \ldots, k$. (Thus, $B_0 = B$ and $B_k = A$.) For $j = 0, \ldots, k$, let $Q_j^N = \rho^N(R_1^N, R_2^N; B_j)$. Then $Q_0^N = R^N$, $Q_k^N = R_1^N$, and Q_{j+1}^N is obtained from Q_j^N by an improvement of the position of a_{j+1}, for $j=0,\ldots,k-1$ (see Definition 2.3.10). Hence,

$$H(Q_{j+1}^N) \subset \{a_{j+1}\} \cup H(Q_j^N) \quad \text{for } j=0,\ldots,k-1$$

(see Definition 2.3.15). Thus,

$$H(R_1^N) = H(Q_k^N) \subset H(R^N) \cup (A-B)$$

and therefore $x \notin H(R_1^N)$.

We now turn to the proof of Theorem 2.4.11.

Proof of Theorem 2.4.11. First, we note the following corollaries of Lemma 2.4.13.

Corollary 2.4.14. If $R_1^N, R_2^N \in L^N$ and $R_1^N \mid A^* = R_2^N \mid A^*$ (see Notation 2.2.4), then $F(R_1^N) = F(R_2^N)$.

Proof: Let $Q^N \in L^N$, and let $R^N = \rho^N(R_1^N, Q^N; A^*)$. By Lemma 2.4.13, $F(R^N) = F(R_1^N)$. Also, by assumption, $R^N = \rho^N(R_2^N, Q^N; A^*)$. Hence, $F(R^N) = F(R_2^N)$, and the proof is complete.

Remark 2.4.15. It follows from Corollary 2.4.14 that we may assume that $A = A^*$.

Corollary 2.4.16. Let $R^N \in L^N$, and let $x \in A$. If xR^iy for all $y \in A$ and all $i \in N$, then $F(R^N) = x$.

Proof: Since $A = A^*$ (see Remark 2.4.15), there exists $R_*^N \in L^N$ such that $F(R_*^N) = x$. Let $B = \{x\}$. Then $R^N = \rho^N(R_*^N, R^N; B)$. By Lemma 2.4.13, $F(R^N) = x$.

Corollary 2.4.16 implies that F is Paretian.

Lemma 2.4.17. *Let* $R^N \in L^N$*, and let* $y \in A$*. If there exists* $x \in A$*,* $x \neq y$*, such that* xR^iy *for all* $i \in N$*, then* $F(R^N) \neq y$*.*

Proof: Let $B = \{x, y\}$. By Corollary 2.4.16, $F(R^N(B)) = x$ (see Notation 2.4.12). By Lemma 2.4.13, it follows that $F(R^N) \neq y$.

We now continue with the proof of Theorem 2.4.11. For each $R^N \in L^N$ we define a binary relation $R = F^*(R^N)$ on A in the following way. Let R_0^N be a fixed member of L^N. If $x, y \in A$ and $x = y$, then we define xRy. If $x \neq y$, then we consider the profile $R_1^N = \rho^N(R^N, R_0^N; \{x, y\})$ (see Notation

2.4.12), and we define xRy if $F(R_1^N)=x$, and yRx if $F(R_1^N)=y$. By Lemma 2.4.17, R is complete (see Definition 2.1.1). It is also clear that R is antisymmetric. The transitivity of R follows easily from the following lemma.

Lemma 2.4.18. *Let* $R^N \in L^N$, *and let* $B \subset A$, $B \neq \emptyset$. *If* $F(R^N(B))=x$ (see Notation 2.4.12), *then* xRy *for all* $y \in B$, *where* $R=F^*(R^N)$.

Proof: By Lemma 2.4.17, $x \in B$. Thus, the lemma is true if $|B|=1$ (see Notation 2.1.7). If $|B| \geqslant 2$, let $y \in B - \{x\}$ and

$$R_1^N = \rho^N(R^N(B), R_0^N; \{x,y\}) = \rho^N(R^N, R_0^N; \{x,y\})$$

Since $F(R^N(B))=x$, it follows from Lemma 2.4.13 that $F(R_1^N)=x$. Thus, xRy.

Corollary 2.4.19. Let $R^N \in L^N$, and let $R=F^*(R^N)$. If $x=F(R^N)$, then xRy for all $y \in A$.

Consider now the SWF $F^*: L^N \to L$ (see Definition 2.2.2). It is clear from the definition of F^* and Corollary 2.4.16 that F^* is Paretian and satisfies the condition of independence of irrelevant alternatives (see Definitions 2.2.3 and 2.2.5, respectively). Hence, by Arrow's Impossibility Theorem (Theorem 2.2.7), F^* is dictatorial (see Definition 2.2.6). Let j be a dictator for F^*. By Corollary 2.4.19, j is a dictator for F (see Definition 2.4.10).

The following result of Muller and Satterthwaite [1977] follows from Theorem 2.4.11 and Lemma 2.3.25.

Corollary 2.4.20. Let F be an SCF, and let $A^*=R(F)$ (see (2.4.1)). If F has the strong positive association property (see Definition 2.3.24), and $|A^*| \geqslant 3$, then F is dictatorial.

2.5   The Gibbard–Satterthwaite Theorem

Let $F: L^N \to A$ be an SCF (see Definition 2.4.1), where $N=\{1,\ldots,n\}$ is a society and A is a set of alternatives. When the members of N choose a member of A according to the rule F, they actually play the following n-person game in normal form. Each member of N declares a member of L (see Definition 2.1.3) as his preference order (i.e., every $R \in L$ is a *legal* strategy for every $i \in N$). Then the outcome is determined by F, and each voter values the outcome according to his *true* preference order. This description is made precise by the following definition.

Definition 2.5.1. Let $R^N \in L^N$. The *game associated with F and R^N* is the n-person game in normal form $g(F, R^N)$, where

$$L \text{ is the set of strategies for each player } i \in N \quad (2.5.1)$$

$$F \text{ is the outcome function} \quad (2.5.2)$$

$$R^i \text{ is the preference relation of player } i \in N \text{ on the}$$
$$\text{outcome space } A \quad (2.5.3)$$

In defining equilibrium points of $g(F, R^N)$, we use the following notation.

Notation 2.5.2. Let $S \subset N$, and let $T \subset S$, $T \neq \varnothing$. For $R^S \in L^S$ (see Notation 2.2.1) we denote by R^T the restriction of R^S to T.

Definition 2.5.3. Let $R^N \in L^N$. $Q^N \in L^N$ is an *equilibrium point* (e.p.) of $g(F, R^N)$ if for each $i \in N$,

$$F(Q^N) R^i F(Q^{N-\{i\}}, T^i) \quad \text{for all } T^i \in L$$

Thus, Q^N is an e.p. of $g(F, R^N)$, if for each $i \in N$, Q^i is a best reply to $Q^{N-\{i\}}$. Hence, if for all $R^N \in L^N$, R^N *itself* is an e.p. of $g(F, R^N)$, then F is nonmanipulable (i.e., there exists no situation in which some voter has an incentive to declare untrue preference order). Formally, we have the following.

Definition 2.5.4. F is *nonmanipulable* if for each $R^N \in L^N$, R^N itself is an e.p. (see Definition 2.5.3) of $g(F, R^N)$.

A fundamental result of Gibbard [1973] and Satterthwaite [1975] is the following.

Theorem 2.5.5. *Let F be an SCF, and $A^* = R(F)$ (see Notation 2.4.9). If F is nonmanipulable and $|A^*| \geq 3$, then F is dictatorial* (see Definition 2.4.10).

Proof: By Theorem 2.4.11, it is sufficient to prove that F is strongly monotonic. Assume, on the contrary, that F is not strongly monotonic. Then there exist $R^N, R_1^N \in L^N$ such that $F(R^N) = t$, R_1^N is obtained from R^N by an elementary improvement of the position of x (see Definition 2.3.17), and $F(R_1^N) = z$, where $z \neq t, x$. By Definition 2.3.17 there exist $y \in A$, $i \in N$, and $1 < h \leq m$ such that $R^j = R_1^j$ if $j \neq i$, and $x = t_h(R^i) = t_{h-1}(R_1^i)$, $y = t_{h-1}(R^i) = t_h(R_1^i)$, and $R^i | A - \{x, y\} = R_1^i | A - \{x, y\}$. We distinguish the following possibilities: (a) $z \neq y$. In this case, $z R^i t$ if and only if $zR_1^i t$. Suppose first that $zR^i t$. Then R^N is not an e.p. of $g(F, R^N)$ (since $F(R_1^N) R^i F(R^N)$). Similarly, if $tR^i z$, R_1^N is not an e.p. of $g(F, R_1^N)$. (b) $z = y$. We distinguish the following subcases: (b.1) $x \neq t$. Then, again, $zR^i t$ if and only if $zR_1^i t$, and the proof is completed as in case (a). (b.2) $x = t$. In this case, $zR^i t$, and R^N is not an e.p. of $g(F, R^N)$.

2.6   Cores of simple games

Definition 2.6.1. A *simple game* is an ordered pair $G = (N, W)$, where N is a society, and W, the set of *winning coalitions,* satisfies

$$S \in W \quad \text{and} \quad T \supset S \Rightarrow T \in W \tag{2.6.1}$$

Remark 2.6.2. Condition (2.6.1) is the *monotonicity* property for simple games.

Remark 2.6.3. Intuitively, a simple game $G = (N, W)$ represents a committee: N is the set of members of the committee, and W is the set of coalitions that fully control the decisions of G. For a comprehensive study of simple games, the reader is referred to Shapley [1962].

We shall be interested in the following properties of simple games.

Definition 2.6.4. Let $G = (N, W)$ be a simple game. G is *proper* if

$$S \in W \Rightarrow N - S \notin W \tag{2.6.2}$$

G is *strong* if

$$S \notin W \Rightarrow N - S \in W \tag{2.6.3}$$

G is *weak* if

$$V = \cap \{S \mid S \in W\} \neq \emptyset \tag{2.6.4}$$

(If G is weak, then the members of V (see (2.6.4)) are called *veto players* (or *vetoers*).) G is *symmetric* if

$$[S \in W, T \subset N, \text{ and } |T| = |S|] \Rightarrow T \in W \tag{2.6.5}$$

(see Notation 2.1.7). (Clearly, a symmetric game is completely described by a pair (n, k) of natural numbers, where $n = |N|$ and $k = \min\{|S| \mid S \in W\}$.) Finally, G is *dictatorial* if there exists $j \in N$ (a *dictator*) such that

$$S \in W \Leftrightarrow j \in S \tag{2.6.6}$$

Remark 2.6.5. Let $G = (N, W)$ be a simple game. If G is weak, then G is proper. G is dictatorial if and only if it is both weak and strong.

Definition 2.6.6. Let $G = (N, W)$ be a simple game. A permutation π of N is a *symmetry* of G if for every $S \in W$, $\pi(S) = \{\pi(i) \mid i \in S\} \in W$. The group of all symmetries of G will be denoted by $\text{SYM}(G)$.

Remark 2.6.7. A simple game $G = (N, W)$ is symmetric (see (2.6.5)) if and only if $\text{SYM}(G) = S_n$, the group of all permutations of N.

Let $G = (N, W)$ be a simple game, and let A be a finite set of alternatives. Further, let $R^N \in L^N$ (see Notation 2.2.1).

Definition 2.6.8. Let $x, y \in A$, $x \neq y$, and let $S \in W$; x *dominates* y (*with respect to* R^N) *via* S, written $x \,\text{Dom}(R^N, S)\, y$, if $x R^i y$ for all $i \in S$; x *dominates* y (*with respect to* R^N), written $x \,\text{Dom}(R^N)\, y$, if there exists $T \in W$ such that $x \,\text{Dom}(R^N, T)\, y$. The *core* of A (*with respect to* G *and* R^N) is the set of undominated alternatives in A and is denoted by $C(N, W, A, R^N) = C(R^N)$.

Remark 2.6.9. Intuitively, $x \in C(N, W, A, R^N)$ if, when the profile of the preferences is R^N, no winning coalition can improve upon x during the process of choosing an alternative (or a set of alternatives) out of A. (Note that $C(N, W, A, R^N)$ is independent of the SCF (or SCC) that "implements" the choice procedure (for the committee G and the set of alternatives A).) Thus, it is interesting to know when $C(R^N) \neq \varnothing$ for all $R^N \in L^N$. This question will be completely answered by the following remarks and theorem.

Remark 2.6.10. Let $G = (N, W)$ be a simple game, and let A be a finite set of alternatives. Then $C(R^N) \neq \varnothing$ for all $R^N \in L^N$ (see Definition 2.6.8) if and only if $\text{Dom}(R^N)$ is acyclic for all $R^N \in L^N$ (see Definition 2.1.1).

As a consequence of Remark 2.6.10, we obtain the following.

Remark 2.6.11. If $G = (N, W)$ is a weak game (see (2.6.4)) and A is a finite set of alternatives, then $C(N, W, A, R^N) \neq \varnothing$ for all $R^N \in L^N$.

For games without vetoers, the solution to the foregoing question is more complicated. We start with a definition.

Definition 2.6.12. Let $G = (N, W)$ be a simple game without veto players. *Nakamura's number* of G, $\nu(G)$, is defined by

$$\nu(G) = \min\{|\sigma| \mid \sigma \subset W \text{ and } \bigcap \{S \mid S \in \sigma\} = \varnothing \} \tag{2.6.7}$$

Remark 2.6.13. As the reader can easily verify, $\nu(G) \leqslant n$ (where $n = |N|$). We are now able to state and prove the following.

Theorem 2.6.14 (Nakamura [1979]). *Let $G = (N, W)$ be a simple game without veto players, and let A be a finite set of alternatives. Then $C(N, W, A, R^N) \neq \varnothing$ for all $R^N \in L^N$ if and only if $|A| < \nu(G)$ (see (2.6.7)).*

Proof: Sufficiency. Assume that $|A| < \nu(G)$. By Remark 2.6.10 we have to show that $\text{Dom}(R^N)$ is acyclic for all $R^N \in L^N$. Assume, on the contrary, that there exists $R^N \in L^N$ such that $\text{Dom}(R^N)$ is cyclic. Then there exist p distinct members of A, $x_1, \ldots, x_p$, and coalitions $S_1, \ldots, S_p \in W$, such that $x_1 \text{Dom}(R^N, S_1) x_2$, $x_2 \text{Dom}(R^N, S_2) x_3, \ldots, x_p \text{Dom}(R^N, S_p) x_1$. We must have $\bigcap_{i=1}^{p} S_i = \varnothing$. Hence, $p \geqslant \nu(G)$. Thus, $|A| \geqslant p \geqslant \nu(G)$, which is the desired contradiction.

Necessity. Assume that for all $R^N \in L^N$, $\text{Dom}(R^N)$ is acyclic. We have to show that $|A| < \nu(G)$. Assume, on the contrary, that $|A| \geqslant \nu(G)$. Let $\sigma \subset W$, $\sigma = \{S_1, \ldots, S_p\}$, satisfy $\bigcap_{i=1}^{p} S_i = \varnothing$, where $p = \nu(G)$, and let $x_1, \ldots, x_p$ be distinct members of A. We now choose $R^N \in L^N$ in the following way. Let $i \in N$. There exists $k = k(i)$ such that $i \notin S_k$. We choose $R^i \in L$ such that

$$x_{k+1} R^i x_{k+2}, \ldots, x_{p-1} R^i x_p, x_p R^i x_1, \ldots, x_{k-1} R^i x_k \qquad (2.6.8)$$

We shall now show that $\text{Dom}(R^N)$ is cyclic (and thereby complete the proof). Let $1 \leqslant j \leqslant p$, and let $i \in S_j$. If $j < p$, then $x_j R^i x_{j+1}$, and if $j = p$, $x_p R^i x_1$ (see (2.6.8)). Hence, $x_j \text{Dom}(R^N) x_{j+1}$ for $j = 1, \ldots, p-1$, and $x_p \text{Dom}(R^N) x_1$, which proves that $\text{Dom}(R^N)$ is cyclic.

Appendix

Proof of Theorem 2.2.7. Let $x, y \in A$, $x \neq y$, and let M be a coalition. We say that M is *decisive for x against y* if for every $R^N \in L^N$, if $x R^i y$ for all $i \in M$ and $y R^i x$ for all $i \in N - M$, then $x F(R^N) y$. Since F is Paretian, N is decisive for every pair of (distinct) alternatives. Also, by independence of irrelevant alternatives, M is decisive for x against y if there exists $R^N \in L^N$ such that $x R^i y$ for all $i \in M$, $y R^i x$ for all $i \in N - M$, and $x F(R^N) y$. Let D be the collection of all coalitions that are decisive for some (ordered) pair of alternatives, and let $V \in D$ satisfy $|V| \leqslant |M|$ for all $M \in D$. Clearly, $V \neq \varnothing$. We claim that $|V| = 1$. Indeed, let $j \in V$, $U = V - \{j\}$, and $W = N - V$. There exist $x, y \in A$ such that V is decisive for x against y. Let $z \in A - \{x, y\}$, and choose $R^N \in L^N$ such that $R^j | \{x, y, z\} = (x, y, z)$, $R^U | \{x, y, z\} = (z, x, y)$, and $R^W | \{x, y, z\} = (y, z, x)$. Since V is decisive for x against y, $xF(R^N)y$. Since $U \notin D$, we must have $yF(R^N)z$. Hence, $xF(R^N)z$, and $\{j\}$ is decisive for x against z. We conclude that $V = \{j\}$ and that j is decisive for x against t for all $t \in A - \{x\}$. We shall now show that j is decisive for every pair of (distinct) alternatives. Let $z, w \in A - \{x\}$, $z \neq w$. Choose first $R^N \in L^N$ such that $R^j \mid \{x, z, w\} = (w, x, z)$ and $R^W \mid \{x, z, w\} = (z, w, x)$. Since j is decisive for x against z, $xF(R^N)z$, and since F is Paretian, $wF(R^N)x$. Hence, $wF(R^N)z$, and j is decisive for w against z. Now choose $R^N \in L^N$ such that $R^j \mid \{x, z, w\} = (w, z, x)$ and $R^W \mid \{x, z, w\} = (z, x, w)$. Since j is decisive for w against z, $wF(R^N)z$, and since F is Paretian, $zF(R^N)x$. Hence, $wF(R^N)x$, and j is decisive for w against x. Thus, j is decisive for every pair of alternatives. We shall show now that j is a dictator. Let $R^N \in L^N$ and $x, y \in A$, $x \neq y$. Assume that xR^jy. We have to show that $xF(R^N)y$. Let $z \in A - \{x, y\}$. By independence of irrelevant alternatives we may assume that xR^jzR^jy, and zR^ix and zR^iy for $i \in W$. Since j is decisive for x against z, $xF(R^N)z$, and since F is Paretian, $zF(R^N)y$. Hence, $xF(R^N)y$.

CHAPTER 3

Representations of committees

This chapter is devoted to a detailed investigation of the relationship between committees (formally, simple games) and social choice correspondences and functions. We begin our investigation in Section 3.1 by associating three simple games, which are derived from three different notions of effectiveness, with every social choice correspondence. These games serve to describe the power distribution induced by a social choice correspondence among the various coalitions of voters. We proceed with a study of the properties of, and the interrelations between, the three simple games. Then we consider several examples, including the Borda rule. A social choice correspondence is *tight* if our three notions of effectiveness coincide for it. We conclude Section 3.1 by demonstrating that certain conditions are sufficient for tightness. In Section 3.2 we consider the converse problem, namely, that of finding representations (i.e., choice procedures or, more formally, social choice correspondences) for committees. We find sufficient conditions for tightness of representations, and we prove, by constructing suitable examples, the existence of tight and "nice" representations. We also find that the solution to the representation problem is closely related to the investigation of cores of simple games. Indeed, the following result is true. Let $G = (N, W)$ be a simple game, and let A be a finite set of m alternatives, $m \geqslant 2$. Then there exists a strongly monotonic representation of G of order m if and only if for every profile of preferences (on A) R^N, the core of G, with respect to A and R^N, is not empty (see Corollary 3.2.10 and Theorem 3.2.13).

In Section 3.3 we investigate the possibility of representing simple games by social choice *functions*. First, we notice that an essential simple game has no representation, by a strongly monotonic social choice function, of order greater than 2 (see p. 53). Then we observe that, under suitable assumptions, a selection from a "nice" representation by a social choice correspondence is, itself, a "nice" representation (by a social choice function; see Lemma 3.3.9). Finally, we investigate, for a given simple game G, the existence of ("nice") *neutral* social choice functions that represent G. It turns out that the solution to that problem depends crucially on the structure of the symmetry group of G (see Lemma 3.3.13, Theorems 3.3.19 and 3.3.35, and Corollary 3.3.30).

Sections 3.1 and 3.2 of this chapter are based mainly on Peleg [1983]. The investigation, in Section 3.3, of the existence of neutral representations by social choice functions has benefited from Moulin [1980]. Finally, we remark that in the last section of Hurwicz and Schmeidler [1978], a theory that pertains to the relationship between "outcome functions" and simple games is outlined. The Hurwicz–Schmeidler theory is similar to our representation theory. Moreover, Hurwicz and Schmeidler emphasize the importance of both the descriptive and normative aspects of the representation problem.

3.1 The simple games associated with an SCC

In this section we associate three simple games with every SCC. The definition of the first game is rather technical and depends on the special game structure of an SCC. The second and the third games are derived from the well-known notions of α- and β-effectivity for cooperative games without side payments (see Aumann [1961]). The three simple games associated with an SCC reflect, quite in detail, the distribution of power among the various coalitions of voters. Such information enables us to analyze and compare SCCs and is also necessary for solving the converse problem – that of associating "faithful" SCCs with committees, which will be investigated later in this chapter.

Let A be a finite set of m alternatives, $m \geqslant 2$, and let N be a society.

Definition 3.1.1. Let $H: L^N \to 2^A$ be an SCC, and let $x \in A$. A coalition S is *winning for x* (with respect to H) if

$$[R^N \in L^N \text{ and } xR^i y \text{ for all } i \in S \text{ and all } y \in A] \Rightarrow H(R^N) = x$$

(see Notation 2.4.3). The set of all winning coalitions for x is denoted by $W^*(H, x)$ or $W^*(x)$.

Remark 3.1.2. Let $H: L^N \to 2^A$ be an SCC, and let $x \in A$. If $S \in W^*(x)$, then S can enforce x *without* knowing the preferences declared (or possessed) by the members of $N - S$.

Definition 3.1.3. Let $H: L^N \to 2^A$ be an SCC. A coalition S is *winning* (with respect to H) if $S \in W^*(H, x)$ for all $x \in A$ (see Definition 3.1.1). The *first simple game associated with H* is the game $G^*(H) = (N, W^*)$, where $W^* = W^*(H)$ is the set of all winning coalitions with respect to H.

Remark 3.1.4. Let $H: L^N \to 2^A$ be an SCC. Then $G^*(H)$ satisfies the monotonicity property (2.6.1). Also, because $m \geqslant 2$, $G^*(H)$ is proper (see (2.6.2)).

Definition 3.1.5. Let $H: L^N \to 2^A$ be an SCC, and let $x \in A$. A coalition S is α-*effective for* x (with respect to H) if there exists $Q^S \in L^S$ such that for all $R^{N-S} \in L^{N-S}$, $H(Q^S, R^{N-S}) = x$. The set of all α-effective coalitions for x is denoted by $W_\alpha(H, x)$ or $W_\alpha(x)$.

Remark 3.1.6. Let $H: L^N \to 2^A$ be an SCC, and let $x \in A$. If $S \in W_\alpha(x)$, then, again, S can enforce x *without* knowing the preferences declared (or possessed) by the members of $N - S$. However, the computational effort needed in order to check whether or not a coalition T belongs to $W_\alpha(x)$ is much greater than that needed in order to check whether or not $T \in W^*(x)$ (see Definition 3.1.1). On the other hand, coalitions in $W_\alpha(x) - W^*(x)$ can hardly be qualified as "ineffective" for x.

Definition 3.1.7. Let $H: L^N \to 2^A$ be an SCC. A coalition S is α-*winning* (with respect to H) if $S \in W_\alpha(H, x)$ for all $x \in A$ (see Definition 3.1.5). The *second simple game associated with* H is the game $G_\alpha(H) = (N, W_\alpha)$, where $W_\alpha = W_\alpha(H)$ is the set of all α-winning coalitions.

Remark 3.1.8. Let $H: L^N \to 2^A$ be an SCC. $G_\alpha(H)$ satisfies the monotonicity property (2.6.1). Also, since $m \geqslant 2$, $G_\alpha(H)$ is proper (see (2.6.2)). Furthermore, $W_\alpha(H) \supset W^*(H)$ (see Definitions 3.1.3 and 3.1.7).

We now introduce the notion of β-effectivity in order to define the third game.

Definition 3.1.9. Let $H: L^N \to 2^A$ be an SCC, and let $x \in A$. A coalition S is β-*effective for* x (with respect to H) if for every $R^{N-S} \in L^{N-S}$ there exists $Q^S \in L^S$ such that $H(Q^S, R^{N-S}) = x$. The set of all β-effective coalitions for x is denoted by $W_\beta(H, x)$ or $W_\beta(x)$.

Remark 3.1.10. Let $H: L^N \to 2^A$ be an SCC, and let $x \in A$. Further, let $S \in W_\beta(x)$ (see Definition 3.1.9). We observe that S may be unable to obtain x without knowing the preferences declared by the members of $N - S$. Thus, if the choice of a profile $R^N \in L^N$ is made by a *secret* ballot, then β-effectivity considerations are inappropriate. However, in open voting processes, β-effectivity arguments may be valid. Another situation in which β-effectivity considerations may appear is the following. Let T be a coalition. When T contemplates what can be achieved by $N - T$, it might happen that it cannot rule out the possibility that $N - T$

will attain an alternative for which it is only β-effective (because, even if T decides to keep its action secret, it may not be completely sure that its choice will not be discovered by the members of $N-T$).

Definition 3.1.11. Let $H: L^N \to 2^A$ be an SCC. A coalition S is β-*winning* (with respect to H) if $S \in W_\beta(H,x)$ for all $x \in A$ (see Definition 3.1.9). The *third simple game associated with* H is the game $G_\beta(H) = (N, W_\beta)$, where $W_\beta = W_\beta(H)$ is the set of all β-winning coalitions.

Remark 3.1.12. Let $H: L^N \to 2^A$ be an SCC. $G_\beta(H) = (N, W_\beta)$ satisfies the monotonicity property (2.6.1), and $W_\beta \supset W_\alpha$ (see Definition 3.1.7). However, G_β may *not* be proper, as is shown by the following example.

Example 3.1.13. Let $A = \{x_1, x_2, x_3, x_4\}$, and let $N = \{1, 2, 3, 4\}$. We define an SCF $F: L^N \to A$ (see Remark 2.4.2) by the following rules. Let $u = (1, 0, 0, 0)$, and let $M = M(R^N; u)$ be the rank-order method that is determined by u (see Example 2.3.12). (Note that M is simply the rule of choice by plurality voting.) Let $R^N \in L^N$. If $|M(R^N)| = 1$, then we define $F(R^N) = M(R^N)$. If $|M(R^N)| \geqslant 2$, let (i, j) be the first pair, in the lexicographic order, of indices of members of $M(R^N)$. Further, let (u, v) be the remaining (ordered) pair in $\{1, 2, 3, 4\}$. We consider now the set

$$S(R^N) = \{h \mid h \in N \text{ and } x_u R^h x_v\} \tag{3.1.1}$$

and define $F(R^N) = x_i$ if $|S(R^N)|$ is odd, and $F(R^N) = x_j$ if $|S(R^N)|$ is even. Before we proceed to investigate several properties of F, we illustrate its definition by computing its value for the following profile:

R^1	R^2	R^3	R^4
x_3	x_3	x_4	x_4
x_1	x_1	x_2	x_2
x_2	x_2	x_1	x_1
x_4	x_4	x_3	x_3

$M(R^N) = \{x_3, x_4\}$. Hence, $(i, j) = (3, 4)$, $(u, v) = (1, 2)$, and

$$S(R^N) = \{h \mid h \in N \text{ and } x_1 R^h x_2\} = \{1, 2\}$$

Thus, $|S(R^N)|$ is even, and therefore $F(R^N) = x_4$.

We now turn to examine some properties of F. It is clear that F is Paretian and anonymous (see Definitions 2.3.4 and 2.3.6). We claim that F is also monotonic (see Definition 2.3.11). Indeed, let $R^N \in L^N$, and let $F(R^N) = x_i$. If $R_1^N \in L^N$ is obtained from R^N by an improvement of the position of x_i (see Definition 2.3.10), then we have to show that $F(R_1^N) = x_i$. If $|M(R_1^N)| = 1$, then $M(R_1^N) = x_i$, and therefore $F(R_1^N) = x_i$. If

$|M(R_1^N)| \geqslant 2$, then $M(R_1^N) = M(R^N)$. Also, $S(R^N) = S(R_1^N)$ (see (3.1.1)). Hence, again, $F(R^N) = F(R_1^N)$.

We conclude by showing that $G_\beta(F) = (4, 2)$ (see Definitions 2.6.4 and 3.1.11). It is sufficient to prove that $T = \{1, 2\}$ is β-effective (see Definition 3.1.9) for x_4. Let $R^{N-T} \in L^{N-T}$. As the reader can easily verify, there exists $Q^T \in L^T$ such that $F(Q^T, R^{N-T}) = x_4$.

Remark 3.1.14. Let F be the SCF of Example 3.1.13, and let $R^N \in L^N$ satisfy $t_1(R^1) = t_1(R^2) = x_1$, and $t_1(R^3) = t_1(R^4) = x_2$ (see Notation 2.1.8). Denote $T_1 = \{1, 2\}$ and $T_2 = \{3, 4\}$. Then $T_1 \cap T_2 = \varnothing$, but in the game $g(F, R^N)$ (see Definition 2.5.1) there exists *no* pair of strategies (Q^{T_1}, Q^{T_2}), where $Q^{T_i} \in L^{T_i}$, $i = 1, 2$, such that Q^{T_1} is a best reply to Q^{T_2} and vice versa. This peculiar phenomenon is due entirely to the discrete character of our model. Indeed, Aumann [1961, Section 9] has proved that the preceding phenomenon is impossible in a cooperative game (in normal form) that is the *mixed* extension of a finite game.

Remark 3.1.15. Let $H: L^N \to 2^A$ be an SCC. If $G_\beta(H)$ is not proper (see Definitions 3.1.11 and 2.6.4), then it is not suitable, from a formal point of view, to serve as a measure of the power distribution induced by H. (See also Remarks 3.1.10 and 3.1.14.)

Remark 3.1.16. Let $H: L^N \to 2^A$ be an SCC. If H is anonymous (see Definition 2.3.6), then $G^*(H)$, $G_\alpha(H)$, and $G_\beta(H)$ (see Definitions 3.1.3, 3.1.7, and 3.1.11, respectively) are symmetric (see Definition 2.6.4). If H is neutral (see Definition 2.3.8), then $W^*(H) = W^*(H, x)$, $W_\alpha(H) = W_\alpha(H, x)$, and $W_\beta(H) = W_\beta(H, x)$ for all $x \in A$. Also, if H is Paretian (see Definition 2.3.4), then $N \in W^*(H)$.

We shall now compute the simple games associated with two well-known SCCs.

Example 3.1.17. Let $u = (1, 0, \ldots, 0)$, and let $M: L^N \to 2^A$ be the rank-order method that is specified by u; that is, M is the rule of choice by plurality voting (see Remark 2.3.13). M is anonymous (see Remark 2.3.14). Hence, by Remark 3.1.16, all the games associated with M are symmetric. Moreover, as the reader can easily verify, $G^*(M) = G_\alpha(M) = G_\beta(M) = (n, [n/2] + 1)$ (see Definition 2.6.4) for all n and all $m \geqslant 2$.

Example 3.1.18. Let $u = (m-1, m-2, \ldots, 0)$, and let $B = B(m, n)$ be the rank-order method that is specified by u. Then B is the well-known Borda rule (see Remark 2.3.13). B is anonymous. Therefore, by Remark 3.1.16, all the games associated with B are symmetric. We show first the following.

Claim 3.1.19. $G^*(B(m,n)) = (n, k(m,n))$, where

$$k(m,n) = [n(m-1)/m]+1$$

Indeed, let $S \subset N$, with $|S| = k$ (see Notation 2.1.7). Then $S \in W^*(B(m,n))$ (see Definition 3.1.3) if and only if

$$k(m-1) > k(m-2) + (n-k)(m-1) \tag{3.1.2}$$

(see Definition 3.1.1 and Remark 3.1.16). Clearly, (3.1.2) is satisfied if and only if $k \geqslant k(m,n)$, which proves our claim.

Next we show the following.

Claim 3.1.20. $G_\alpha(B(m,n)) = (n, k_\alpha(m,n))$, where

$$k_\alpha(m,n) = [(2(m-1)n+1)/(3m-2)]+1$$

First we prove the following lemma.

Lemma 3.1.21. *Let $S \subset N$, with $|S| = k \geqslant 2$, and let $A^* \subset A$, with $|A^*| = r$. Then there exists $P^S \in L^S$ such that for all $y \in A^*$, $w(P^S, y) \leqslant k(r-1)/2 + 1/2$, where $w(\cdot, \cdot)$ is defined by (2.3.5) (see Example 2.3.12).*

It is useful to introduce at this point the following notation.

Notation 3.1.22. Let $R \in L$. By $_*R$ we denote the reverse order to R. (Thus, for $x, y \in A$, x_*Ry if and only if yRx.)

Proof of Lemma 3.1.21. Clearly, we may assume that $S = N$ and $A^* = A$. Thus, $k = n$ and $r = m$. We distinguish the following possibilities:

(a) n is even.

Let $R \in L$, and let $P^i = R$ for $1 \leqslant i \leqslant n/2$, and $P^i = {}_*R$ for $n/2 < i \leqslant n$ (see Notation 3.1.22). As the reader can easily verify, $w(P^N, y) = n(m-1)/2$ for all $y \in A$.

(b) n is odd.

Thus, $n \geqslant 3$ and $n = 3 + n^*$, where n^* is even (or zero). By the proof of (a), it is sufficient to prove (b) for $n = 3$. We further distinguish the following subcases:

(b.1) m is odd.

Let $A = \{x_1, \ldots, x_m\}$, $P^1 = (x_1, x_2, \ldots, x_m)$, $P^2 = (x_m, x_{m-2}, \ldots, x_1, x_{m-1}, x_{m-3}, \ldots, x_2)$, and $P^3 = (x_{m-1}, x_{m-3}, \ldots, x_2, x_m, x_{m-2}, \ldots, x_1)$. Then $w(P^1, x_i) + w(P^2, x_i) + w(P^3, x_i) = 3(m-1)/2$ for $i = 1, \ldots, m$. Indeed, for $i = m - 2t$ (where $0 \leqslant t \leqslant (m-1)/2$),

$$w(P^1, x_i) + w(P^2, x_i) + w(P^3, x_i) = m - (m - 2t) + m - (t + 1)$$
$$+ m - ((m-1)/2 + t + 1) = 3(m-1)/2$$

Similarly, for $i = m - 2t - 1$ (where $0 \leqslant t \leqslant (m-3)/2$),

$$w(P^1, x_i) + w(P^2, x_i) + w(P^3, x_i) = m - (m - 2t - 1)$$
$$+ m - ((m-1)/2 + t + 1) + m - (t + 1)$$
$$= 3(m-1)/2$$

(b.2) m is even.

Let $A = \{x_1, \ldots, x_m\}$, $P^1 = (x_1, x_2, \ldots, x_m)$, $P^2 = (x_m, x_{m-2}, \ldots, x_2, x_{m-1}, x_{m-3}, \ldots, x_1)$, and $P^3 = (x_{m-1}, x_{m-3}, \ldots, x_1, x_m, x_{m-2}, \ldots, x_2)$. Then, for $i = m - 2t$ (where $0 \leqslant t \leqslant m/2 - 1$),

$$w(P^1, x_i) + w(P^2, x_i) + w(P^3, x_i) = m - (m - 2t) + m - (t + 1)$$
$$+ m/2 - (t + 1) = 3(m-1)/2 - 1/2$$

and for $i = m - 1 - 2t$ (where $0 \leqslant t \leqslant m/2 - 1$),

$$w(P^1, x_i) + w(P^2, x_i) + w(P^3, x_i) = m - (m - 1 - 2t) + m/2 - (t + 1)$$
$$+ m - (t + 1) = 3(m-1)/2 + 1/2$$

We are now able to prove Claim 3.1.20.

Proof of Claim 3.1.20. Let $S \subset N$, with $|S| = k$, let $T = N - S$, and let $x \in A$. If $S \in W_\alpha$, then there exists $P^S \in L^S$ such that for all $Q^T \in L^T$, $B(P^S, Q^T) = x$. We may assume that $t_1(P^i) = x$ for all $i \in S$ (see Notation 2.1.8). The remaining $m - 1$ alternatives get together $k(m-1)(m-2)/2$ points. Hence, there exists $y \in A$, $y \neq x$, such that

$$w(P^S, y) \geqslant [(k(m-2) - 1)/2] + 1$$

Since k is an integer, the inequalities

$$w(P^S, x) > w(P^S, y) + w(Q^T, y) \quad \text{for all } Q^T \in L^T$$

imply that

$$k(m-1) > k(m-2)/2 + 1/2 + (n-k)(m-1) \tag{3.1.3}$$

Inequality (3.1.3) implies that $k \geqslant [(2(m-1)n + 1)/(3m - 2)] + 1$. Thus, $k_\alpha(m, n) \geqslant [(2(m-1)n + 1)/(3m - 2)] + 1$.

In order to prove the reverse inequality, assume that $k \geqslant [(2(m-1)n + 1)/(3m - 2)] + 1$. We shall prove that $S \in W_\alpha(x) = W_\alpha$. Clearly, we may assume that $n \geqslant 2$. Hence, $k \geqslant 2$. Thus, by Lemma 3.1.21, there exists $P^S \in L^S$ such that $w(P^S, y) \leqslant k(m-2)/2 + 1/2$ for all $y \in A - \{x\}$, and $t_1(P^i) = x$ for all $i \in S$ (see Notation 2.1.8). By (3.1.3),

$B(P^S, Q^T) = x$ for all $Q^T \in L^T$. Thus, $S \in W_\alpha$, and the reverse inequality is proved.

We conclude the discussion of Example 3.1.18 with a computation of $G_\beta(B(m, n))$.

Claim 3.1.23. $G_\beta(B(m, n)) = (n, [n/2] + 1)$.

Let $G_\beta(B(m, n)) = (n, k_\beta(m, n))$. Clearly, $k_\beta(m, n) \geqslant [n/2] + 1$. Thus, we have to show the reverse inequality. Assume first that n is odd. Let $n = 2k + 1$, $S = \{1, 2, \ldots, k + 1\}$, $T = N - S$, and $x \in A$. By Remark 3.1.16, it is sufficient to prove that S is β-effective for x. Let $R^T \in L^T$. We have to show that there exists $Q^S \in L^S$ such that $B(Q^S, R^T) = x$. For $i = 2, \ldots, k + 1$, let $Q^i = {}_*R^{k+i}$ (see Notation 3.1.22), and let $Q^1 \in L$ satisfy $t_1(Q^1) = x$. As the reader can easily verify, $B(Q^S, R^T) = x$. The proof when n is even is similar.

Remark 3.1.24. Similar investigations of the strategical properties of Borda's rule are contained in Gardner [1977] and Moulin [1982a].

Let $H: L^N \to 2^A$ be an SCC. It follows from Remarks 3.1.2, 3.1.6, and 3.1.10 that if the three notions of effectiveness we have discussed coincide for H, then the analysis of H, from the strategical and informational pionts of view, is greatly simplified. This observation leads to the following investigation.

Definition 3.1.25. Let $H: L^N \to 2^A$ be an SCC. H is *tight* if for every $x \in A$, $W_\beta(x) = W^*(x)$ (see Definitions 3.1.1 and 3.1.9).

Remark 3.1.26. If an SCC H is tight, then $G^*(H) = G_\beta(H)$ (see Definitions 3.1.3 and 3.1.11). Hence, in particular, $G_\beta(H)$ *is proper* (see Remark 3.1.12). The converse is not true, as is shown by the following example.

Example 3.1.27. Let $A = \{x_1, x_2, x_3\}$, and let $N = \{1, 2\}$. We define an SCF $F: L^N \to A$ by the following rule. For $R^N \in L^N$, $F(R^N)$ is the first alternative in $B(R^N)$, where $B(\cdot)$ is the Borda rule (see Example 3.1.18). As the reader can easily verify, $G^*(F) = G_\beta(F) = (2, 2)$. However, $\{1\} \in W_\beta(x_1)$, whereas $\{1\} \notin W^*(x_1)$.

The following simple result is true.

Theorem 3.1.28. *Let* $H: L^N \to 2^A$ *be an SCC. If* $G^*(H)$ *is strong* (see (2.6.3)), *then* H *is tight.*

Proof: Let $x \in A$, and let S be a coalition. If $S \notin W^*(x)$, then we have to show that $S \notin W_\beta(x)$. Let $T = N - S$. Since $G^*(H)$ is strong and $S \notin W^*(H)$ (see Definition 3.1.3), $T \in W^*(H)$. Let $a \in A - \{x\}$ (recall that $|A| \geqslant 2$), and let $P^T \in L^T$ satisfy $t_1(P^i) = a$ for all $i \in T$ (see Notation 2.1.8). Then $H(Q^S, P^T) = a$ for all $Q^S \in L^S$. Thus, $S \notin W_\beta(x)$.

We conclude this section with the following lemma and corollary.

Lemma 3.1.29. *Let $H: L^N \to 2^A$ be a monotonic SCC. If H depends only on top alternatives (i.e., there exists a function $h: A^N \to 2^A$ such that $H(R^N) = h(t_1(R^1), \ldots, t_1(R^n))$ for every $R^N = (R^1, \ldots, R^n)$ in L^N), then H is tight.*

Proof: Let $x \in A$, and let $S \subset N$, $S \notin W^*(x)$. We have to show that $S \notin W_\beta(x)$. Assume, on the contrary, that $S \in W_\beta(x)$. Since $S \notin W^*(x)$, there exists $R^N \in L^N$ such that $x R^i y$ for all $i \in S$ and all $y \in A$, and $H(R^N) \neq x$. Now, since $S \in W_\beta(x)$, there exists $Q^S \in L^S$ such that $H(Q^S, R^T) = x$, where $T = N - S$. Since H is monotonic, we may assume that $t_1(Q^i) = x$ for all $i \in S$ (see Definition 2.3.11). Hence, by assumption, $H(R^N) = H(Q^S, R^T) = x$, which is the desired contradiction.

Corollary 3.1.30. Choice by plurality voting (see Example 3.1.17) is tight. (We remark that this corollary can also be deduced directly from Remarks 3.1.16 and 2.3.14.)

3.2   Representations of simple games by SCCs

Definition 3.2.1. Let $G = (N, W)$ be a proper simple game (see (2.6.2)), and let A be a set of m alternatives, $m \geqslant 2$. An SCC $H: L^N \to 2^A$ is a *representation of G of order m* if $G^*(H) = G$ (see Definition 3.1.3).

Intuitively, if $G = (N, W)$ is a committee that has to choose a (nonempty) subset of a set A of alternatives, then a representation $H: L^N \to 2^A$ is a feasible choice procedure that reflects "faithfully" the distribution of power in G. We shall now investigate the problem of the existence of representations. It turns out that the solution to this problem is closely related to the investigation of cores of simple games. We start with the following definitions.

Let $G = (N, W)$ be a proper simple game, and let A be a finite set of m alternatives, $m \geqslant 2$.

Definition 3.2.2. Let $R^N \in L^N$. An alternative $c \in A$ is a *Condorcet alternative* (with respect to R^N) if $c \operatorname{Dom}(R^N) x$ for all $x \in A - \{c\}$ (see Definition 2.6.8).

Let $R^N \in L^N$. If c is a Condorcet alternative with respect to R^N, then it is a natural candidate for choice by the committee G. This remark leads to the following definition.

Definition 3.2.3. An SCC $H: L^N \to 2^A$ satisfies the *Condorcet condition* if for every $R^N \in L^N$, if c is a Condorcet alternative with respect to R^N (see Definition 3.2.2), then $H(R^N) = c$.

We also need the following definition.

Definition 3.2.4. An SCC $H: L^N \to 2^A$ is *core-inclusive* if for every $R^N \in L^N$, $H(R^N) \supset C(N, W, A, R^N)$ (see Definition 2.6.8).

The following interesting result is true.

Theorem 3.2.5. *Let $H: L^N \to 2^A$ be an SCC. If H satisfies the Condorcet condition and is core-inclusive* (see Definitions 3.2.3 and 3.2.4, respectively), *then H is a tight representation of G* (see Definitions 3.2.1 and 3.1.25).

Proof: Let $G^*(H) = (N, W^*(H))$ (see Definition 3.1.3). We shall prove first that $W \subset W^*(H)$. Let $S \in W$. If $R^N \in L^N$, $x \in A$, and $x R^i y$ for all $i \in S$ and all $y \in A$, then x is a Condorcet alternative with respect to R^N (see Definition 3.2.2). Since H satisfies the Condorcet condition, $H(R^N) = x$. Hence, $S \in W^*(H, x)$ (see Definition 3.1.1). Since x is arbitrary, $S \in W^*(H)$. We shall complete the proof by showing that $W_\beta(H, x) \subset W$ for all $x \in A$ (see Definition 3.1.9). Indeed, let $x \in A$. If $S \notin W$, let $T = N - S$. Further, let $y \in A - \{x\}$ and $R^T \in L^T$ satisfy $t_1(R^i) = y$ for all $i \in T$ (see Notation 2.1.8). Then, for every $Q^S \in L^S$, $y \in C(Q^S, R^T)$ (see Definition 2.6.8). Since H is core-inclusive, $y \in H(Q^S, R^T)$ for all $Q^S \in L^S$. Hence, $S \notin W_\beta(H, x)$.

Remark 3.2.6. An SCC $H: L^N \to 2^A$ is a *core extension* (for the game $G = (N, W)$ and the set of alternatives A) if $H(R^N) = C(N, W, A, R^N)$ whenever $C(N, W, A, R^N) \neq \emptyset$. By Theorem 3.2.5, every core extension for G is a tight representation of G.

Remark 3.2.6 implies that if $C(N, W, A, R^N) \neq \emptyset$ for all $R^N \in L^N$, then $C(N, W, A, \cdot)$ is a tight representation of G. This important result will now be formulated in detail. First we need the following definition and lemmata.

Definition 3.2.7. Let the SCC $H: L^N \to 2^A$ be a representation of G (see Definition 3.2.1). H is a *faithful* representation of G if $\mathrm{SYM}(H) = \mathrm{SYM}(G)$ (see Definitions 2.3.5 and 2.6.6).

Lemma 3.2.8. *If* $H: L^N \to 2^A$ *is a representation of* G, *then* $\mathrm{SYM}(H) \subset \mathrm{SYM}(G)$ *(see Definitions 2.3.5 and 2.6.6).*

Proof: Let π be a permutation of N such that $\pi \notin \mathrm{SYM}(G)$. There exists $S \in W$ such that $\pi(S) = T \notin W$. Since H is a representation of G, $G^*(H) = G$. Hence, $T \notin W^*(H)$ (see Definition 3.1.3). Thus, there exist $b \in A$ and $R^N \in L^N$ such that $t_1(R^i) = b$ for all $i \in T$ and $H(R^N) \neq \{b\}$. Let $Q^N = (R^{\pi(1)}, \ldots, R^{\pi(n)})$. If $j \in S$, then $\pi(j) \in T$. Hence, for $j \in S$, $t_1(Q^j) = t_1(R^{\pi(j)}) = b$. Since $S \in W^* = W^*(H)$, $H(Q^N) = b$. Denote $\tau = \pi^{-1}$. Then

$$H(Q^{\tau(1)}, \ldots, Q^{\tau(n)}) = H(R^N) \neq \{b\}$$

Thus, $\pi^{-1} \notin \mathrm{SYM}(H)$, and therefore $\pi \notin \mathrm{SYM}(H)$.

Lemma 3.2.9. *Let* $\pi \in \mathrm{SYM}(G)$, $R^N \in L^N$, *and* $Q^N = (R^{\pi(1)}, \ldots, R^{\pi(n)})$. *Then, for all* $x, y \in A$, $x \, \mathrm{Dom}(R^N) \, y$ *if and only if* $x \, \mathrm{Dom}(Q^N) \, y$.

The proof is left to the reader.

Corollary 3.2.10. Assume that for every $R^N \in L^N$, $C(N, W, A, R^N) = C(R^N) \neq \varnothing$. Then $C(\cdot)$ is a tight and faithful (see Definition 3.2.7) representation of G. Furthermore, $C(\cdot)$ is neutral and strongly monotonic (see Definitions 2.3.8 and 2.3.15), and if G is non-null (i.e., $N \in W$), then $C(\cdot)$ is also Paretian (see Definition 2.3.4).

Proof: $C(\cdot)$ is faithful by Lemmata 3.2.8 and 3.2.9. The rest of the proof is left to the reader.

Remark 3.2.11. If G is weak (see (2.6.4)), then $C(N, W, A, \cdot)$ is a representation of G for every A such that $2 \leqslant |A| < \infty$ (see Remark 2.6.11). If G has no veto players, then $C(N, W, A, \cdot)$ is a representation of G if and only if $2 \leqslant |A| < \nu(G)$ (see Theorem 2.6.14).

Let $G = (N, W)$ be a proper simple game without veto players. Before we proceed to construct representations of G of every order, we prove an impossibility theorem for representations. Our theorem is a corollary of the following lemma.

Lemma 3.2.12. *Let* $G = (N, W)$ *be a proper simple game, and let* A *be a set of* m *alternatives,* $m \geqslant 2$. *Further, let* $H: L^N \to 2^A$ *be a strongly monotonic SCC (see Definition 2.3.15). If* H *is a representation of* G, *then* $H(R^N) \subset C(N, W, A, R^N)$ *for all* $R^N \in L^N$.

Proof: Let $R^N \in L^N$, and let $x \notin C(R^N)$. There exist $y \in A$, $y \neq x$, and $S \in W$ such that $y R^i x$ for all $i \in S$. Let $B = \{x, y\}$, and let $Q^N = R^N(B)$ (see

Notation 2.4.12). Clearly, $yQ^i z$ for all $i \in S$ and for all $z \in A$. Since H is a representation of G, $S \in W^*(H)$ (see Definitions 3.1.3 and 3.2.1). Hence, $H(R^N(B)) = y$. By Lemma 2.4.13, $x \notin H(R^N)$. Thus, $H(R^N) \subset C(R^N)$.

Our impossibility theorem for representations is as follows.

Theorem 3.2.13. *Let* $G = (N, W)$ *be a proper simple game without veto players. If* $m \geqslant \nu(G)$ *(see Definition 2.6.12), then* G *has no strongly monotonic representation of order* m.

Proof: Theorem 2.6.14 and Lemma 3.2.12.

We now present three generalizations of the core that are defined for every simple game and any number of alternatives. These generalizations will yield tight and "nice" representations of simple games.

Let $G = (N, W)$ be a non-null (i.e., $N \in W$) proper simple game, and let A be a set of m alternatives, $m \geqslant 2$. Our first example is due to Gillies [1959].

Example 3.2.14. Let $R^N \in L^N$, and let $x, y \in A$, $x \neq y$; x *majorizes* y (with respect to R^N), written $x \, \mathrm{Maj}(R^N) y$, if (a) $x \, \mathrm{Dom}(R^N) y$ (see Definition 2.6.8) and (b) if $w \, \mathrm{Dom}(R^N) x$, then $w \, \mathrm{Dom}(R^N) y$. The set of unmajorized alternatives is denoted by $\mathrm{GIL}(R^N) = \mathrm{GIL}(N, W, A, R^N)$. Since $\mathrm{Maj}(R^N)$ is transitive, $\mathrm{GIL}(R^N) \neq \emptyset$ for all $R^N \in L^N$. Thus, $\mathrm{GIL}(\cdot)$ is an SCC. Clearly, $\mathrm{GIL}(\cdot)$ satisfies the Condorcet condition and is core-inclusive (see Definitions 3.2.3 and 3.2.4). Hence, by Theorem 3.2.5, $\mathrm{GIL}(\cdot)$ is a tight representation of G. Since G is non-null, $\mathrm{GIL}(\cdot)$ is Paretian (see Definition 2.3.4). Also, it can be verified that $\mathrm{GIL}(\cdot)$ is neutral and faithful (see Definitions 2.3.8 and 3.2.7). However, $\mathrm{GIL}(\cdot)$ is *not* monotonic, as is shown by the following example.

Example 3.2.15. Let $G = (4, 3)$ (see Definition 2.6.4), and let $A = \{a, b, c\}$. Consider the situations

R^1	R^2	R^3	R^4
a	a	c	b
b	b	b	c
c	c	a	a

and

Q^1	Q^2	Q^3	Q^4
a	a	c	b
b	b	a	c
c	c	b	a

Then Q^N is obtained from R^N by an improvement of the position of a (see Definition 2.3.10), and GIL$(R^N) = \{a, b\}$ and GIL$(Q^N) = \{a, c\}$. Hence, GIL$(\cdot)$ is not monotonic (see Definition 2.3.11).

Remark 3.2.16. We may have GIL$(R^N) \neq C(R^N)$ even if $m < \nu(G)$. Indeed, in Example, 3.2.15, $\nu(G) = 4$ and $m = |A| = 3$, whereas GIL$(Q^N) \neq C(Q^N)$ $(C(Q^N) = a)$.

GIL$(\cdot)$ has the following monotonicity property.

Definition 3.2.17. Let $H: L^N \to 2^A$ be an SCC. H is *weakly monotonic* if it satisfies the following:

> If $R^N \in L^N$, $x \in H(R^N)$, and R_1^N is obtained from R^N by an improvement of the position of x (see Definition 2.3.10), then $x \in H(R_1^N)$. $\qquad(3.2.1)$

Clearly, a monotonic SCC (see Definition 2.3.11) is weakly monotonic.

Remark 3.2.18. GIL$(\cdot)$ is weakly monotonic.

Remark 3.2.19. Intuitively, GIL$(\cdot)$ is the "largest" solution that is based solely on the binary relation Dom$(\cdot)$. More precisely, if $U = U(R^N)$ is a solution that is derived from Dom(R^N), and if $x, y \in A$ and x Maj$(R^N)y$, then we should have $y \notin U(R^N)$.

Our next two examples are ad hoc constructions.

Example 3.2.20. Let $R^N \in L^N$, and let $x \in A$. We denote

$$\text{Dom}^{-1}(x) = \text{Dom}^{-1}(x, R^N) = \{y \mid y \in A \text{ and } y \text{ Dom}(R^N)x\} \qquad(3.2.2)$$

We define

$$\theta(R^N) = \{x \in A \mid |\text{Dom}^{-1}(x)| \leqslant |\text{Dom}^{-1}(y)| \text{ for all } y \in A\}$$

(see (3.2.2)). Clearly, $\theta(\cdot)$ is a core extension (see Remark 3.2.6). Hence, $\theta(\cdot)$ is a tight representation of G. Furthermore, it can be verified that $\theta(\cdot)$ is Paretian, neutral, monotonic, and faithful.

Remark 3.2.21. $\theta(R^N) \subset \text{GIL}(R^N)$ for all $R^N \in L^N$ (see Examples 3.2.14 and 3.2.20). Since $\theta(\cdot)$ is monotonic, it has a monotonic selection (see Lemma 2.4.8). Hence, GIL$(\cdot)$ has a monotonic selection. (For an example of a weakly monotonic SCC that admits no monotonic selection, the reader is referred to Example 5.7 in Peleg [1979]. Notice that a weakly monotonic SCC is called "monotonic" in Peleg [1979].)

Example 3.2.22. For $1 \leqslant k \leqslant n$ we denote

$$W_k = \{ S \mid S \in W \text{ and } |S| \geqslant k \}$$

Now let $R^N \in L^N$. We define

$$C_k(R^N) = C(N, W_k, A, R^N)$$

(see Definition 2.6.8). Further, let

$$h = h(R^N) = \min\{ k \mid C_k(R^N) \neq \varnothing \} \tag{3.2.3}$$

Clearly, $C_n(R^N) \neq \varnothing$. Hence, $h(R^N)$ is well defined. Let $\sigma(R^N) = C_h(R^N)$, where $h = h(R^N)$ (see (3.2.3)). Clearly, $\sigma(\cdot)$ is a core extension (see Remark 3.2.6). Hence, $\sigma(\cdot)$ is a tight representation of G. Furthermore, it can be verified that $\sigma(\cdot)$ is Paretian, neutral, monotonic, and faithful.

We remark that $\sigma(R^N)$ may not be a subset of $\mathrm{GIL}(R^N)$. Indeed, this is shown by the following example.

Example 3.2.23. Let $G = (5, 3)$, and let $A = \{a, b, c, d\}$. Consider the following situation:

R^1	R^2	R^3	R^4	R^5
a	c	b	d	d
b	a	c	a	c
c	b	a	b	a
d	d	d	c	b

As the reader can easily verify, $\mathrm{GIL}(R^N) = \{a, b, c\}$. Now, $h(R^N) = 4$. Hence, $\sigma(R^N) = \{a, c, d\}$.

Remark 3.2.24. The SCCs θ and σ have already been used to analyze voting in committees. Indeed, they appear, among other solution concepts, in McKelvey and Ordeshook [1979]. The reader is referred to that study for further discussion and references concerning Examples 3.2.20 and 3.2.22.

Whereas the Condorcet condition (see Definition 3.2.3) is well known, core inclusion (see Definition 3.2.4) is a new condition. The following example serves to illuminate the role of core inclusion.

Example 3.2.25. Let $G = (8, 7)$ (see Definition 2.6.4), and let $|A| = 3$. By Theorem 2.6.14, $C(R^N) \neq \varnothing$ for all $R^N \in L^N$. We define an SCC $H: L^N \to 2^A$ by the following rule. Let $R^N \in L^N$. An alternative $x \in A$ is *blocked* (relative to R^N) if

$$|\{i \mid i \in N \text{ and } t_3(R^i) = x\}| \geqslant 3$$

(see Notation 2.1.8). We now define $H(R^N)$ to be the set of unblocked alternatives in $C(R^N)$. As the reader can easily verify, $H(R^N) \neq \varnothing$ for all $R^N \in L^N$. Thus, H satisfies the Condorcet condition. Also, H is Paretian, anonymous, and neutral, and $G^*(H) = G$ (see Definition 3.1.3). Thus, H is a faithful representation of G. Furthermore, one can show that H has the SPA property (see Definition 2.3.24). Hence, H is strongly monotonic (see Lemma 2.3.25). However, as the reader can easily verify, $G_\alpha(H) = (8, 6)$ (see Definition 3.1.7). Thus, H is a representation of G that has all the desirable properties except tightness (see Definition 3.1.25). Clearly, H violates core inclusion.

We conclude this section with the following remark.

Remark 3.2.26. Lemma 3.1.29 can be used to construct tight representations of committees that violate the Condorcet condition (see Theorem 4.11 and Example 4.12 in Peleg [1980]).

3.3   Representations by SCFs

Let $G = (N, W)$ be a committee (i.e., a proper simple game), and let A be a set of alternatives. The choice of a single alternative out of A can be achieved in two different ways. The first is to choose an SCC $H: L^N \to 2^A$ that is a "nice" representation of G. Then, if $R^N \in L^N$ and $H(R^N)$ contains more than one alternative, an alternative $a \in H(R^N)$ is chosen by some ad hoc method like a chance mechanism or a second round of voting. The second possibility to guarantee the choice of a single alternative is to choose an SCF $F: L^N \to A$ that is, itself, a "nice" representation of G. In this section we shall investigate the second approach. Because some of our results are of a negative type (i.e., impossibility results for single-valued representations), our investigation serves as a (partial) justification for the first approach.

We start with the following lemma.

Lemma 3.3.1. *Let A be a set of alternatives, and let N be a society. Further, let $F: L^N \to A$ be an SCF. If $G^*(F)$ is dictatorial (see Definitions 3.1.3 and 2.6.4), then F is dictatorial (see Definition 2.4.10). Conversely, if F is dictatorial and the range of F, $R(F) = A$, then $G^*(F)$ is dictatorial.*

Proof: Assume first that $G^*(F) = (N, W^*(F))$ is dictatorial, and let j be a dictator for $G^*(F)$. Thus, $\{j\} \in W^*(F)$. Let $R^N \in L^N$. By Definitions 3.1.1 and 3.1.3, $F(R^N) = t_1(R^j)$ (see Notation 2.1.8). Hence, j is a dictator for F.

Assume now that F is dictatorial and $R(F)=A$ (see Notation 2.4.9). Let j be a dictator for F. By Definition 2.4.10, $F(R^N)=t_1(R^j)$ for every $R^N \in L^N$. Hence, $\{j\} \in W^*(F)$. Since $G^*(F)=(N, W^*(F))$ is monotonic and proper (see Remark 3.1.4), j is a dictator for $G^*(F)$.

Invoking Theorem 2.4.11, we obtain the following impossibility result for representation by SCFs. First we introduce the following definition.

Definition 3.3.2. A simple game $G=(N, W)$ is *essential* if it is non-null (i.e., $N \in W$) and nondictatorial (see Definition 2.6.4).

Corollary 3.3.3. Let $G=(N, W)$ be an essential simple game (see Definition 3.3.2), and let A be a set of m alternatives, $m \geqslant 3$. Then there exists no strongly monotonic SCF $F: L^N \to A$ that is a representation of G (see Definitions 2.3.15 and 3.2.1).

Proof: Let $F: L^N \to A$ be a strongly monotonic SCF. Assume, on the contrary, that F is a representation of G. Since G is non-null, $N \in W$. Hence, $N \in W^*(F)$. It follows now from Definition 3.1.3 that $R(F)=A$. Hence, by Theorem 2.4.11, F is dictatorial. Therefore, by Lemma 3.3.1, $G^*(F)$ is dictatorial. Since $G^*(F)=G$, we have reached the desired contradiction.

Remark 3.3.4. Corollary 3.3.3 should be compared with Corollary 3.2.10, Remark 3.2.11, and Theorem 3.2.13.

We now turn to investigate the existence of representations of simple games by SCFs. We start with the following remarks.

Remark 3.3.5. Let N be a society, and let A be a set of alternatives. If $H: L^N \to 2^A$ is an SCC and the SCF $F: L^N \to A$ is a selection from H (see Definition 2.4.4), then for every $x \in A$, $W^*(H, x) \subset W^*(F, x)$, $W_\alpha(H, x) \subset W_\alpha(F, x)$, and $W_\beta(H, x) \subset W_\beta(F, x)$ (see Definitions 3.1.1, 3.1.5, and 3.1.9).

Remark 3.3.6. Let $G=(N, W)$ be a simple game, and let A be a set of alternatives. If $H: L^N \to 2^A$ is a representation of G and F is a selection from H, then F may *not* be a representation of G. For example, let $G=(n, n)$ (see Definition 2.6.4). Then PAR$(\cdot)$ (see Definition 2.3.3) is a representation of G. However, $F(R^N)=t_1(R^1)$ is a selection from PAR$(\cdot)$ that is not a representation of G (provided that $n \geqslant 2$).

We shall now show the existence of representations by "nice" SCFs. Let $G=(N, W)$ be a proper simple game, and let A be a finite set of m alternatives, $m \geqslant 2$. We need the following definition.

Definition 3.3.7. A coalition $S \subset N$ is *blocking* if $N - S \notin W$. We denote by $B = B(G)$ the set of all blocking coalitions.

Remark 3.3.8. A winning coalition is blocking; that is, $B \supset W$ (see (2.6.2)). Also, G is strong if and only if $B = W$ (see (2.6.3)).

Lemma 3.3.9. *Let* $H: L^N \to 2^A$ *be an SCC that satisfies the Condorcet condition and that is core-inclusive (see Definitions 3.2.3 and 3.2.4). If* $F = F(H, R)$ *is a selection from H according to the order R (see Definition 2.4.6), then F is a tight representation of G that satisfies the Condorcet condition. Furthermore, if H is faithful (respectively monotonic, Paretian), then F is faithful (respectively monotonic, Paretian).*

Proof: Let $s = t_1(R)$ (see Notation 2.1.8). Our first claim is

$$W^*(F, s) = W_\beta(F, s) = B \tag{3.3.1}$$

(see Definition 3.3.7).

Indeed, let $S \in B$. Choose $Q^S \in L^S$ such that $t_1(Q^i) = s$ for all $i \in S$. If $T = N - S$, then $s \in C(Q^S, R^T)$ for all $R^T \in L^T$ (see Definition 2.6.8). Since H is core-inclusive, $s \in H(Q^S, R^T)$ for all $R^T \in L^T$. Hence, $F(Q^S, R^T) = s$ for all $R^T \in L^T$, and $S \in W^*(F, s)$. Now, if $S \notin B$, then $T = N - S$ is in $W = W^*(H)$ (see Theorem 3.2.5). Let $a \in A - \{s\}$. Since $W^*(F, a) \supset W^*(F) \supset W^*(H)$ (see Remark 3.3.5), $T \in W^*(F, a)$. Hence, $S \notin W_\beta(F, s)$. (We note that (3.3.1) implies that s plays the role of the status quo.)

Our second claim is

$$W^*(F, x) = W_\beta(F, x) = W \quad \text{for all } x \in A - \{s\} \tag{3.3.2}$$

Indeed, let $x \in A - \{s\}$. $W^*(F, x) \supset W^*(F) \supset W^*(H) = W$. On the other hand, if $S \notin W$, then $T = N - S$ is, by (3.3.1) in $W^*(F, s)$. Hence, $S \notin W_\beta(F, x)$.

It follows now from (3.3.1) and (3.3.2) that F is a tight representation of G. Also, by Remark 2.4.7, $SYM(F) \supset SYM(H)$, and by Lemma 3.2.8, $SYM(F) \subset SYM(G)$. Hence, if H is faithful (i.e., $SYM(H) = SYM(G)$), then F is faithful. Our last two claims follow from Lemma 2.4.8 and Remark 2.4.5, respectively.

Remark 3.3.10. It follows now from Lemma 3.3.9 and Examples 3.2.14, 3.2.20, and 3.2.22 that G has tight, faithful, monotonic, and Paretian representations (which also satisfy the Condorcet condition) of every order $m \geqslant 2$. (*Henceforth in this chapter, by a "representation," we mean a "representation by an SCF."*)

We turn now to investigate the problem of the existence of representations of simple games by neutral SCFs. The solution to this problem depends crucially on the structure of the symmetry group of the game for which we look for representations. It will be helpful to recall the following simple property of permutations.

Remark 3.3.11. Let G be a simple game, and let $\pi \in \text{SYM}(G)$ (see Definition 2.6.6). Then π can be represented (in essentially a unique way) as a product of disjoint cycles (see Biggs and White [1979]): $\pi = c_1 \ldots c_k$. If γ_i is the length of the cycle c_i, $i = 1, \ldots, k$, then we shall denote by $d(\pi)$ the greatest common divisor (GCD) of $\gamma_1, \ldots, \gamma_k$ (i.e., $d(\pi) = (\gamma_1, \ldots, \gamma_k)$).

The following notation will be useful in the sequel.

Notation 3.3.12. Let $t \geq 1$ be a natural number. If $t \geq 2$, we denote by m.p.(t) the minimum prime number that divides t. For $t = 1$, we define m.p.$(1) = \infty$.

The following lemma illustrates the restrictions, which are imposed by the symmetry group of a game, on possible representations of the game by neutral SCFs.

Lemma 3.3.13. *Let $G = (N, W)$ be a proper simple game* (see Definition 2.6.4), *and let $\pi \in \text{SYM}(G)$. If $d(\pi) \geq 2$ (see Remark 3.3.11) and $t \geq$ m.p.$(d(\pi))$ (see Notation 3.3.12), then there exists no SCF F that satisfies the following: (a) F is a representation of G of order t (see Definition 3.2.1), (b) F is Paretian (see Definition 2.3.4), (c) F is faithful (see Definition 3.2.7), and (d) F is neutral (see Definition 2.3.8).*

Proof: Let $c_1, \ldots, c_k$ be the (disjoint) cycles of π, and let γ_i be the length of c_i for $i = 1, \ldots, k$. Since $t \geq$ m.p.$(d(\pi))$, there exists a prime number p such that $t \geq p$ and $p \mid \gamma_i$ (i.e., p divides γ_i) for $i = 1, \ldots, k$. Without loss of generality we may assume that

$$c_i = (h_{i-1}p + 1, h_{i-1}p + 2, \ldots, h_i p) \quad \text{for } i = 1, \ldots, k$$

where $0 = h_0 < h_1 < \cdots < h_k = n/p$. Now let A be a set of t alternatives (i.e., $|A| = t$), and let an SCF $F: L^N \to A$ be a Paretian and faithful representation of G. We have to show that F is not neutral. So let $R = (x_1, \ldots, x_p, x_{p+1}, \ldots, x_t)$ be a linear order of A (i.e., $R \in L$). Now let σ be a permutation of A that is given (in the *cyclic form*) by $\sigma = (x_1, \ldots, x_p)(x_{p+1}) \ldots (x_t)$. We now consider the following profile $R^N \in L^N$: for $i = 1, \ldots, n$, let $R^i = \sigma^{i-1}(R)$ (see Section 2.3). Since F is Paretian, $F(R^N) \in \{x_1, \ldots, x_p\}$. By our construction, $\sigma(R^i) = R^{\pi(i)}$ for $i = 1, \ldots, n$. Since we have assumed that F is faithful, $F(R^{\pi(1)}, \ldots, R^{\pi(n)}) = F(R^N)$. Hence,

$$F(\sigma(R^1), \ldots, \sigma(R^n)) = F(R^{\pi(1)}, \ldots, R^{\pi(n)}) = F(R^N) \neq \sigma(F(R^N))$$

and F is *not* neutral (see Definition 2.3.8).

Remark 3.3.14. Let $N = \{1, \ldots, n\}$ be a society, and let Γ be a group of permutations of N. We define

$$\delta^*(\Gamma) = \min\{\text{m.p.}(d(\pi)) \mid \pi \in \Gamma\}$$

(see Notations 3.3.11 and 3.3.12). If G is a simple game, then we denote $\delta^*(G) = \delta^*(\text{SYM}(G))$ (see Definition 2.6.6). Let G be a proper simple game, and let $t \geqslant \delta^*(G)$. By Lemma 3.3.13, there exists no Paretian, neutral, and faithful representation of G of order t. In particular, if $G = (n, k)$ (i.e., G is symmetric; see Definition 2.6.4), then G has no Paretian, neutral, and anonymous representations of order $t \geqslant \text{m.p.}(n)$. Thus, if n is even, then G has no Paretian, neutral, and anonymous representations at all.

We shall now prove a lemma that is very useful for constructions of neutral representations (by SCFs). We start with the following remark.

Remark 3.3.15. Let $w = [w^1, \ldots, w^n]$ be an n-tuple of real numbers. A permutation π of $N = \{1, \ldots, n\}$ is a *symmetry* of w if

$$w_\pi = [w^{\pi(1)}, \ldots, w^{\pi(n)}] = w$$

The group of all symmetries of w will be denoted by $\text{SYM}(w)$.

The following notation will be useful in the sequel.

Notation 3.3.16. Let $w = [w^1, \ldots, w^n]$ be an n-tuple of real numbers. For a set $S \subset \{1, \ldots, n)$ we denote $w(S) = \sum_{i \in S} w^i$.

Lemma 3.3.17. *Let $w = [w^1, \ldots, w^n]$ be an n-tuple of non-negative integers and let $s = w(N)$, where $N = \{1, \ldots, n\}$ (see Notation 3.3.16). Furthermore, let $2 \leqslant t < \text{m.p.}(s)$ (see Notation 3.3.12), and let A be a set of t alternatives. Then there exists an SCF $F^* = \phi(w, A)$ from L^N to A that is monotonic, Paretian, and neutral and that satisfies, in addition, $\text{SYM}(F^*) \supset \text{SYM}(w)$ (see Definition 2.3.5 and Remark 3.3.15).*

Proof: We prove the lemma by induction on t. Let $A = \{x_1, \ldots, x_t\}$ be a set of t alternatives, and let $R^N \in L^N$. For each $x \in A$, let

$$S(x) = \{j \mid j \in N \text{ and } t_1(R^j) = x\}$$

(see Notation 2.1.8). Now let

$$A_1 = \{x \mid x \in A \text{ and } w(S(x)) \geqslant w(S(y)) \text{ for all } y \in A\} \qquad (3.3.3)$$

(see Notation 3.3.16). Since $t < \text{m.p.}(s)$, we have $|A_1| < t$ (see Notation 2.1.7). If $|A_1| = 1$, then we define $F^*(R^N) = \phi(w, A; R^N) = x$, where $A_1 = \{x\}$. If $|A_1| > 1$, then we may define, by our induction hypothesis,

$$F^*(R^N) = \phi(w, A; R^N) = \phi(w, A_1; R^N \mid A_1)$$

(see Notation 2.2.4). Clearly, for $t=2$, our construction yields an SCF that possesses all the required properties. For $t>2$, Pareto optimality follows directly from (3.3.3). Monotonicity and neutrality of F^* may be verified by direct inspection. Finally, $\text{SYM}(F^*) \supset \text{SYM}(w)$ is obvious.

Remark 3.3.18. Let $N = \{1, \ldots, n\}$ be a society, and let Γ be a group of permutations of N. We denote by $T_1, \ldots, T_k$ the *orbits* of Γ. (Two voters i and j belong to the same orbit if there exists a permutation $\pi \in \Gamma$ such that $\pi(i) = j$; see Biggs and White [1979].) Clearly, $T_1, \ldots, T_k$ is a partition of N. The GCD of $|T_1|, \ldots, |T_k|$ (see Notation 2.1.7) is denoted by $d(\Gamma)$. If $G = (N, W)$ is a simple game, then we denote $d(G) = d(\text{SYM}(G))$ (see Definition 2.6.6).

We are now ready to state the following theorem.

Theorem 3.3.19. *Let $G = (N, W)$ be a strong and proper simple game, and let $d = d(G)$ (see Remark 3.3.18). If $2 \leqslant t < m.p.(d)$ (see Notation 3.3.12) and A is a set of t alternatives, then there exists an SCF $F: L^N \to A$ that is a Paretian, monotonic, faithful, and neutral representation of G (see Definitions 2.3.4, 2.3.11, 3.2.7, 3.2.8, and 3.2.1, respectively). Furthermore, F satisfies the Condorcet condition (see Definition 3.2.3).*

Our proof of Theorem 3.3.19 relies on the following lemma.

Lemma 3.3.20. *Let $t_1, \ldots, t_k$ be non-negative integers. If the GCD $(t_1, \ldots, t_k) = 1$, then there exists a natural number T with the following property: Every natural number $t \geqslant T$ can be written as a linear combination of $t_1, \ldots, t_k$ with non-negative integer coefficients (i.e., $t = \sum_{i=1}^{k} a_i t_i$, where $a_1, \ldots, a_k$ are non-negative integers).*

We postpone the proof of Lemma 3.3.20 and start with the proof of Theorem 3.3.19.

Proof of Theorem 3.3.19. We distinguish the following possibilities:

(a) $d(G) = 1$.

Let $T_1, \ldots, T_k$ be the orbits of $\text{SYM}(G)$, and let $t_i = |T_i|$, $i = 1, \ldots, k$. Now let $t \geqslant 2$ be a natural number. By Lemma 3.3.20, there exists a prime number $p > t$ such that $p = \sum_{i=1}^{k} a_i t_i$, where $a_1, \ldots, a_k$ are non-negative integers. Now let $w = [w^1, \ldots, w^n]$ be defined by $w^j = a_i$ for all $j \in T_i$ and for $i = 1, \ldots, k$. Note that $w(N) = p$ (see Notation 3.3.16). We are now able to define an SCF $F: L^N \to A$ by the following rules. Let $R^N \in L^N$. If there exists a Condorcet alternative x (with respect to R^N; see

Definition 3.2.2), then we define $F(R^N) = x$. Otherwise, (i.e., if there is no Condorcet alternative), we define $F(R^N) = \phi(w, A; R^N)$ (see Lemma 3.3.17). Clearly, F satisfies the Condorcet condition (see Definition 3.2.3). Hence, because G is strong (see (2.6.3)), $G^*(F) = G$; that is, F is a representation of G (see Definitions 3.1.3 and 3.2.1). It follows now from the definition of F and Lemma 3.3.17 that F is Paretian and monotonic. The neutrality of F follows from the following two facts: (1) $\phi(w, A)$ is neutral (see Lemma 3.3.17). (2) If $R^N \in L^N$ and x is a Condorcet alternative with respect to R^N (see Definition 3.2.2), and if σ is a permutation of A, then $\sigma(x)$ is a Condorcet alternative with respect to $\sigma(R^N) = (\sigma(R^1), \ldots, \sigma(R^N))$ (see Section 2.3). To see that F is faithful, we notice first the following two facts: (1) If $R^N \in L^N$ and x is a Condorcet alternative with respect to R^N, and if $\pi \in \mathrm{SYM}(G)$ (see Definition 2.6.6), then x is a Condorcet alternative with respect to $R_\pi^N = (R^{\pi(1)}, \ldots, R^{\pi(n)})$. (2) $\mathrm{SYM}(\phi(w, A)) \supset \mathrm{SYM}(w)$ (see Lemma 3.3.17), and, obviously, $\mathrm{SYM}(w) \supset \mathrm{SYM}(G)$. Hence, $\mathrm{SYM}(F) \supset \mathrm{SYM}(G)$. Since F is a representation of G, $\mathrm{SYM}(G) \supset \mathrm{SYM}(F)$ (see Lemma 3.2.8). Thus, F is faithful, and the proof of case (a) is complete.

(b) $d(G) > 1$.

Let, again, $T_1, \ldots, T_k$ be the orbits of $\mathrm{SYM}(G)$, and let $t_i = |T_i|$, $i = 1, \ldots, k$. Furthermore, let $\theta_i = t_i / d(G)$, $i = 1, \ldots, k$. Then, $(\theta_1, \ldots, \theta_k) = 1$. Now let $2 \leqslant t < \mathrm{m.p.}(d)$. By Lemma 3.3.20, there exists a prime number $p > d$ such that $p = \sum_{i=1}^k a_i \theta_i$, where $a_1, \ldots, a_k$ are non-negative integers. Thus, $s = pd = \sum_{i=1}^k a_i t_i$. Since $\mathrm{m.p.}(s) = \mathrm{m.p.}(pd) = \mathrm{m.p.}(d)$, it follows that $t < \mathrm{m.p.}(s)$. Hence, we can now construct an SCF $F: L^N \to A$ that satisfies all the properties of the theorem, in exactly the same way as in case (a).

Proof of Lemma 3.3.20. Since $(t_1, \ldots, t_k) = 1$, there exist integers $z_1, \ldots, z_k$ such that $\sum_{i=1}^k z_i t_i = 1$. Let $Q = \{i \mid 1 \leqslant i \leqslant k \text{ and } z_i < 0\}$, and let $s = -\sum_{i \in Q} z_i t_i$. Now define $T = s(s - 1)$. If $t \geqslant T$, then $t = qs + r$, where $q \geqslant s - 1$ and $0 \leqslant r < s$. Hence,

$$t = -q \sum_{i \in Q} z_i t_i + r \sum_{i=1}^k z_i t_i = \sum_{i \in Q} (r - q) z_i t_i + \sum_{i \notin Q} r z_i t_i$$

Thus, $(r - q) z_i \geqslant 0$ for $i \in Q$, and $r z_i \geqslant 0$ for $i \notin Q$, and the proof is complete.

Remark 3.3.21. Lemma 3.3.20 is a well-known result in the theory of numbers. We have proved it here for the sake of completeness.

Remark 3.3.22. Let $N = \{1, \ldots, n\}$ be a society, and let Γ be a group of permutations of N. We denote $\delta_*(\Gamma) = $ m.p. $(d(\Gamma))$ (see Remark 3.3.18). We remark that $\delta_*(\Gamma) \leqslant \delta^*(\Gamma)$ (see Remark 3.3.14). (Indeed, let $T_1, \ldots, T_k$ be the orbits of Γ. If $\pi \in \Gamma$ is a product of disjoint cycles $c_1, \ldots, c_h$, then each T_i, $i = 1, \ldots, k$, is a union of some subset of $c_1, \ldots, c_h$. Hence, if $p \mid d(\pi)$ (see Remark 3.3.11), then $p \mid d(\Gamma)$.) For a simple game G, we denote $\delta_*(G) = \delta_*(\text{SYM}(G))$ (see Definition 2.6.6). Clearly, $\delta_*(G) \leqslant \delta^*(G)$. We shall now show that there exists a strong and proper simple game G that satisfies $\delta^*(G) > \delta_*(G)$. First we need the following lemma.

Lemma 3.3.23. *If* $G = (N, W)$ *is a proper and strong simple game, then* $\delta^*(G) \geqslant 3$ (see Remark 3.3.14 and Definition 2.6.4).

Proof: Let $G = (N, W)$ be a proper and strong simple game. Now let π be a permutation of N such that m.p. $(d(\pi)) = 2$ (see Remark 3.3.11 and Notation 3.3.12). We shall prove that $\pi \notin \text{SYM}(G)$. Indeed, let $c_1, \ldots, c_k$ be the disjoint cycles of π. Then each c_i, $i = 1, \ldots, k$, is of even length. Hence, n is even, and there exists a coalition S of $n/2$ players such that $\pi(S) = N - S$. Because G is proper and strong, exactly one of the coalitions S or $N - S$ is in W. Hence, $\pi \notin \text{SYM}(G)$.

Remark 3.3.24. Let $G = (N, W)$ be a proper simple game. Following Isbell [1957], we call G *homogeneous* if $\text{SYM}(G)$ is *transitive* (i.e., if it has only one orbit). Clearly, if G is homogeneous, then $\delta_*(G) = $ m.p.(n) (see Remark 3.3.22). Hence, if $G = (N, W)$ is a homogeneous, proper, and strong simple game and n is even, then $\delta_*(G) = 2 < 3 \leqslant \delta^*(G)$ (see Lemma 3.3.23). Now, by Theorem 1 in Isbell [1957], there exist infinitely many homogeneous, proper, and strong simple games with even numbers of players.

We shall now introduce an important class of simple games, namely, the weighted majority games, for which the structure of the symmetry group can be easily determined. We start with the following definition.

Definition 3.3.25. Let $G = (N, W)$ be a simple game. G is a *weighted majority* game if there exist a *quota* $q > 0$ and *weights* $w^1 \geqslant 0, \ldots, w^n \geqslant 0$ such that

$$S \in W \Leftrightarrow w(S) \geqslant q$$

(see Notation 3.3.16). The $(n + 1)$-tuple $[q; w^1, \ldots, w^n]$ is called a representation of G (*not to be confused with Definition 3.2.1*), and we write $G = [q; w^1, \ldots, w^n]$.

The following notation will be useful in the sequel.

Notation 3.3.26. Let T be a finite set. We denote by $\Sigma(T)$ the group of all permutations of T. (Thus, e.g., if $N = \{1, \ldots, n\}$, then $\Sigma(N) = S_n$ (see Definition 2.3.6).)

Lemma 3.3.27. *Let $G = (N, W)$ be a weighted majority game. If $T_1, \ldots, T_k$ are the orbits of* SYM(G) *(see Definition 2.6.6), then* SYM(G) *is the direct product $\Sigma(T_1) \times \cdots \times \Sigma(T_k)$ (see Notation 3.3.26).*

Proof: We observe first that if $[q_i; w_i^1, \ldots, w_i^n]$, $i = 1, \ldots, h$, are representations of G (see Definition 3.3.25), then the (vectorial) sum $\Sigma_{i=1}^h [q_i; w_i^1, \ldots, w_i^n]$ is a representation of G. Second, we notice that if $\pi \in$ SYM(G) and $[q; w^1, \ldots, w^n]$ is a representation of G, then $[q; w^{\pi(1)}, \ldots, w^{\pi(n)}]$ is a representation of G. Now let $[q; w^1, \ldots, w^n]$ be a representation of G. It follows from the two preceding remarks that

$$[q_*; w_*^1, \ldots, w_*^n] = \Sigma\{[q; w^{\pi(1)}, \ldots, w^{\pi(n)}] \mid \pi \in \text{SYM}(G)\}$$

is a representation of G. Clearly, if i and j are in the same orbit of G, then $w_*^i = w_*^j$. Hence, the transposition (i, j) is a symmetry of G and the proof is complete.

Remark 3.3.28. Lemma 3.3.27 is a well-known result in game theory; its proof is included here only for the sake of completeness.

Corollary 3.3.29. If $G = (N, W)$ is a weighted majority game, then $\delta^*(G) = \delta_*(G)$ (see Remarks 3.3.14 and 3.3.22).

Corollary 3.3.30. Let $G = (N, W)$ be a proper and strong weighted majority game, and let A be a set of t alternatives. Then there exists a Paretian and neutral SCF $F: L^N \to A$ that is a faithful representation of G if and only if $2 \leqslant t < \delta^*(G)$.

Proof: Remark 3.3.14, Theorem 3.3.19, and Corollary 3.3.29.

Remark 3.3.31. Let $G = (N, W)$ be a proper simple game. If G is strong, then G has a Paretian, monotonic, neutral, and faithful representation of order 2. (Indeed, if $A = \{a, b\}$ is a set of two alternatives, then we can define an SCF $F: L^N \to A$ by the following rule. Let $R^N \in L^N$. If $\{i \mid aR^ib\} \in W$, let $F(R^N) = a$, and let $F(R^N) = b$ otherwise. Then F has all the previously mentioned properties.) We shall prove now that if G is not strong, then the foregoing claim is not true.

Lemma 3.3.32. *Let $G = (N, W)$ be a proper simple game. If G is not strong, then it has no monotonic and neutral representation of order 2.*

Proof: Let $A = \{a, b\}$ be a set of two alternatives, and let $F: L^N \to A$ be a neutral and monotonic SCF. We have to show that F is not a representation of G. Now, since G is not strong, there exists a coalition S such that both S and $N - S$ are blocking (see Definition 3.3.7). Let $R^N \in L^N$ satisfy aR^ib for $i \in S$, and bR^ia for $i \in N - S$. If $F(R^N) = a$, then (since F is monotonic and neutral) $S \in W^*(F)$ (see Definition 3.1.3 and Remark 3.1.16). Similarly, if $F(R^N) = b$, then $N - S \in W^*(F)$. Hence, in both cases, $W^*(F) \neq W$. Thus, F is not a representation of G.

The following definition is needed for further investigation of representations (by SCFs) of non-strong simple games.

Definition 3.3.33. Let $G = (N, W)$ be a simple game. A partition $P = \{S_1, \ldots, S_h\}$ of N is a *blocking partition* if each of the coalitions $S_1, \ldots, S_h$ is blocking (see Definition 3.3.7). The *blocking coefficient* of G, $\beta(G)$, is defined by

$$\beta(G) = \max\{|P| \mid P \text{ is a blocking partition}\} \tag{3.3.4}$$

Remark 3.3.34. If G is a strong simple game (see (2.6.3)), then $\beta(G) = 1$. If $G = (n, k)$ is a symmetric simple game (see Definition 2.6.4), then $\beta(G) = [n/b]$, where $b = n - k + 1$ is the size of a *minimal* blocking coalition. We are now able to state and prove the following theorem.

Theorem 3.3.35. *Let $G = (N, W)$ be a proper simple game. If $\beta(G) < t < \delta_*(G)$ (see Definition 3.3.33 and Remark 3.3.22) and A is a set of t alternatives, then there exists an SCF $F: L^N \to A$ that is a Paretian, faithful, and neutral representation of G (see Definitions 2.3.4, 3.2.7, 2.3.8, and 3.2.1, respectively). Furthermore, F satisfies the Condorcet condition (see Definition 3.2.3).*

Proof: The proof consists of a modification of the proof of Theorem 3.3.19. As in that proof, we distinguish the following possibilities

    (a) $d(G) = 1$ (see Remark 3.3.18).

Let $T_1, \ldots, T_k$ be the orbits of SYM(G), and let $t_i = |T_i|$, $i = 1, \ldots, k$. Now let $t > \beta(G)$ be a natural number. By Lemma 3.3.20, there exists a prime number $p > t$ such that $p = \sum_{i=1}^k a_i t_i$, where $a_1, \ldots, a_k$ are non-negative integers. Now let $w = [w^1, \ldots, w^n]$ be defined by $w^j = a_i$ for all $j \in T_i$ and for $i = 1, \ldots, k$. Note that $w(N) = p$ (see Notation 3.3.16). We are now able to define an SCF $F: L^N \to A$ by the following rules. Let $R^N \in L^N$. An alternative $b \in A$ is *blocked at R^N* if

$$\{i \mid i \in N \text{ and } aR^i b \text{ for all } a \in A\}$$

is blocking in G (see Definition 3.3.7). Denote by A^* the set of all *unblocked* alternatives at R^N. Because $t > \beta(G)$, $A^* \neq \varnothing$ (see Definition 3.3.33). Now, if there exists a Condorcet alternative x (with respect to R^N; see Definition 3.2.2), then we define $F(R^N) = x$. Otherwise (i.e., if there is no Condorcet alternative), we define $F(R^N) = \phi(w, A^*; R^N)$ (see Lemma 3.3.17). We shall prove now that $W^*(F) = W$ (see Definition 3.1.3). Indeed, let $S \in W$. Since F (by its construction) satisfies the Condorcet condition (see Definition 3.2.3), $S \in W^*(F)$. Also, if $T \notin W$, then $N - T$ can block every alternative. Hence, since for each $R^N \in L^N$, $F(R^N)$ is unblocked at R^N, $T \notin W^*(F)$. Thus, F is a representation of G (see Definition 3.2.1) that satisfies the Condorcet condition. Following the proof (of case (a)) of Theorem 3.3.19, the reader can verify that F is a Paretian, neutral, and faithful representation of G.

(b) $d(G) > 1$.

The proof of this case is left to the reader.

Remark 3.3.36. The SCF F that is constructed in the proof of Theorem 3.3.35 is a *tight* representation of the game G (see Definition 3.1.25).

Remark 3.3.37. Let $G = (n, k)$ be a proper and symmetric simple game, and let $b = n - k + 1$. If $[n/b] < t < \text{m.p.}(n)$, then G has a Paretian, anonymous, and neutral representation of order t (see Remarks 3.3.34 and 3.3.24 and Theorem 3.3.35). Thus, for example, if $G = (7, 6)$, then $b = 2$, $[7/2] = 3$, and m.p.$(7) = 7$. Hence, $(7, 6)$ has representations with the aforementioned properties of orders 4, 5, and 6.

Example 3.3.38. Let $G = [3; 2, 1, 1]$ (see Definition 3.3.25). Then, as the reader can easily verify, $\beta(G) = 2$ and $\delta_*(G) = \infty$. Hence, by Theorem 3.3.35, G has a Paretian, neutral, and faithful representation of every order $t \geqslant 3$.

CHAPTER 4

Strong and dynamic representations

Let $G = (N, W)$ be a proper simple game. A strong representation of G is, intuitively, a representation of G that is not distorted by manipulation of preferences by coalitions of voters. In the first two sections of this chapter we investigate the existence of strong representations of committees. First we note that every representation of a nontrivial committee of an order greater than or equal to 3 is manipulable (see Lemma 4.1.1). Then we argue that an SCF $F: L^N \to A$ that is not distorted by manipulation of preferences by coalitions should have the following property: For each $R^N \in L^N$, the game $g(F, R^N)$ has a strong e.p. Q^N such that $F(Q^N) = F(R^N)$. An SCF is *exactly and strongly consistent* if it has the foregoing property. We observe that if $F: L^N \to A$ is an exactly and strongly consistent SCF, then for each $R^N \in L^N$, $F(R^N)$ is in the β-core of $g(F, R^N)$ (see Lemma 4.1.25). Also, F satisfies a strong tightness condition (see Corollary 4.1.29).

Let, again, $G = (N, W)$ be a proper simple game. The *capacity* of G, $\mu(G)$, is the maximum order of an exactly and strongly consistent representation of G. We prove that if G has no vetoers, then $\mu(G) < \nu(G)$ (see Theorem 4.1.34). Then we show that if G is strong (and essential), then $\mu(G) = 2$ (see Theorem 4.1.35). In Section 4.2 we prove that if G is weak, then $\mu(G) = \infty$ (see Theorem 4.2.1).

The discussion in the first two sections leads to the following problem: Is it possible to increase capacities of committees by using dynamic voting procedures? In Section 4.3 we provide a negative answer to the foregoing question. Our main result can be described as follows. Let N be a society, and let A be a set of m alternatives, $m \geq 2$. A voting procedure $K: 2^A \times L^N \to A$ is exactly and strongly consistent in the limited sense if for every $B \in 2^A$ such that $|B| = 2$, $K(B, \cdot)$ is exactly and strongly consistent. Let $K: 2^A \times L^N \to A$ be a binary and Paretian voting procedure. Because K is binary, it has a rationalization $\phi: L^N \to L$ (see Remark 4.3.5). We prove that *K is exactly and strongly consistent in the* limited sense if and only if ϕ satisfies the condition of independence of irrelevant alternatives (see Theorem 4.3.13). This result can be easily translated to a negative result on dynamic representations of committees (see Corollary 4.3.17). It also provides a game theoretic interpretation of Arrow's condition of independence of irrelevant alternatives.

Section 4.4 is devoted to an axiomatic characterization of the core of a simple game. We obtain the following characterization. Let $G = (N, W)$ be a proper simple game. Furthermore, let A be a set of m alternatives, $m \geq 2$, such that $C(N, W, A, R^N) \neq \varnothing$ for all $R^N \in L^N$. We define the core correspondence $C: 2^A \times L^N \rightarrow 2^A$ by $C(B, R^N) = C(N, W, B, R^N \mid B)$. Then the core correspondence $C(\cdot, \cdot)$ is the unique dynamic representation of G that satisfies (1) pairwise rejection, (2) reward for pairwise optimality, (3) neutrality, (4) independence of irrelevant alternatives, and (5) monotonicity (see Remark 4.4.13 and Theorem 4.4.14). Moreover, the foregoing five axioms are independent.

The first three sections of this chapter are based mainly on Peleg [1978b]. The investigation in Section 4.4 has benefited from Pattanaik [1978].

4.1   Consistent SCFs

This section is devoted to an investigation of the problem of manipulability of choice procedures (i.e., representations) of committees. First we show that every nontrivial committee that has to choose one alternative out of a set that contains at least three alternatives has no representative nonmanipulable voting procedure.

Lemma 4.1.1. Let $G = (N, W)$ be an essential simple game (see Definition 3.3.2), and let A be a set of m alternatives, $m \geq 3$. If an SCF $F: L^N \rightarrow A$ is a representation of G (see Definition 3.2.1), then F is manipulable (see Definition 2.5.4).

Proof: Since F is a representation of G, $G^*(F) = (N, W^*(F)) = G$ (see Definition 3.1.3). Hence, since G is essential, $N \in W^*(F)$. Therefore, the range of F, $R(F) = A$. Also, $G^*(F)$ is not dictatorial. By Lemma 3.3.1, F is not dictatorial. Since $|R(F)| \geq 3$, F is manipulable (see Theorem 2.5.5).

Remark 4.1.2. Let $G = (N, W)$ be a simple game, let A be a set of alternatives, and let $F: L^N \rightarrow A$ be a *manipulable* representation of G. Then there exists $R^N \in L^N$ such that R^N is *not* an e.p. of $g(F, R^N)$ (see Definitions 2.5.3 and 2.5.1). We consider now the situation in which R^N is the profile of *true* preferences of the voters in N. The outcome in this case is determined by a play of $g(F, R^N)$. (We assume that R^N is common knowledge. This assumption is acceptable if, for example, the committee has held open and frequent discussions during the period of formation of R^N.) If $g(F, R^N)$ has no e.p., then there is no consistent way of playing $g(F, R^N)$, and F should be rejected. If $g(F, R^N)$ has an e.p., then we inquire whether or not it possesses an *exact* e.p. (i.e., an e.p. $Q^N \in L^N$ such that $F(Q^N) = F(R^N)$). If $g(F, R^N)$ has no exact e.p., then, accepting the dictate of (normative) game theory that games (in normal form) should be resolved by a choice of an e.p., F is not a reliable predictor of the outcome of the voting process that it represents. Hence, again, F should be rejected. Thus, a *necessary* condition for F to be acceptable is that for every $P^N \in L^N$, $g(F, P^N)$ has an exact e.p.

Remark 4.1.2 leads to the following definitions.

Definition 4.1.3. Let N be a society, and let A be a finite set of alternatives. Further, let $F: L^N \to A$ be an SCF, and let $R^N \in L^N$. $Q^N \in L^N$ is an *exact e.p.* of $g(F, R^N)$ (see Definition 2.5.1) if (a) Q^N is an e.p. of $g(F, R^N)$ (see Definition 2.5.3) and (b) $F(Q^N) = F(R^N)$.

Definition 4.1.4. Let N be a society, and let A be a finite set of alternatives. An SCF $F: L^N \to A$ is *exactly consistent* if for every $R^N \in L^N$, $g(F, R^N)$ has an exact e.p. (see Definition 4.1.3).

Remark 4.1.5. Clearly, an SCF $F: L^N \to A$ is exactly consistent if and only if there exists a function $E: L^N \to L^N$ such that (a) for each $R^N \in L^N$, $E(R^N)$ is an e.p. of $g(F, R^N)$ and (b) the composition $F \circ E = F$ (see Definition 4.1.4).

Remark 4.1.6. Let $F: L^N \to A$ be an exactly consistent SCF. Then there may exist $Q^N, R^N \in L^N$ such that Q^N is an e.p. of $g(F, R^N)$ and $F(Q^N) \neq F(R^N)$. Thus, exact consistency of F may not be a sufficient condition for "reliable prediction" of the outcome of the voting process (which is specified by F).

Remark 4.1.7. Let $F: L^N \to A$ be an exactly consistent SCF, and let $R^N \in L^N$. Assume now that R^N itself is an e.p. of $g(F, R^N)$ and that $F(R^N)$ is the unique equilibrium outcome of $g(F, R^N)$. Then, still there may exist (exact) e.p.'s of $g(F, R^N)$ that are different from R^N. For example, even when F is dictatorial (see Definition 2.4.10), if $|A| \geqslant 3$ (see Notation 2.1.7) or $|N| \geqslant 2$, then, as the reader can easily verify, for every $R^N \in L^N$, $g(F, R^N)$ has e.p.'s different from R^N.

Remark 4.1.8. Let $F: L^N \to A$ be an SCF. We conclude from Remark 4.1.7 that it is practically impossible to guarantee "sincere voting" (i.e., the choice of R^N in the voting game $g(F, R^N)$ for every $R^N \in L^N$) by purely strategic considerations. (Other considerations, e.g., ethical considerations, may dictate sincere voting.) Thus, the only part of the sincere situation that may be saved by a theory of strategic voting is the *sincere outcome*. Hence, our approach, which concentrates on establishing the sincere outcome as an equilibrium outcome, is justified.

The existence of exactly consistent representations for (proper) simple games is guaranteed by the following lemma and remark.

Lemma 4.1.9. *Let $G = (N, W)$ be a proper simple game without veto players (see Definition 2.6.4), and let A be a set of m alternatives, $m \geq 2$. If an SCF $F: L^N \to A$ is a representation of G (see Definition 3.2.1), then F is exactly consistent.*

Proof: Let $R^N \in L^N$, and let $x = F(R^N)$. Further, let $Q^N \in L^N$ satisfy $xQ^i y$ for all $y \in A$ and all $i \in N$. Since F is a representation of G, $G^*(F) = G$. Thus, $G^*(F)$ has no veto players. Hence, $N - \{i\} \in W^*(F)$ for every $i \in N$. By monotonicity, $N \in W^*(F)$ (see (2.6.1)). Thus, $F(Q^N) = x$ (see Definition 3.1.1). Furthermore, for every $i \in N$,

$$F(Q^{N-\{i\}}, P^i) = x \quad \text{for all } P^i \in L$$

(see Notation 2.5.2). Thus, Q^N is an exact e.p. of $g(F, R^N)$ (see Definition 4.1.3). ∎

A proof of a more general result is contained in Dutta and Pattanaik [1978].

Remark 4.1.10. Let $G = (N, W)$ be a weak game (see Definition 2.6.4). Then G may have "nice" representations that are *not* exactly consistent (see the next example). However, as we shall prove in the next section, G has always ("nice") exactly consistent representations of every order $m \geq 2$. Hence, the problem of the existence of exactly consistent representations for committees is, actually, solved by Lemma 4.1.9.

Example 4.1.11. Let $G = [3; 2, 1, 1]$ (see Definition 3.3.25). Then G is weak, and player 1 is a vetoer. Let $A = \{x_1, x_2, x_3\}$. By Remark 2.6.11, the core $C(R^N) \neq \varnothing$ for all $R^N \in L^N$. We now define an SCF $F: L^N \to A$ by the following rule. Let $R = (x_1, x_2, x_3)$. Then $F = F(C(\cdot), R)$; that is, for every $R^N \in L^N$, $F(R^N)$ is the first alternative in $C(R^N)$. By Lemma 3.3.9, F is a "nice" representation of G. Now let $R^N \in L^N$ be defined by

$R^1 = (x_3, x_1, x_2)$ and $R^2 = R^3 = (x_2, x_3, x_1)$. Clearly, $C(R^N) = \{x_2, x_3\}$. Hence, $F(R^N) = x_2$. Let $Q^1 = (x_1, x_3, x_2)$ and $S = \{2, 3\}$. Then, as the reader can easily verify, for every $P^S \in L^S$ (see Notation 2.2.1), $F(Q^1, P^S) = x_1$. Since $x_1 R^1 x_2$, $g(F, R^N)$ has no *exact* e.p. Thus, F is *not* exactly consistent.

Remark 4.1.12. From a game theoretic point of view, Lemma 4.1.9 is "uninteresting." Indeed, under the assumptions of that lemma, *every* alternative is always an equilibrium outcome. More precisely, let $F: L^N \to A$ be an SCF. Assume that $G^*(F)$ (see Definition 3.1.3) has not veto players (see Definition 2.6.4). If $a \in A$ and $Q^N(a) \in L^N$ satisfies $t_1(Q^i(a)) = a$ for all $i \in N$ (see Notation 2.1.8), then for every $R^N \in L^N$, $Q^N(a)$ is an e.p. of $g(F, R^N)$ (see Definitions 2.5.3 and 2.5.1), and $F(Q^N(a)) = a$. (See also Remark 3 in Dutta and Pattanaik [1978].) The elimination of "uninteresting" e.p.'s can be achieved by the following strengthening of the notion of an e.p.

Notation 4.1.13. Let K be a finite set. We denote by 2^K the set of all *nonempty* subsets of K.

Notation 4.1.13 generalizes Notation 2.3.1.

Definition 4.1.14. Let $F: L^N \to A$ be an SCF, $R^N \in L^N$, and $M \subset 2^N$, $M \ne \varnothing$ (see Notation 4.1.13). $Q^N \in L^N$ is an *M-e.p.* of $g(F, R^N)$ (see Definition 2.5.1) if for every $S \in M$ and for every $P^S \in L^S$ there exists $i \in S$ such that

$$F(Q^N) R^i F(Q^{N-S}, P^S)$$

(see Notation 2.5.2).

Remark 4.1.15. If $M = M_1 = \{\{i\} \mid i \in N\}$, then an *M*-e.p. is an e.p. according to Definition 2.5.3. An M_1-e.p. is also called a *Nash e.p.* If $M = M_r = \{S \mid S \in 2^N$ and $|S| = r\}$ for some $1 \le r \le n$, then an *M*-e.p. is an *r*-e.p. (see Farquharson [1969]).

Remark 4.1.16. In interpreting Definition 4.1.14, M is to be considered as the set of all coalitions that are allowed to *coordinate* strategies. More precisely, if $S \in M$, then the members of S can jointly choose, using direct or indirect communication, a member of L^S (i.e., a coordinated strategy of S). Thus, an *M*-e.p. is a situation that is stable when only coalitions in M are able to coordinate their choices. The case of unrestricted coordination is particularly interesting. Hence, we introduce the following definition.

Definition 4.1.17. A *strong e.p.* is a 2^N-e.p.

We are now able to generalize Definition 4.1.4.

Definition 4.1.18. Let $F: L^N \to A$ be an SCF, and let $M \subset 2^N$, $M \neq \emptyset$. F is *exactly M-consistent* if for each $R^N \in L^N$, $g(F, R^N)$ has an M-e.p. Q^N (see Definition 4.1.14) such that $F(Q^N) = F(R^N)$. In particular, if F is exactly 2^N-consistent, then F is called *exactly and strongly consistent*.

Let $F: L^N \to A$ be an exactly and strongly consistent SCF. We shall show that for every $R^N \in L^N$, $F(R^N)$ is a "strongly stable" outcome relative to the game $g(F, R^N)$ (see Definition 2.5.1). First we need the following definitions.

Definition 4.1.19. Let $H: L^N \to 2^A$ be an SCC, let $S \in 2^N$, and let $B \in 2^A$. S is *winning for B* if

$$[R^N \in L^N \text{ and } xR^i y \text{ for all } x \in B, y \notin B, \text{ and } i \in S] \Rightarrow H(R^N) \subset B$$

S is *α-effective for B* if there exists $R^S \in L^S$ such that for all $Q^{N-S} \in L^{N-S}$, $H(R^S, Q^{N-S}) \subset B$. S is *β-effective for B* if for every $Q^{N-S} \in L^{N-S}$ there exists $R^S \in L^S$ such that $H(R^S, Q^{N-S}) \subset B$.

Clearly, Definition 4.1.19 consists of a generalization of Definitions 3.1.1, 3.1.5, and 3.1.9.

Notation 4.1.20. Let K be a finite set. We denote by $P(2^K)$ the set of all *nonempty* subsets of 2^K (see Notation 4.1.13).

Definition 4.1.21. Let $H: L^N \to 2^A$ be an SCC. The *first effectivity function* associated with H is the function $E^* = E^*(H): 2^N \to P(2^A)$ (see Notation 4.1.20) defined by

$$E^*(S) = \{B \mid B \in 2^A, \text{ and } S \text{ is winning for } B\} \tag{4.1.1}$$

(see Definition 4.1.19) for each $S \in 2^N$. The *α-effectivity function* associated with H, $E_\alpha = E_\alpha(H): 2^N \to P(2^A)$, is given by

$$E_\alpha(S) = \{B \mid B \in 2^A, \text{ and } S \text{ is α-effective for } B\} \tag{4.1.2}$$

(see Definition 4.1.19) for each $S \in 2^N$. The *β-effectivity function* associated with H, $E_\beta = E_\beta(H): 2^N \to P(2^A)$, is given by

$$E_\beta(S) = \{B \mid B \in 2^A, \text{ and } S \text{ is β-effective for } B\} \tag{4.1.3}$$

(see Definition 4.1.19) for each $S \in 2^N$.

The α-effectivity function was introduced in Moulin and Peleg [1982].

Remark 4.1.22. Let $H: L^N \to 2^A$ be an SCC. Then

$$W^*(H) \supset \{S \mid S \in 2^N \text{ and } E^*(S) = 2^A\} \tag{4.1.4}$$

$$W_\alpha(H) = \{S \mid S \in 2^N \text{ and } E_\alpha(S) = 2^A\} \tag{4.1.5}$$

$$W_\beta(H) = \{S \mid S \in 2^N \text{ and } E_\beta(S) = 2^A\} \tag{4.1.6}$$

(see Definitions 4.1.21, 3.1.3, 3.1.7, and 3.1.11).

Definition 4.1.23. Let N be a society, and let A be a finite set of alternatives. Further, let $E: 2^N \to P(2^A)$, $R^N \in L^N$, $x \in A$, and $B \subset A - \{x\}$. B *dominates* x *via a coalition* S, written $B \, \mathrm{Dom}(R^N, S)x$, if (a) $B \in E(S)$ and (b) $bR^i x$ for all $b \in B$ and all $i \in S$. B *dominates* x, written $B \, \mathrm{Dom}(R^N)x$, if there exists $T \in 2^N$ such that $B \, \mathrm{Dom}(R^N, T)x$. The *core* of A (*with respect to E and R^N*) is the set of undominated alternatives in A and is denoted by $C(E, A, R^N) = C(E, R^N)$.

Remark 4.1.24. Let $H: L^N \to 2^A$ be an SCC, and let $R^N \in L^N$. Then

$$C(E^*, R^N) \supset C(E_\alpha, R^N) \supset C(E_\beta, R^N) \tag{4.1.7}$$

$$C(E^*, A, R^N) \subset C(N, W^*, A, R^N) \tag{4.1.8}$$

$$C(E_\alpha, A, R^N) \subset C(N, W_\alpha, A, R^N) \tag{4.1.9}$$

$$C(E_\beta, A, R^N) \subset C(N, W_\beta, A, R^N) \tag{4.1.10}$$

(see Definitions 4.1.21, 4.1.23, 2.6.8, 3.1.3, 3.1.7, and 3.1.11).
We are now able to state the following lemma.

Lemma 4.1.25. *Let $F: L^N \to A$ be an exactly and strongly consistent SCF, and let $E_\beta = E_\beta(F)$ (see Definition 4.1.21). Then, for every $R^N \in L^N$, $F(R^N) \in C(E_\beta, R^N)$ (see Definition 4.1.23).*

Proof: Let $R^N \in L^N$, and let $x = F(R^N)$. Assume, on the contrary, that $x \notin C(E_\beta, R^N)$. Then there exist $B \subset A - \{x\}$ and $S \in 2^N$ such that $B \in E_\beta(S)$ and $bR^i x$ for all $b \in B$ and all $i \in S$. Because F is exactly and strongly consistent, there exists a strong e.p. Q^N (see Definition 4.1.17) of $g(F, R^N)$ such that $F(Q^N) = x$. Now, since S is β-effective for B, there exists $P^S \in L^S$ such that $F(P^S, Q^{N-S}) = y$, where $y \in B$. By our assumption, $yR^i x$ for all $i \in S$, contradicting the fact that Q^N is a strong e.p.

Corollary 4.1.26. Let $G = (N, W)$ be a proper simple game (see Definition 2.6.4). If an exactly and strongly consistent SCF $F: L^N \to A$ is a representation of G (see Definition 3.2.1), then $F(R^N) \in C(N, W, A, R^N)$ for all $R^N \in L^N$.

Proof: Lemma 4.1.25, statements (4.1.7) and (4.1.8), and Definition 3.2.1.

Applying Lemma 4.1.25, we shall also show that exactly and strongly consistent SCFs (see Definition 4.1.18) satisfy the following strong tightness condition.

Definition 4.1.27. An SCC $H: L^N \to 2^A$ is *strongly tight* if $E^*(S) = E_\beta(S)$ for every $S \in 2^N$ (see Definition 4.1.21).

Remark 4.1.28. A strongly tight SCC is tight (see Definitions 4.1.27 and 3.1.25).

Corollary 4.1.29. Let $F: L^N \to A$ be an SCF. If F is exactly and strongly consistent, then it is strongly tight.

Proof: Let $S \in 2^N$, and let $B \in E_\beta(S)$ (see Definition 4.1.21). We have to show that $B \in E^*(S)$. Thus, let $R^N \in L^N$ satisfy $x R^i y$ for all $x \in B$, $y \in A - B$, and $i \in S$. Since $F(R^N)$ is in $C(E_\beta, R^N)$, $F(R^N) \in B$ (see Lemma 4.1.25 and Definition 4.1.23). Hence, $B \in E^*(S)$ (see Definition 4.1.19).

We conclude our discussion of the definition of exactly and strongly consistent SCFs with the following remark.

Remark 4.1.30. Let $F: L^N \to A$ be an SCF, and let $R^N \in L^N$. A strong e.p. Q^N of $g(F, R^N)$ has the following stability property. Suppose that while the players are communicating with each other in order to coordinate their strategies, the members of some coalition S *have committed themselves publicly* to choose Q^S. Then $T = N - S$ has no possible jointly profitable deviation from Q^T. Hence, any deviation from Q^N can involve only the members of a proper subset of T. Using backward recursion, we conclude that no (jointly profitable) deviation from Q^N is possible.

Clearly, if $g(F, R^N)$ has several strong e.p.'s yielding *different outcomes,* then it is not clear which strong e.p. will be adopted at the end of the communication period. However, if F is exactly and strongly consistent, then there is always a distinguished set of strong e.p.'s, namely, the *exact* strong e.p.'s; and it is our feeling that such e.p.'s have a better chance to be adopted because of nonstrategic (e.g., ethical) considerations. Indeed, if $R^N \in L^N$ and Q^N is a *strong* e.p. of $g(F, R^N)$ such that $F(Q^N) = F(R^N)$, then, according to the foregoing discussion, it takes only one voter (a "zealot of truth") to enforce $F(R^N)$.

We now turn to investigate the existence of exactly and strongly consistent representations of simple games. We start with the following definition.

Definition 4.1.31. Let $G = (N, W)$ be a proper simple game, and let A be a finite set of m alternatives, $m \geq 2$. An SCF $F: L^N \to A$ is a *strong representation* of G (of *order m*) if (a) F is a representation of G (i.e., $G^*(F) = G$; see Definition 3.1.3) and (b) F is exactly and strongly consistent (see Definition 4.1.18).

We now prove the following simple result.

Lemma 4.1.32. *Let $G = (N, W)$ be a simple game. If G is proper, then G has a faithful and monotonic strong representation of order 2* (see Definition 4.1.31).

Proof: Let $A = \{x_1, x_2\}$. Since G is proper, $v(G) \geq 3$ (see (2.6.2) and (2.6.7)). Hence, $C(N, W, A, R^N) \neq \varnothing$ for all $R^N \in L^N$ (see Theorem 2.6.14). Now let $R = (x_1, x_2)$, and consider the SCF $F = F(C(N, W, A, \cdot), R)$ (i.e., $F(R^N)$ is the first alternative in $C(N, W, A, R^N)$ for all $R^N \in L^N$; see Definition 2.4.6). By Lemma 3.3.9, F is a monotonic and faithful representation of G. Furthermore, as the reader can easily verify, R^N is a strong e.p. of $g(F, R^N)$ (see Definitions 4.1.17 and 2.5.1) for every $R^N \in L^N$.

We remark that if G is strong, then (the foregoing) F is also neutral (see Remark 3.3.31).

Lemma 4.1.32 enables us to formulate the following definition.

Definition 4.1.33. Let G be a proper simple game. The *capacity* of G, $\mu(G)$, is defined as follows. If G has a *strong* representation of maximum order m (see Definition 4.1.31), then we define $\mu(G) = m$. Otherwise (i.e., if the orders of the strong representations of G are not bounded), we define $\mu(G) = \infty$.

Thus, the capacity of a committee is the maximum number of alternatives that the members of the committee can deal with simultaneously in a (strongly) consistent way. Hence, it is a (purely combinatorial) measure of the complexity of the choice problems that lead to voting games that possess strong e.p.'s.

We now prove the existence of an upper bound for the capacity of a simple game without veto players.

Theorem 4.1.34. *Let $G = (N, W)$ be a proper simple game. If G has no vetoers, then $\mu(G) < v(G)$.*

Proof: Let A be a finite set of m alternatives, $m \geq 2$. If an SCF $F: L^N \to A$ is a strong representation of G, then, by Corollary 4.1.26, $C(N, W, A, R^N) \neq \emptyset$ for all $R^N \in L^N$. Therefore, by Theorem 2.6.14, $m < \nu(G)$. Hence, we have $\mu(G) < \nu(G)$.

Lemma 4.1.32 and Theorem 4.1.34 determine the capacity of strong simple games.

Theorem 4.1.35. *Let $G = (N, W)$ be a proper and strong game. If G is also essential* (see Definition 3.3.2), *then $\mu(G) = 2$* (see Definition 4.1.33).

Proof: By Lemma 4.1.32, $\mu(G) \geq 2$. Hence, by Theorem 4.1.34, it is sufficient to prove that $\nu(G) \leq 3$. Since G is strong, $W \neq \emptyset$. Let S be a *minimal* winning coalition. If $j \in S$, then $S - \{j\}$ is losing. Hence, since G is strong, $T = (N - S) \cup \{j\} \in W$. Now, since G is nondictatorial, j is not a vetoer (see Remark 2.6.5). Hence, there exists $U \in W$ such that $j \notin U$. Clearly, $S \cap T \cap U = \emptyset$. Thus, $\nu(G) \leq 3$.

4.2   Strong representations of weak games

In this section we present a complete solution to the problem of the existence of strong representations for weak games. Indeed, the following theorem is proved.

Theorem 4.2.1. *Every weak game has monotonic and faithful strong representations of every order greater than or equal to 2.*

Proof: Let $G = (N, W)$ be a weak game (see Definition 2.6.4), and let V be the set of vetoers of G (i.e., $V = \cap \{S \mid S \in W\}$). Clearly, $V \neq \emptyset$. Also, we may assume that $W \neq \emptyset$. Now let A be a set of m alternatives, $m \geq 2$, and let $R_0 = (x_1, \ldots, x_m)$ be a fixed linear order of A (see Definition 2.1.3). We denote $s = x_1$ and $e = x_m$. Clearly, $s \neq e$. We shall define now an SCF $F: L^N \to A$ by the following rules. Let $R^N \in L^N$. We consider the following (auxiliary) simple game $G_a = (N, W_a)$, where

$$W_a = \{S \mid S \subset N \text{ and } S \supset V\}$$

Let

$$B(A, R^N) = \{x \mid x \in C(N, W_a, A, R^N) \text{ and } xR^is \text{ for all } i \in V\}$$

As the reader can easily verify, $B(A, R^N) \neq \emptyset$. Let $f = f(R^N)$ be the first alternative, according to the order R_0, in $B(A, R^N)$. If $f \neq e$, then we define $F(R^N) = f$. If $f = e$, then let $A_* = A - \{e\}$. Furthermore, let $h =$

$h(R^N)$ be the first alternative, according to R_0, in $B(A_*, R^N | A_*)$ (see Notation 2.2.4). We consider now the set

$$S = S(R^N) = \{i \mid i \in N \text{ and } eR^i h\} \tag{4.2.1}$$

and define $F(R^N) = e$ if $S \in W$, and $F(R^N) = h$ if $S \notin W$. The following remark is now in order.

Remark 4.2.2. The foregoing construction of an SCF has the following simple interpretation. The state s, which can be enforced by every vetoer, may be considered to represent the status quo. By unanimous voting, the vetoers can attain every alternative except e; e may be considered as an "emergency state." Indeed, it takes a winning coalition to ratify the choice of e.

We shall now prove that $W^*(F) = W$ (see Definition 3.1.3). Clearly, $W^*(F) \supset W$. Now let $S \notin W$. Consider a profile $R^N \in L^N$ that satisfies $t_1(R^i) = e$ and $t_2(R^i) = s$ for $i \in S$, and $t_1(R^i) = s$ for $i \in N - S$ (see Notation 2.1.8). If $S \supset V$, then $f(R^N) = e$ and $h(R^N) = s$. Since S is losing, $F(R^N) = s$ (see (4.2.1)). If $V - S \neq \varnothing$, then $f(R^N) = s$. Hence, again $F(R^N) = s$. Therefore, $S \notin W^*(F)$. Thus, $W \supset W^*(F)$. So we have proved that F is a representation of G (see Definition 3.2.1). Now, it is clear that $\text{SYM}(F) \supset \text{SYM}(G)$. By Lemma 3.2.8, $\text{SYM}(G) \supset \text{SYM}(F)$. Hence, F is a faithful representation of G (see Definition 3.2.7). Also, as the reader can easily verify, F is monotonic (see Definition 2.3.11).

We shall now prove that F is exactly and strongly consistent (see Definition 4.1.18). We start with the following remarks.

Remark 4.2.3. Let $R^N \in L^N$ and $i \in V$. If $s = t_k(R^i)$ and $F(R^N) = t_h(R^i)$ (see Notation 2.1.8), then $h \leq k$.

Remark 4.2.4. Let $R^N \in L^N$. If there exists a blocking coalition T (see Definition 3.3.7) such that $t_m(R^i) = e$ for all $i \in T$, then $F(R^N) \neq e$.

The proof of Remarks 4.2.3 and 4.2.4 is left to the reader. Now let $R^N \in L^N$. We have to show that there exists a strong e.p. Q^N of the game $g(F, R^N)$ (see Definitions 4.1.17 and 2.5.1) such that $F(Q^N) = F(R^N)$. We distinguish the following possibilities.

$$f = f(R^N) = s \tag{4.2.2}$$

In this case, $F(R^N) = s$. Let $Q^N \in L^N$ satisfy $t_1(Q^i) = s$ for all $i \in N$. Clearly, $F(Q^N) = s$. We shall prove that Q^N is a strong e.p. of $g(F, R^N)$. Assume, on the contrary, that Q^N is not a strong e.p. of $g(F, R^N)$. Then there exist a coalition T and $P^T \in L^T$ such that $F(Q^{N-T}, P^T) = x$, $x \neq s$, and xR^is for all $i \in T$. Since $s \in C(N, W_a, A, R^N)$, we must have $V - T \neq \varnothing$.

Let $j \in V-T$; $t_1(Q^j)=s$. Hence, $s=f(Q^{N-T},P^T)$. Thus, $F(Q^{N-T},P^T)=s$, and the desired contradiction has been obtained.

$$f=f(R^N) \notin \{s,e\} \tag{4.2.3}$$

In this case, $F(R^N)=f$. Let $Q^N \in L^N$ satisfy $t_1(Q^i)=f$ and $t_2(Q^i)=s$ for all $i \in N$. Clearly, $F(Q^N)=f$. We shall prove that Q^N is a strong e.p. of $g(F,R^N)$. Assume, on the contrary, that Q^N is not a strong e.p. of $g(F,R^N)$. Then there exist a coalition T and $P^T \in L^T$ such that $F(Q^{N-T},P^T)=x$, $x \neq f$, and $xR^i f$ for all $i \in T$. Since $f \in C(N,W_a,A,R^N)$, we must have $V-T \neq \varnothing$. Let $j \in V-T$; $t_1(Q^j)=f$ and $t_2(Q^j)=s$. It follows now from Remark 4.2.3 that $F(Q^{N-T},P^T)=s$. Now, since $s \neq f$, $fR^i s$ for all $i \in V$. Hence, $T \cap V = \varnothing$. Now, since $f \neq e$, $F(Q^{N-T},P^T)=f$, and the desired contradiction has been obtained.

$$f=f(R^N)=e \tag{4.2.4}$$

We further distinguish the following subcases.

$$S=S(R^N) \notin W \text{ (see (4.2.1))} \quad \text{and} \quad h(R^N)=s \tag{4.2.5}$$

In this case, $F(R^N)=s$. Let $Q^N \in L^N$ satisfy $t_1(Q^i)=s$ and $t_m(Q^i)=e$ for all $i \in N$. Clearly, $F(Q^N)=s$. We shall prove that Q^N is a strong e.p. of $g(F,R^N)$. Assume, on the contrary, that Q^N is not a strong e.p. of $g(F,R^N)$. Then there exist a coalition T and $P^T \in L^T$ such that $F(Q^{N-T},P^T)=x$, $x \neq s$, and $xR^i s$ for all $i \in T$. Now, $s=h(R^N)$. Hence, if $x \neq e$, then $V-T \neq \varnothing$. Let $j \in V-T$; $t_1(Q^j)=s$. Hence, $F(Q^{N-T},P^T)=s$, and the desired contradiction has been obtained. If $x=e$, then $T \subset S$ (see (4.2.5) and (4.2.1)). Since $S \notin W$, $T \notin W$. Hence, $N-T$ is blocking. For all $i \in N-T$, $t_m(Q^i)=e$. Hence, by Remark 4.2.4, $F(Q^{N-T},P^T) \neq e$, and, again, the desired contradiction has been obtained.

$$S=S(R^N) \notin W \quad \text{and} \quad h=h(R^N) \neq s \tag{4.2.6}$$

In this case, $F(R^N)=h$. Let $Q^N \in L^N$ satisfy $t_1(Q^i)=h$, $t_2(Q^i)=s$, and $t_m(Q^i)=e$ for all $i \in N$. Clearly, $F(Q^N)=h$. We shall prove that Q^N is a strong e.p. of $g(F,R^N)$. Assume, on the contrary, that Q^N is not a strong e.p. of $g(F,R^N)$. Then there exist a coalition T and $P^T \in L^T$ such that $F(Q^{N-T},P^T)=x$, $x \neq h$, and $xR^i h$ for all $i \in T$. Now, $h \in C(N,W_a,A_*,R^N|A_*)$. Hence, if $x \neq e$, then $V-T \neq \varnothing$. Let $j \in V-T$. Then $t_1(Q^j)=h$ and $t_2(Q^j)=s$. Hence, by Remark 4.2.3, $x=s$. Because $h \neq s$, $hR^i s$ for all $i \in V$. Hence, $V \cap T = \varnothing$. Since $h \neq e$, $F(Q^{N-T},P^T)=h$, and the desired contradiction has been obtained. If $x=e$, then $T \subset S$ (see (4.2.6) and (4.2.1)). Hence, $N-T$ is blocking. For all $i \in N-T$, $t_m(Q^i)=e$. Hence, by Remark 4.2.4, $F(Q^{N-T},P^T) \neq e$, and, again, the desired contradiction has been obtained.

$$S = S(R^N) \in W \quad \text{and} \quad h(R^N) = s \tag{4.2.7}$$

In this case, $F(R^N) = e$. Let $Q^N \in L^N$ satisfy $t_1(Q^i) = e$ and $t_2(Q^i) = s$ for all $i \in N$. Clearly, $F(Q^N) = e$. We shall prove that Q^N is a strong e.p. of $g(F, R^N)$. Assume, on the contrary, that Q^N is not a strong e.p. of $g(F, R^N)$. Then there exist a coalition T and $P^T \in L^T$ such that $F(Q^{N-T}, P^T) = x$, $x \neq e$, and $xR^i e$ for all $i \in T$. Now, $e \in C(N, W_a, A, R^N)$. Hence, $V - T \neq \emptyset$. Let $j \in V - T$. Then $t_1(Q^j) = e$ and $t_2(Q^j) = s$. By Remark 4.2.3, $x = s$. Therefore, $S \cap T = \emptyset$ (see (4.2.1) and (4.2.7)). Hence, $N - T \in W$. Because F is a representation of G, $N - T \in W^*(F)$. Therefore, $F(Q^{N-T}, P^T) = e$, and the desired contradiction has been obtained.

$$S = S(R^N) \in W \quad \text{and} \quad h = h(R^N) \neq s \tag{4.2.8}$$

In this case, $F(R^N) = e$. Let $Q^N \in L^N$ satisfy $t_1(Q^i) = e$, $t_2(Q^i) = h$, and $t_3(Q^i) = s$ for all $i \in N$. Clearly, $F(Q^N) = e$. We shall prove that Q^N is a strong e.p. of $g(F, R^N)$. Assume, on the contrary, that Q^N is not a strong e.p. of $g(F, R^N)$. Then there exist a coalition T and $P^T \in L^T$ such that $F(Q^{N-T}, P^T) = x$, $x \neq e$, and $xR^i e$ for all $i \in T$. Now, $e = f(R^N)$ (see (4.2.4)). Hence, $V - T \neq \emptyset$. Let $j \in V - T$. Then $t_1(Q^j) = e$, $t_2(Q^j) = h$, and $t_3(Q^j) = s$. Hence, by Remark 4.2.3, $x \in \{h, s\}$. If $x = h$, then $S \cap T = \emptyset$ (see (4.2.1) and (4.2.8)). Hence, $N - T \in W^*(F)$. Therefore, $F(Q^{N-T}, P^T) = e$, and the desired contradiction has been obtained. Thus, $x = s$. Because $e = f(R^N)$, $T \cap V = \emptyset$. Now, $h \neq s$ and $hQ^i s$ for all $i \in V$. Therefore, $F(Q^{N-T}, P^T) \neq s$, and the desired contradiction has, again, been obtained.

4.3 Voting procedures and Arrow's conditions

We have proved in Section 4.1 that capacities of games without veto players are bounded (see Theorem 4.1.34). In particular, by Theorem 4.1.35, the capacity of an essential, proper, and strong game is 2. Now, usually committees use *dynamic* procedures in order to choose one alternative out of a large set of alternatives. In each step of such a procedure, an alternative is chosen from a small set, and the final outcome is determined by a sequence of such choices. (The reader is referred to Black [1958, p. 21] for a description of several dynamic procedures of voting.) The foregoing remarks motivate the investigation of the following problem. Let $G = (N, W)$ be an essential and proper simple game, and let A be a set of alternatives. We shall inquire whether or not it is possible to devise a dynamic voting procedure such that (a) the choice from every subset of A can be always reduced to a sequence of binary choices and (b) binary choices are made by using exactly and strongly consistent representations of G. As we shall prove in this section, the answer to the foregoing question is negative. Indeed, very surprisingly, our impossibility result for voting procedures is equivalent to Arrow's Impossibility Theorem (see Section 2.2). We start with the following definitions.

Let $N = \{1, \ldots, n\}$ be a society, and let A be a set of m alternatives, $m \geqslant 3$.

Definition 4.3.1. A *voting procedure* (VP) is a function $K: 2^A \times L^N \to A$ that satisfies $K(B, R^N) \in B$ for all $B \in 2^A$ and $R^N \in L^N$.

Definition 4.3.1 is due to Blin and Satterthwaite [1978].

Let $K: 2^A \times L^N \to A$ be a VP (see Definition 4.3.1). K is "binary" if it satisfies the following condition. Let $R^N \in L^N$. We define a binary relation $R = \phi(R^N)$ in the following way. Let $x, y \in A$, $x \neq y$. Then xRx, and

$$xRy \quad \text{if and only if} \quad x = K(\{x, y\}, R^N) \tag{4.3.1}$$

Clearly, R is complete and antisymmetric (see Definition 2.1.1). We are now able to state the following definition.

Definition 4.3.2. K is *binary* if for all $B \in 2^A$ and all $R^N \in L^N$,

$$K(B, R^N) = x \quad \text{if and only if} \quad xRy \text{ for all } y \in B \tag{4.3.2}$$

(see Pattanaik [1978, p. 25]).

Lemma 4.3.3. *Let* $K: 2^A \times L^N \to A$ *be a binary VP (see Definition 4.3.2). Then, for every* $R^N \in L^N$, $R = \phi(R^N)$ *(see (4.3.1)) is transitive.*

Proof: Let $R^N \in L^N$, and let $x, y,$ and z be three distinct members of A. If xRy and yRz, then, by (4.3.2), $K(\{x, y, z\}, R^N) = x$. Hence, xRz.

We shall now characterize the class of binary VPs.

Definition 4.3.4. Let $K: 2^A \times L^N \to A$ be a VP. An SWF $\phi: L^N \to L$ (see Definition 2.2.2) is a *rationalization* of K if for all $B \in 2^A$ and all $R^N \in L^N$, $K(B, R^N)$ is the maximum of B with respect to $\phi(R^N)$.

Remark 4.3.5. A VP is binary if and only if it has a rationalization. Furthermore, the correspondence between binary VPs and their rationalizations is one-to-one.

It is worthwhile to mention the following fact.

Remark 4.3.6. Let $K: 2^A \times L^N \to A$ be a VP. K is *path-independent* if for all $B_1, B_2 \in 2^A$ and all $R^N \in L^N$,

$$K(B_1 \cup B_2, R^N) = K(\{K(B_1, R^N)\} \cup \{K(B_2, R^N)\}, R^N)$$

By Theorem 5 of Plott [1973], K is path-independent if and only if it has a rationalization.

We shall now consider the Pareto condition for VPs.

Definition 4.3.7. Let $K: 2^A \times L^N \to A$ be a VP. K is *Paretian in the limited sense* if it satisfies the following condition: For each pair of distinct alternatives $x, y \in A$, and for each $R^N \in L^N$, if $x R^i y$ for all $i \in N$, then $x = K(\{x, y\}, R^N)$.

Remark 4.3.8. Let $K: 2^A \times L^N \to A$ be a binary VP, and let the SWF $\phi: L^N \to L$ be the rationalization of K. Then K is Paretian in the limited sense (see Definition 4.3.7) if and only if ϕ is Paretian (see Definition 2.2.3).

We now define (limited) exact consistency of VPs.

Definition 4.3.9. Let $K: 2^A \times L^N \to A$ be a VP. K is *exactly and strongly consistent in the limited sense* if for each $B \in 2^A$ such that $|B| = 2$ (see Notation 2.1.7), the SCF $K(B, \cdot)$ is exactly and strongly consistent (see Definition 4.1.18).

We shall now prove the main result of this section, namely, that limited consistency of a binary VP is equivalent to the independence of irrelevant alternatives of its rationalization.

We start with the following definition and remarks.

Definition 4.3.10. A binary VP is *dictatorial* if it has a dictatorial rationalization (see Definitions 4.3.4 and 2.2.6).

Remark 4.3.11. Let $K: 2^A \times L^N \to A$ be a VP. If K is dictatorial, then for each $B \in 2^A$, the SCF $K(B, \cdot)$ is dictatorial (see Definitions 4.3.10 and 2.4.10).

Remark 4.3.12. A dictatorial SCF is exactly and strongly consistent (see Definitions 2.4.10 and 4.1.18).

Theorem 4.3.13. *Let $K: 2^A \times L^N \to A$ be a binary VP, and let the SWF $\phi: L^N \to L$ be the rationalization of K (see Definitions 4.3.2 and 4.3.4). Assume that K is Paretian in the limited sense (see Definition 4.3.7). Then K is exactly and strongly consistent in the limited sense (see Definition 4.3.9) if and only if ϕ satisfies the condition of independence of irrelevant alternatives (see Definition 2.2.5).*

Proof: Sufficiency. If ϕ satisfies the condition of independence of irrelevant alternatives, then, by Remark 4.3.8 and Theorem 2.2.7, ϕ is dictatorial. By Remark 4.3.11, for all $B \in 2^A$, the SCF $K(B, \cdot)$ is dictatorial. Hence, by Remark 4.3.12, K is exactly and strongly consistent in the limited sense.

Necessity. Assume now that K is exactly and strongly consistent in the limited sense. Let $x, y \in A$, $x \neq y$, and let $R^N, T^N \in L^N$ such that $R^N \mid \{x, y\} = T^N \mid \{x, y\}$ (see Notation 2.2.4). We have to show that $\phi(R^N) \mid \{x, y\} = \phi(T^N) \mid \{x, y\}$ (see Definition 2.2.5). Assume, on the contrary, that, say, $x\phi(R^N)y$ and $y\phi(T^N)x$. Let $B = \{x, y\}$. Since ϕ is a rationalization of K, $K(B, R^N) = x$ and $K(B, T^N) = y$. Since $K(B, \cdot)$ is, by our assumption, exactly and strongly consistent, the game $g(K(B, \cdot), R^N)$ (see Definition 2.5.1) has a strong e.p. Q^N such that $K(B, Q^N) = x$. Similarly, the game $g(K(B, \cdot), T^N)$ has a strong e.p. P^N such that $K(B, P^N) = y$. Now let

$$S = \{i \mid i \in N \text{ and } xR^iy\} = \{i \mid i \in N \text{ and } xT^iy\}$$

Because K is Paretian in the limited sense (see Definition 4.3.7), $S \neq \varnothing$ and $S \neq N$. Now let $z = K(B, (Q^S, P^{N-S}))$. If $z = x$, then, because xT^iy for all $i \in S$, P^N is not a strong e.p. of $g(K(B, \cdot), T^N)$. Similarly, if $z = y$, then Q^N is not a strong e.p. of $g(K(B, \cdot), R^N)$. Thus, the desired contradiction has been obtained.

We shall now examine the implications of Theorem 4.3.13 for the theory of representation of committees. We start with the following definitions.

Definition 4.3.14. A *voting correspondence* (VC) is a function $D: 2^A \times L^N \to 2^A$ that satisfies $D(B, R^N) \subset B$ for all $B \in 2^A$ and $R^N \in L^N$.

Definition 4.3.15. Let $D: 2^A \times L^N \to 2^A$ be a VC (see Definition 4.3.14), and let $B \in 2^A$, with $|B| \geqslant 2$ (see Notation 2.1.7). A coalition S is *winning for* $x \in B$ (with respect to D and B) if

$$[R^N \in L^N \text{ and } xR^iy \text{ for all } i \in S \text{ and all } y \in B] \Rightarrow D(B, R^N) = x$$

(see Notation 2.4.3). The set of all winning coalitions for x is denoted by $W^*(D, B, x)$ or $W^*(B, x)$. The *first simple game associated with D and B* is the game $G^*(D, B) = (N, W^*(D, B))$, where $W^*(D, B) = \bigcap \{W^*(D, B, x) \mid x \in B\}$.

In the next section we shall develop a theory of dynamic representations (i.e., representations by VCs) of committees. Here the following definition is sufficient.

Definition 4.3.16. Let $G = (N, W)$ be a proper simple game, and let A be a finite set of m alternatives, $m \geq 3$. A VP $K: 2^A \times L^N \to A$ is a *strong and dynamic representation of G in the limited sense* if (a) K is exactly and strongly consistent in the limited sense (see Definition 4.3.9) and (b) for every $B \in 2^A$ such that $|B| = 2$ (see Notation 2.1.7), $W^*(K, B) = W$ (see Definition 4.3.15).

We are now able to prove the following.

Corollary 4.3.17. Let $G = (N, W)$ be a proper and essential simple game (see Definition 3.3.2). Then G has no strong and dynamic representation in the limited sense by means of a binary VP (see Definition 4.3.2).

Proof: Let A be a set of m alternatives, $m \geq 3$, and let $K: 2^A \times L^N \to A$ be a binary voting procedure. Assume, on the contrary, that K is a strong and dynamic representation of G in the limited sense (see Definition 4.3.16). Then K is exactly and strongly consistent in the limited sense. Furthermore, let $B \in 2^A$ such that $|B| = 2$. Then $W^*(K, B) = W$. Since G is essential, $N \in W$. Hence, K is Paretian in the limited sense (see Definitions 4.3.15 and 4.3.7). By Theorem 4.3.13, K is dictatorial (see Definition 4.3.10). Let, again, $B \in 2^A$ such that $|B| = 2$. By Remark 4.3.11, $K(B, \cdot)$ is dictatorial. Hence, as the reader can easily verify, $G^*(K, B)$ is dictatorial (see Definitions 2.4.10, 4.3.15, and 2.6.4). Since $W^*(K, B) = W$ and G is nondictatorial, the desired contradiction has been obtained.

4.4 Dynamic representations and the core

Definition 4.4.1. Let $G = (N, W)$ be a proper simple game (see Definition 2.6.4), and let A be a finite set of m alternatives, $m \geq 2$. A VC $D: 2^A \times L^N \to 2^A$ (see Definition 4.3.14) is a *dynamic representation* of G of order m if for all $B \in 2^A$ such that $|B| \geq 2$ (see Notation 2.1.7), $W^*(D, B) = W$ (see Definition 4.3.15). D is a dynamic representation of G in the *limited sense* if $W^*(D, B) = W$ for all $B \in 2^A$ such that $|B| = 2$.

Let $G = (N, W)$ be a committee, and let A be a set of alternatives. A dynamic representation $D: 2^A \times L^N \to 2^A$ of G is, intuitively, a feasible choice procedure that (a) reflects "faithfully" the distribution of power in G and (b) can be applied to every possible agenda (i.e., a sequence of choices from subsets of A that determines a choice of a member $B \in 2^A$ (when A is the issue under consideration)).

We shall now investigate the relationship between the core of a simple game and the dynamic representations of the game. We start with the following definition.

Definition 4.4.2. Let $D: 2^A \times L^N \to 2^A$ be a VC (see Definition 4.3.14), and let $R^N \in L^N$. The *base relation* $R = \phi(R^N)$ is defined by the following rule. Let $x, y \in A$, $x \neq y$. Then xRx, and

$$xRy \quad \text{if and only if} \quad x \in D(\{x, y\}, R^N) \tag{4.4.1}$$

Clearly, R is complete (see Definition 2.1.1). Also, (4.4.1) generalizes (4.3.1) to VCs.

Notation 4.4.3. Let $D: 2^A \times L^N \to 2^A$ be a VC, and $R^N \in L^N$. Furthermore, let $x, y \in A$, $x \neq y$. Then

$$x\psi(R^N)y \quad \text{if} \quad x = D(\{x, y\} R^N) \tag{4.4.2}$$

(see Notation 2.4.3). Clearly, $x\psi(R^N)y$ if and only if $[x\phi(R^N)y$ and not $y\phi(R^N)x]$. We also denote $P = \psi(R^N)$.

We are now able to define the following property of VCs.

Definition 4.4.4. Let $D: 2^A \times L^N \to 2^A$ be a VC (see Definition 4.3.14). D satisfies *pairwise rejection* if for all $R^N \in L^N$, $B \in 2^A$, and $x, y \in B$, $x \neq y$, if yPx (see Notation 4.4.3), then $x \notin D(B, R^N)$.

Remark 4.4.5. Definition 4.4.4 is due to Pattanaik [1978].

We are now able to establish the following connection between the core and dynamic representations.

Lemma 4.4.6. *Let* $G = (N, W)$ *be a proper simple game, and let* $D: 2^A \times L^N \to 2^A$ *be a dynamic representation of G in the limited sense* (see Definition 4.4.1). *If D satisfies pairwise rejection* (see Definition 4.4.4), *then*

$$D(B, R^N) \subset C(N, W, B, R^N \mid B) \quad \text{for all } B \in 2^A \text{ and } R^N \in L^N$$

(see Definition 2.6.8 and Notation 2.2.4).

Proof: Let $B \in 2^A$ and $R^N \in L^N$. Furthermore, let $x \in B$. If $x \notin C(N, W, B, R^N \mid B)$, then there exists $y \in B - \{x\}$ such that

$$S = \{i \mid i \in N \text{ and } yR^ix\} \in W$$

Let $B_* = \{x, y\}$. Since D is a dynamic representation of G in the limited sense, $S \in W^*(D, B_*)$. Hence, $x \notin D(B_*, R^N)$ (see Definition 4.3.15). Thus, yPx (where $P = \psi(R^N)$; see Notation 4.4.3). Since D satisfies pairwise rejection, it follows that $x \notin D(B, R^N)$.

We continue with the following definitions.

Definition 4.4.7. Let $D: 2^A \times L^N \to 2^A$ be a VC (see Definition 4.3.14). D satisfies *reward for pairwise optimality* if for all $R^N \in L^N$, $B \in 2^A$, and $x \in B$,

$$[xRy \text{ for all } y \in B] \Rightarrow x \in D(B, R^N)$$

(see (4.4.1)).

Remark 4.4.8. Definition 4.4.7 is also due to Pattanaik [1978].

Definition 4.4.9. Let $D: 2^A \times L^N \to 2^A$ be a VC (see Definition 4.3.14), and let $B \in 2^A$. D is *neutral with respect to* B if for every permutation σ of A that satisfies $\sigma(x) = x$ for all $x \in A - B$, and for every $R^N \in L^N$,

$$D(B, (\sigma(R^1), \ldots, \sigma(R^N))) = \sigma(D(B, R^N))$$

(see Section 2.3 for our notation). D is *neutral* if it is neutral with respect to every $B \in 2^A$. D satisfies *limited neutrality* if it is neutral with respect to every $B \in 2^A$ such that $|B| = 2$.

Definition 4.4.10. Let $D: 2^A \times L^N \to 2^A$ be a VC (see Definition 4.3.14), and let $B \in 2^A$. D satisfies *independence of irrelevant alternatives with respect to* B (IIA(B)) if for all $R^N, Q^N \in L^N$,

$$[R^N | B = Q^N | B] \Rightarrow D(B, R^N) = D(B, Q^N)$$

(see Notation 2.2.4). D satisfies *universal* independence of irrelevant alternatives (UIIA) if it satisfies IIA(B) for all $B \in 2^A$. D satisfies *limited* independence of irrelevant alternatives (LIIA) if it satisfies IIA(B) for every B such that $|B| = 2$ (see Notation 2.1.7).

Remark 4.4.11. Definition 4.4.10 should not be confused with Definition 2.2.5. The first definition applies to VCs, whereas the second applies to SWFs.

Definition 4.4.12. A VC $D: 2^A \times L^N \to 2^A$ is *monotonic* if for every $B \in 2^A$ the SCC $D^*(B, \cdot)$ that is defined by $D^*(B, R^N) = D(B, R^N(B))$ for all $R^N \in L^N$ (see Notation 2.4.12) is monotonic (see Definition 2.3.11). D is monotonic in the *limited sense* if $D^*(B, \cdot)$ is monotonic for every $B \in 2^A$ such that $|B| = 2$ (see Notation 2.1.7).

Remark 4.4.13. Let $G = (N, W)$ be a proper simple game, and let A be a set of m alternatives, $m \geq 2$, such that $C(N, W, A, R^N) \neq \varnothing$ for all $R^N \in L^N$ (see Definitions 2.6.4 and 2.6.8). Then the VC D that is defined by

$$D(B, R^N) = C(N, W, B, R^N | B) \quad \text{for all } B \in 2^A \text{ and } R^N \in L^N \qquad (4.4.3)$$

(see Notation 2.2.4) is a dynamic representation of G (see Definitions 4.4.1 and 4.3.15 and Corollary 3.2.10). Furthermore, $D(B, R^N) = C(B, R^N | B)$ satisfies pairwise rejection, reward for pairwise optimality, neutrality, and UIIA (see Definitions 4.4.4, 4.4.7, 4.4.9, and 4.4.10). Also, D is monotonic (see Definition 4.4.12). The converse result is proved by the following theorem.

Theorem 4.4.14. *Let $G = (N, W)$ be a proper simple game, and let the VC $D: 2^A \times L^N \to 2^A$ be a dynamic representation of G in the limited sense (see Definition 4.4.1). If D is monotonic in the limited sense and satisfies pairwise rejection, reward for pairwise optimality, limited neutrality, and LIIA (see Definitions 4.4.12, 4.4.4, 4.4.7, 4.4.9, and 4.4.10), then $D(B, R^N) = C(N, W, B, R^N | B)$ for all $R^N \in L^N$ and all $B \in 2^A$.*

Proof: Let $R^N \in L^N$ and $B \in 2^A$. Since D satisfies pairwise rejection, by Lemma 4.4.6, $D(B, R^N) \subset C(N, W, B, R^N | B)$. We shall now show that if $|B| = 2$, then $D(B, R^N) = C(N, W, B, R^N | B) = C(B, R^N | B)$. Indeed, let $B = \{x, y\}$. If $|C(B, R^N | B)| = 1$ (see Notation 2.1.7), then, clearly, our claim is true. So let $C(B, R^N | B) = B$. Assume now, on the contrary, that, say, $D(B, R^N) = x$. Let $S = \{i | i \in N \text{ and } x R^i y\}$. Since $y \in C(B, R^N | B)$, $S \notin W$. On the other hand, let σ be a permutation of A that is specified by $\sigma(x) = y$, $\sigma(y) = x$, and $\sigma(z) = z$ for all $z \in A - B$. Then, by limited neutrality, $D(B, \sigma(R^N)) = \sigma(D(B, R^N)) = y$ (where $\sigma(R^N) = (\sigma(R^1), \ldots, \sigma(R^n)))$. Now, $S = \{i | i \in N \text{ and } y \sigma(R^i) x\}$. Hence, since D is monotonic in the limited sense and satisfies LIIA, $S \in W^*(D, B)$ (see Definition 4.3.15). Since D is a dynamic representation of G in the limited sense, $W^*(D, B) = W$. Hence, the desired contradiction has been obtained. Thus, if $|B| = 2$, then $D(B, R^N) = C(B, R^N | B)$. Using now our assumption of reward for pairwise optimality, we conclude that $D(B, R^N) \supset C(N, W, B, R^N | B)$ for every $B \in 2^A$.

We shall now prove, by constructing suitable examples, that the five axioms that characterize the core are independent.

Example 4.4.15. Let $G = (3, 3)$ (see Definition 2.6.4), and let $A = \{x, y, z\}$. We define a VC $D: 2^A \times L^N \to 2^A$ by the following rules. Let $R^N \in L^N$. If there is no Condorcet alternative with respect to R^N (see Definition 3.2.2), then we define $D(B, R^N) = C(N, W, B, R^N | B)$ for all $B \in 2^A$ (see Definition 2.6.8). If there exists a Condorcet alternative $u = u(R^N)$, then we consider the set $B_0 = B_0(R^N) = A - \{u\}$. Let $G_0 = (N, W_0) = (3, 2)$. We define $D(B_0, R^N) = C(N, W_0, B_0, R^N | B_0)$ and

$D(B, R^N) = C(N, W, B, R^N \mid B)$ for all $B \neq B_0$. For example, consider the following situation:

R^1	R^2	R^3
y	y	y
z	z	x
x	x	z

$y = u(R^N)$ and $B_0(R^N) = \{x, z\}$. Also, $D(B_0, R^N) = z$. As the reader can easily verify, D is a dynamic representation of G. Also, D satisfies pairwise rejection, reward for pairwise optimality, neutrality, and monotonicity. Clearly, the VC D is different from the core VC. We observe that D violates LIIA (see Definition 4.4.10).

Example 4.4.16. Let $G = (N, W)$ be an essential *strong* and proper simple game, and let A be a set of m alternatives, $m \geq 3$. Furthermore, let $B \in 2^A$ and $R^N \in L^N$; $a \in B$ is a *Condorcet alternative with respect to B and R^N* if $a \operatorname{Dom}(R^N) b$ for all $b \in B - \{a\}$ (see Definition 2.6.8). We now define a VC $D: 2^A \times L^N \to 2^A$ by the following rules. Let, again, $B \in 2^A$ and $R^N \in L^N$. If there exists a Condorcet alternative a with respect to B and R^N, then we define $D(B, R^N) = a$. Otherwise (i.e., if there exists no Condorcet alternative with respect to B and R^N), we define $D(B, R^N) = B$. Clearly, D is a dynamic representation of G. Also, as the reader can easily verify, D satisfies UIIA, reward for pairwise optimality, neutrality, and monotonicity. Because G is strong and essential and $m \geq 3$, the VC D is different from the core VC (see the proof of Theorem 4.1.35). We observe that D violates pairwise rejection (see Definition 4.4.4).

Example 4.4.17. Let $G = (8, 7)$, and let A be a set of three alternatives. We define a VC $D: 2^A \times L^N \to 2^A$ by the following rules. Let $R^N \in L^N$ and $B \in 2^A$. If $|B| \leq 2$, then we define $D(B, R^N) = C(N, W, B, R^N \mid B)$. If $B = A$, then we define $D(A, R^N) = H(R^N)$, where $H(R^N)$ is defined in Example 3.2.25. Clearly, D is a dynamic representation of G. Furthermore, D is neutral and monotonic and satisfies UIIA and pairwise rejection. By Example 3.2.25, D is different from the core VC. We observe that D violates reward for pairwise optimality (see Definition 4.4.7).

Example 4.4.18. Let $G = (3, 3)$ (see Definition 2.6.4), and let $A = \{x, y\}$. We define a VC $D: 2^A \times L^N \to 2^A$ by the following rules. Let $R^N \in L^N$, and let $S(R^N) = \{i \mid i \in N \text{ and } x R^i y\}$. We define

$$D(A, R^N) = x \quad \text{if } |S(R^N)| \geqslant 2$$

$$= A \quad \text{if } |S(R^N)| = 1$$

$$= y \quad \text{if } |S(R^N)| = 0$$

(see Notation 2.1.7). Clearly, D is a dynamic representation of G that is monotonic and that satisfies UIIA, pairwise rejection, and reward for pairwise optimality. Also, D is different from the core VC. We observe that D violates neutrality (see Definition 4.4.9).

Example 4.4.19. Let $G = (5, 5)$ (see Definition 2.6.4), and let $A = \{x, y\}$. We define a VC $D: 2^A \times L^N \to 2^A$ by the following rules. Let $R^N \in L^N$, and let $S(R^N) = \{i \mid i \in N \text{ and } x R^i y\}$. We define

$$D(A, R^N) = x \quad \text{if } |S(R^N)| \in \{5, 3\}$$

$$= y \quad \text{if } |S(R^N)| \in \{0, 2\}$$

$$= A \quad \text{if } |S(R^N)| \in \{1, 4\}$$

Clearly, D is a dynamic representation of G. Furthermore, D is neutral, and it satisfies UIIA, pairwise rejection, and reward for pairwise optimality. Also, D is different from the core VC. We observe that D is not monotonic (see Definition 4.4.12).

Definition 4.4.20. Let $D: 2^A \times L^N \to 2^A$ be a VC (see Definition 4.3.14). D is *binary* if for all $B \in 2^A$ and all $R^N \in L^N$,

$$D(B, R^N) = \{x \mid x \in B \text{ and } x R y \text{ for all } y \in B\} \tag{4.4.4}$$

(see Definition 4.4.2).

Remark 4.4.21. Clearly, Definition 4.4.20 generalizes Definition 4.3.2. Also, a VC $D: 2^A \times L^N \to 2^A$ is binary if and only if it satisfies pairwise rejection and reward for pairwise optimality (see Definitions 4.4.4 and 4.4.7).

Remark 4.4.22. Let $G = (N, W)$ be a proper simple game, and let A be a set of m alternatives, $m \geqslant 2$, such that $C(N, W, A, R^N) \neq \emptyset$ for all $R^N \in L^N$ (see Definitions 2.6.4 and 2.6.8). Then the core VC of G and A, which is defined by (4.4.3), is the unique dynamic representation of G that satisfies *binariness* (see Definition 4.4.20) and NIM (neutrality, universal independence of irrelevant alternatives, and monotonicity).

Remark 4.4.22 follows from Remark 4.4.13, Theorem 4.4.14, and Remark 4.4.21.

We conclude this section with some remarks on path independence of VCs.

Definition 4.4.23. Let $D: 2^A \times L^N \to 2^A$ be a VC. D is *path-independent* if for all $B_1, B_2 \in 2^A$ and all $R^N \in L^N$,

$$D(B_1 \cup B_2, R^N) = D(D(B_1, R^N) \cup D(B_2, R^N), R^N)$$

The core does not satisfy path independence, as is shown by the following example.

Example 4.4.24. Let $G = (4, 3)$ (see Definition 2.6.4), and let $A = \{x, y, z\}$. Consider the following situation:

R^1	R^2	R^3	R^4
x	x	z	y
y	y	x	z
z	z	y	x

Let $B_1 = \{x, y\}$ and $B_2 = \{z\}$. Then

$$C(C(B_1, R^N \mid B_1) \cup C(B_2, R^N \mid B_2), R^N) = C(\{x, z\}, R^N \mid \{x, z\}) = \{x, z\}$$

and $C(A, R^N) = x$ (see Definition 2.6.8 and Notation 2.4.3).

However, the core satisfies the weaker condition of *upper* path independence.

Definition 4.4.25. Let $D: 2^A \times L^N \to 2^A$ be a VC. D satisfies *upper path independence* if for all $B_1, B_2 \in 2^A$ and all $R^N \in L^N$,

$$D(B_1 \cup B_2, R^N) \subset D(D(B_1, R^N) \cup D(B_2, R^N), R^N)$$

Remark 4.4.26. Let $D: 2^A \times L^N \to 2^A$ be a VC. If D satisfies upper path independence (see Definition 4.4.25), then, as the reader can easily verify, D satisfies pairwise rejection (see Definition 4.4.4).

Corollary 4.4.27. Let $G = (N, W)$ be a proper simple game, and let $D: 2^A \times L^N \to 2^A$ be a dynamic representation of G in the limited sense (see Definition 4.4.1). If D satisfies upper path independence (see Definition 4.4.25), then

$$D(B, R^N) \subset C(N, W, B, R^N \mid B) \quad \text{for all } B \in 2^A \text{ and } R^N \in L^N$$

(see Definition 2.6.8 and Notation 2.2.4).

Corollary 4.4.27 follows from Remark 4.4.26 and Lemma 4.4.6.

CHAPTER 5

Exactly and strongly consistent anonymous social choice functions

This chapter consists of a detailed presentation of almost all significant results on exactly and strongly consistent anonymous SCFs. We open our investigation in Section 5.1 by introducing the more general class of partially implementable SCCs. An SCC $H: L^N \to 2^A$ is partially implementable if there exists a game form Γ such that for each $R^N \in L^N$, every $a \in H(R^N)$ is the outcome of a strong e.p. of Γ (see Definition 5.1.8). Thus, an SCF is exactly and strongly consistent if and only if it is partially self-implementable (see Remark 5.1.9). We prove that partially implementable SCCs share the tightness and stability properties of exactly and strongly consistent SCFs (see Lemmata 5.1.14 and 5.1.20). In Section 5.2 we define and investigate the blocking coefficients of partially implementable and anonymous SCCs. Let $H: L^N \to 2^A$ be a partially implementable and anonymous SCC, and let $B \in 2^A$. The blocking coefficient of B, $\beta(B)$, is the size of a minimal blocking coalition of B. We find sharp bounds for the function $\beta(\cdot)$ (see Theorem 5.2.16). Clearly, $\beta(\cdot)$ is subadditive. We also find necessary and sufficient conditions for $\beta(\cdot)$ to be additive (see Lemma 5.2.18). Section 5.3 is devoted to a complete characterization of the class of exactly and strongly consistent anonymous SCFs whose blocking function is additive. Let $N = \{1, \ldots, n\}$ be a society, and let $A = \{x_1, \ldots, x_m\}$ be a set of m alternatives, where $2 \leqslant m \leqslant n+1$. Furthermore, let $\beta_*: A \to \{1, \ldots, n\}$ satisfy $\sum_{i=1}^{m} \beta_*(x_i) = n+1$. We define a function $E_*: 2^N \to P(2^A)$ as follows: $B \in E_*(S)$ if and only if $|S| \geqslant \beta_*(A-B)$ (i.e., $S \in 2^N$ is "winning" for $B \in 2^A$ if and only if it "blocks" $A-B$). Then the following result is true. Let $F: L^N \to A$ be an anonymous SCF. Then F is exactly and strongly consistent, and $\beta(F; x_i) = \beta_*(x_i)$ for $i = 1, \ldots, m$, if and only if F is a selection from the core $C(E_*, \cdot)$. Moreover, $C(E_*, \cdot)$ admits anonymous and monotonic selections (see Theorem 5.3.7, Remark 5.3.11, and Corollary 5.3.13). Section 5.4 is devoted to further investigation of the core correspondence $C(E_*, \cdot)$. We prove that an alternative $x \in C(E_*, R^N)$ if and only if it can be reached by a feasible elimination procedure (see Definition 5.3.8 and Theorem 5.4.2). In Section 5.5 we investigate possible constructions of exactly and strongly consistent anonymous SCFs whose blocking function is not additive. Finally, in Section 5.6, we discuss possible applications of our results to mass elections and representation of symmetric simple games.

Section 5.1 is based on Moulin and Peleg [1982]. Section 5.2 consists of a generalization of some of the results in Oren [1981]. Section 5.3 is based on Peleg [1978a] and Oren [1981]. The investigation in Sections 5.4 and 5.5 has greatly benefited from Polishchuk [1978].

5.1 Partial implementation

In this section we generalize the notion of exact M-consistency (see Definition 4.1.18). Our generalization will enable us to define exactly M-consistent SCCs and to prove (in the next chapter) the existence of "exactly and strongly consistent" (in our new generalized sense) SCCs. We start with the following definition.

Let A be a finite set of m alternatives, $m \geq 2$, and let $N = \{1, \ldots, n\}$ be a society. If S is a coalition, and for each $i \in S$, Σ^i is a nonempty set, then we denote by Σ^S the Cartesian product $\times_{i \in S} \Sigma^i$.

Definition 5.1.1. A *game form* (GF) is an $(n+1)$-tuple $\Gamma = (\Sigma^1, \ldots, \Sigma^n; \pi)$, where Σ^i, $i = 1, \ldots, n$, is a nonempty finite set, and π is a function from Σ^N to A.

Remark 5.1.2. Let $\Gamma = (\Sigma^1, \ldots, \Sigma^n; \pi)$ be a GF (see Definition 5.1.1). Σ^i is called the set of *strategies* of player $i \in N$, and π is the *outcome function*. Intuitively, Γ is a "generalized voting scheme" that enables the members of N to choose one alternative out of A.

Remark 5.1.3. Let $F: L^N \to A$ be an SCF (see Definition 2.4.1). Then F is, essentially, equivalent to the GF $(L, \ldots, L; F)$.

We now generalize Definition 2.5.1.

Definition 5.1.4. Let $\Gamma = (\Sigma^1, \ldots, \Sigma^n; \pi)$ be a GF (see Definition 5.1.1), and let $R^N \in L^N$. The *game associated with Γ and R^N* is the n-person game in normal form

$$g(\Gamma, R^N) = (\Sigma^1, \ldots, \Sigma^n; \pi; R^1, \ldots, R^n)$$

where R^i is the preference relation of player i on the outcome space A. (See also Remark 5.1.2.)

Notation 5.1.5. Let $\Gamma = (\Sigma^1, \ldots, \Sigma^n; \pi)$ be a GF, and let $S, T \in 2^N$, $T \subset S$. For $y^S \in \Sigma^S$, we denote by y^T the restriction of y^S to T.

We are now able to generalize Definition 4.1.14.

Definition 5.1.6. Let $\Gamma = (\Sigma^1, \ldots, \Sigma^n; \pi)$ be a GF, let $R^N \in L^N$, and let $M \subset 2^N$, $M \neq \varnothing$ (see Notation 4.1.13); $e^N \in \Sigma^N$ is an *M-e.p.* of $g(\Gamma, R^N)$ (see Definition 5.1.4) if for every $S \in M$ and for every $y^S \in \Sigma^S$ there exists a player $i \in S$ such that $\pi(e^N) R^i \pi(e^{N-S}, y^S)$ (see Notation 5.1.5). The set of all M-e.p.'s of $g(\Gamma, R^N)$ will be denoted by e.p.(M, Γ, R^N).

Remark 5.1.7. Let $\Gamma = (\Sigma^1, \ldots, \Sigma^n; \pi)$ be a GF, and let $R^N \in L^N$. If $M = 2^N$, then an M-e.p. is called a *strong* e.p. (See also Definition 4.1.17.) The set of strong e.p.'s of $g(\Gamma, R^N)$ is denoted by s.e.p.(Γ, R^N) $(= \text{e.p.}(2^N, \Gamma, R^N))$.

We are now able to generalize Definition 4.1.18.

Definition 5.1.8. Let $H: L^N \to 2^A$ be an SCC, let $\Gamma = (\Sigma^1, \ldots, \Sigma^n; \pi)$ be a GF, and let $M \subset 2^N$, $M \neq \varnothing$. Γ *(partially) M-implements H* if for every $R^N \in L^N$,

$$H(R^N) = \pi(\text{e.p.}(M, \Gamma, R^N))(H(R^N) \subset \pi(\text{e.p.}(M, \Gamma, R^N)))$$

We shall say that Γ *(partially) implements H* if Γ (partially) 2^N-implements H.

Remark 5.1.9. Let $F: L^N \to A$ be an SCF, and let $M \subset 2^N$, $M \neq \varnothing$. Then F is exactly M-consistent (see Definition 4.1.18) if and only if the GF $(L, \ldots, L; F)$ partially M-implements F (i.e., F partially M-implements itself). In particular, F is exactly and strongly consistent if and only if F is partially self-implementable (see Definitions 5.1.8 and 4.1.18).

Remark 5.1.10. Let $H: L^N \to 2^A$ be an SCC, and let $\Gamma = (\Sigma^1, \ldots, \Sigma^n; \pi)$ be a GF (see Definition 5.1.1). Further, let $M \subset 2^N$ such that $\{i\} \in M$ for all $i \in N$. If the choice from A is performed by a play of Γ, and M is the set of all coalitions that are allowed to coordinate their strategies, then a *necessary* condition for H to be "acceptable" is that it is partially M-implementable by Γ. (See also Remarks 4.1.2 and 4.1.16.)

Remark 5.1.11. Let H be an SCC, and let Γ be a GF that M-implements H. Then, in order for H to be "acceptable," Γ has to be "acceptable" in the first place (i.e., Γ has to be a "reasonable" (generalized) voting scheme).

We shall now investigate some basic properties of implementable SCCs. First, however, we need the following definitions.

Definition 5.1.12. Let $\Gamma = (\Sigma^1, \ldots, \Sigma^n; \pi)$ be a GF (see Definition 5.1.1), let $S \in 2^N$, and let $B \in 2^A$. S is α-*effective for* B if there exists $x^S \in \Sigma^S$ such that for all $y^{N-S} \in \Sigma^{N-S}$, $\pi(x^S, y^{N-S}) \in B$. S is β-*effective for* B if for every $y^{N-S} \in \Sigma^{N-S}$ there exists $x^S \in \Sigma^S$ such that $\pi(x^S, y^{N-S}) \in B$.

Definition 5.1.13. Let $\Gamma = (\Sigma^1, \ldots, \Sigma^n; \pi)$ be a GF. The α-*effectivity function* associated with Γ, $E_\alpha = E_\alpha(\Gamma): 2^N \to P(2^A)$ (see Notation 4.1.20), is given by

$$E_\alpha(S) = \{B \mid B \in 2^A, \text{ and } S \text{ is } \alpha\text{-effective for } B\} \tag{5.1.1}$$

for every $S \in 2^N$ (see Definition 5.1.12). The β-*effectivity function* associated with Γ, $E_\beta = E_\beta(\Gamma): 2^N \to P(2^A)$, is given by

$$E_\beta(S) = \{B \mid B \in 2^A, \text{ and } S \text{ is } \beta\text{-effective for } B\} \tag{5.1.2}$$

for every $S \in 2^N$ (see Definition 5.1.12).

We are now able to prove the following lemma.

Lemma 5.1.14. *Let* $H: L^N \to 2^A$ *be an SCC, and let* $\Gamma = (\Sigma^1, \ldots, \Sigma^n; \pi)$ *be a GF. If* H *is partially implemented by* Γ *(see Definition 5.1.8), then* $E_\alpha(\Gamma) = E_\beta(\Gamma) = E^*(H) = E_\alpha(H) = E_\beta(H)$ *(see Definitions 5.1.13 and 4.1.21).*

Proof: Let $S \in 2^N$ and $B \in 2^A$. Assume first that $B \in E_\beta(H; S)$ (i.e., S is β-effective for B with respect to H). Let $Q^{N-S} \in L^{N-S}$ satisfy $aQ^i b$ for all $a \in A - B$, $b \in B$, and $i \in N - S$. By assumption, there exists $R^S \in L^S$ such that $H(R^S, Q^{N-S}) \subset B$. Let $x^N \in \Sigma^N$ be a strong e.p. of $g(\Gamma, (R^S, Q^{N-S}))$ (see Remark 5.1.7 and Definition 5.1.4) such that $\pi(x^N) \in B$. Then, for every $y^{N-S} \in \Sigma^{N-S}$, $\pi(x^S, y^{N-S}) \in B$. Hence, $B \in E_\alpha(\Gamma; S)$ (i.e., S is α-effective for B with respect to Γ).

Assume now that $B \in E_\beta(\Gamma; S)$. Let $R^S \in L^S$ satisfy $bR^i a$ for all $b \in B$, $a \in A - B$, and $i \in S$. We claim that $H(R^S, Q^{N-S}) \subset B$ for all $Q^{N-S} \in L^{N-S}$. Indeed, assume, on the contrary, that there exist $P^{N-S} \in L^{N-S}$ and $a \in A$ such that $a \in H(R^S, P^{N-S})$ and $a \notin B$. Let x^N be a strong e.p. of $g(\Gamma, (R^S, P^{N-S}))$ such that $\pi(x^N) = a$. Since S is β-effective for B (with respect to Γ), there exists $y^S \in \Sigma^S$ such that $\pi(y^S, x^{N-S}) \in B$. Let $\pi(y^S, x^{N-S}) = b$. Then $bR^i a$ for all $i \in S$. Thus, x^N is not a strong e.p. of $g(\Gamma, (R^S, P^{N-S}))$, and the desired contradiction has been obtained. We conclude that $B \in E^*(H; S)$.

We have shown that for every $S \in 2^N$, $E_\beta(H; S) \subset E_\alpha(\Gamma; S)$ and $E^*(H; S) \supset E_\beta(\Gamma; S)$. Since $E_\alpha(\Gamma; S) \subset E_\beta(\Gamma; S)$, $E^*(H; S) \subset E_\alpha(H; S)$, and $E_\alpha(H; S) \subset E_\beta(H; S)$, the proof is complete.

Corollary 5.1.15. Let $H: L^N \rightarrow 2^A$ be an SCC. If H is partially implementable, then H is strongly tight.

Proof: Definitions 5.1.8 and 4.1.27 and Lemma 5.1.14.

Corollary 5.1.15 consists of a generalization of Corollary 4.1.29.
The following definition will be useful in the sequel.

Definition 5.1.16. A function $E: 2^N \rightarrow P(2^A)$ is *maximal* if for every $S \in 2^N$ and $B \in 2^A$,

$$B \notin E(S) \Rightarrow A - B \in E(N-S) \tag{5.1.3}$$

Lemma 5.1.17. *Let Γ be a GF (see Definition 5.1.1). Then $E_\alpha(\Gamma) = E_\beta(\Gamma)$ if and only if $E_\alpha(\Gamma)$ is maximal (see Definitions 5.1.13 and 5.1.16).*

Proof: Let $S \in 2^N$ and $B \in 2^A$. Then $B \notin E_\alpha(S)$ if and only if $A - B \in E_\beta(N-S)$. Suppose now that $E_\alpha(\Gamma)$ is maximal. Let $S \in 2^N$ and $B \in E_\beta(S)$. Then, by the foregoing remark, $A - B \notin E_\alpha(N-S)$. By (5.1.3), $B \in E_\alpha(S)$. Thus, $E_\alpha(S) \supset E_\beta(S)$ (and therefore $E_\alpha(S) = E_\beta(S)$) for all $S \in 2^N$.

Assume now that $E_\alpha(\Gamma) = E_\beta(\Gamma)$, and let $S \in 2^N$ and $B \in 2^A$. If $B \notin E_\alpha(S)$, then, again by our first remark, $A - B \in E_\beta(N-S)$. Hence, by assumption, $A - B \in E_\alpha(N-S)$. Thus, E_α is maximal.

Corollary 5.1.18. Let H be an SCC. If H is partially implementable (see Definition 5.1.8), then $E^*(H)$ is maximal (see Definitions 4.1.21 and 5.1.16).

Proof: Lemmata 5.1.14 and 5.1.17.

We now generalize Lemma 4.1.25 to partially implementable SCCs. We start with the following definition.

Definition 5.1.19. An SCC $H: L^N \rightarrow 2^A$ is *stable* if for every $R^N \in L^N$, $H(R^N) \subset C(E^*, R^N)$, where $E^* = E^*(H)$ (see Definitions 4.1.21 and 4.1.23).

Lemma 5.1.20. *Let $H: L^N \to 2^A$ be an SCC. If H is partially implementable, then H is stable* (see Definitions 5.1.8 and 5.1.19).

Proof: Let $R^N \in L^N$. We have to show that $H(R^N) \subset C(E^*, R^N)$ (where $E^* = E^*(H)$). Assume, on the contrary, that there exists $a \in H(R^N)$ such that $a \notin C(E^*, R^N)$. Now, H is partially implemented by a GF $\Gamma = (\Sigma^1, \ldots, \Sigma^n; \pi)$. Hence, there exists a strong e.p. x^N of the game $g(\Gamma, R^N)$ such that $\pi(x^N) = a$. Now, by our assumption, there exist $S \in 2^N$ and $B \in E^*(H; S)$ such that $a \notin B$ and $bR^i a$ for all $b \in B$ and $i \in S$. By Lemma 5.1.14, $B \in E_\beta(\Gamma; S)$. Hence, there exists $y^S \in \Sigma^S$ such that $\pi(y^S, x^{N-S}) \in B$. Let $b = \pi(y^S, x^{N-S})$. Then $bR^i a$ for all $i \in S$. Thus, x^N is not a strong e.p. of $g(\Gamma, R^N)$, and the desired contradiction has been obtained.

The following two examples show that maximality and stability are independent properties (of SCCs).

Example 5.1.21. Let $G = (3, 2)$ (see Definition 2.6.4), and let A be a set of three alternatives. We define an SCC $H: L^N \to 2^A$ by the following rule. Let $R^N \in L^N$. If $C(N, W, A, R^N) \neq \varnothing$, then we define $H(R^N) = C(N, W, A, R^N)$ (see Definition 2.6.8). Otherwise (i.e., if $C(N, W, A, R^N) = \varnothing$), we define $H(R^N) = A$. Let $S \subset N$. If $|S| \geq 2$ (see Notation 2.1.7), then $E^*(S) = E_\alpha(S) = E_\beta(S) = 2^A$, and if $|S| = 1$, then $E^*(S) = E_\alpha(S) = E_\beta(S) = \{A\}$. Thus, $E^*(H)$ is maximal (see Definition 5.1.16). By the proof of Theorem 4.1.35, there exists $R^N \in L^N$ such that $C(N, W, A, R^N) = \varnothing$. By Theorem 3.2.5 and Remark 4.1.24, $C(E^*, R^N) = \varnothing$. Hence, H is not stable (see Definition 5.1.19).

Example 5.1.22. Let $N = \{1, 2, 3\}$, and let $A = \{x_1, x_2, x_3\}$. Consider the Borda correspondence $B(3, 3)$ (see Example 3.1.18). Let $S \subset N$. If $|S| = 1$, then $E^*(S) = E_\alpha(S) = E_\beta(S) = \{A\}$. If $|S| = 2$, then $E_\alpha(S) = E_\beta(S) = 2^A$, and $E^*(S) = \{B \mid B \in 2^A \text{ and } |B| \geq 2\}$. Also, $E^*(N) = E_\alpha(N) = E_\beta(N) = 2^A$. Thus, $E^*(B(3, 3))$ is *not* maximal (see Definition 5.1.16). However, as the reader can easily verify, $B(3, 3)$ is stable (see Definition 5.1.19).

5.2 The coefficients of a partially implementable and anonymous SCC

Let N be a society, and let A be a finite set of alternatives.

Definition 5.2.1. A function $E: 2^N \to P(2^A)$ (see Notation 4.1.20) is *regular* if it satisfies

$$S \in 2^N \quad \text{and} \quad B \in E(S) \Rightarrow A - B \notin E(N - S)$$

Remark 5.2.2. If $H: L^N \to 2^A$ is an SCC, then $E^*(H)$ and $E_\alpha(H)$ are regular (see Definitions 4.1.21 and 5.2.1), whereas $E_\beta(H)$ may not be regular (see Definition 4.1.21, Remark 4.1.22, and Example 3.1.13).

Remark 5.2.3. A systematic investigation of the properties of the effectivity functions $E^*(H)$, $E_\alpha(H)$, and $E_\beta(H)$ of an SCC H will be presented in the next chapter.

Definition 5.2.4. A function $E: 2^N \to P(2^A)$ (see Notation 4.1.20) is *monotonic with respect to the players* (i.e., the members of N) if for every $S \in 2^N$ and $B \in E(S)$, if $T \supset S$ ($T \in 2^N$), then $B \in E(T)$.

Remark 5.2.5. If $H: L^N \to 2^A$ is an SCC, then $E^*(H)$, $E_\alpha(H)$, and $E_\beta(H)$ are monotonic with respect to the players (see Definitions 4.1.21 and 5.2.4).

Definition 5.2.6. An SCC $H: L^N \to 2^A$ satisfies *nonimposition* (NI) if for every $a \in A$ there exists $R^N \in L^N$ such that $H(R^N) = a$ (see Notation 2.4.3).

Remark 5.2.7. Let H be an SCC. If H is Paretian (see Definition 2.3.4), then it satisfies NI (see Definition 5.2.6).

Definition 5.2.8. Let $H: L^N \to 2^A$ be a strongly tight and anonymous SCC that satisfies NI (see Definitions 4.1.27, 2.3.6, and 5.2.6), and let $B \subset A$, $B \neq \varnothing, A$. The *winning coefficient* of B is defined by

$$w(H; B) = w(B) = \min\{|S| \mid B \in E^*(H; S)\} \tag{5.2.1}$$

(see Notation 2.1.7 and Definition 4.1.21). We also define $w(\varnothing) = n + 1$ and $w(A) = 0$. Let, again, $B \subset A$. The *blocking coefficient* of B is defined by $\beta(B) = w(A - B)$.

Remark 5.2.9. Since H is strongly tight, $E^*(H) = E_\alpha(H)$. Hence, because H satisfies NI, $w(B)$ is well defined for all B (see (5.2.1)).

Remark 5.2.10. For $B \subset A$, $B \neq \varnothing, A$, $w(B)$ is the size of a minimal winning coalition for B (see Definition 4.1.19 and Remark 5.2.5).

Lemma 5.2.11. *Let $H: L^N \to 2^A$ be a partially implementable SCC* (see Definition 5.1.8). *If H is anonymous and satisfies NI, then for all $B \subset A$,*

$$w(B) + \beta(B) = n + 1 \qquad (5.2.2)$$

(see Definition 5.2.8).

Proof: Clearly, we may assume $B \neq \emptyset, A$. Since $E^*(H)$ is regular, we must have

$$w(B) + \beta(B) = w(B) + w(A - B) \geqslant n + 1$$

To prove the reverse inequality, let $S \subset N$ such that $|S| = \beta(B) - 1$. Then S is not winning for $A - B$. Since H is partially implementable, $E^*(H)$ is maximal (see Corollary 5.1.18). Hence, $B \in E^*(N - S)$. Thus,

$$w(B) \leqslant |N - S| = n - \{\beta(B) - 1\} = n + 1 - \beta(B)$$

Therefore, $w(B) + \beta(B) \leqslant n + 1$, and the proof is complete.

Remark 5.2.12. Let $H: L^N \to 2^A$ be a strongly tight SCC (see Definition 4.1.27). If H is anonymous and satisfies NI (see Definition 5.2.6), then for all $B_1, B_2 \in 2^A$, $\beta(B_1 \cup B_2) \leqslant \beta(B_1) + \beta(B_2)$ (see Definition 5.2.8).

Lemma 5.2.13. *Let $H: L^N \to 2^A$ be a partially implementable and anonymous SCC* (see Definition 5.1.8). *Assume also that H satisfies NI* (see Definition 5.2.6). *If $B_1, B_2 \in 2^A$ and $B_1 \cap B_2 = \emptyset$, then*

$$\beta(B_1 \cup B_2) \geqslant \beta(B_1) + \beta(B_2) - 1 \qquad (5.2.3)$$

(see Definition 5.2.8).

It is convenient to introduce at this point the following notation.

Notation 5.2.14. Let $B_1, B_2 \in 2^A$ such that $B_1 \cap B_2 = \emptyset$, and let $S \in 2^N$. We write $B_1 R^S B_2$ (for $R^S \in L^S$) if $x R^i y$ for all $x \in B_1$, $y \in B_2$, and $i \in S$.

Proof of Lemma 5.2.13. Assume, on the contrary, that $\beta(B_1 \cup B_2) < \beta(B_1) + \beta(B_2) - 1$. Then there exists a partition (S, T, V) of N such that $|S| < \beta(B_1)$, $|T| < \beta(B_2)$, and $|S \cup T| = \beta(B_1 \cup B_2)$. Let $B_3 = A - (B_1 \cup B_2)$, and let $R^N \in L^N$ satisfy

$$B_3 R^S B_2 R^S B_1 \qquad (5.2.4)$$

$$B_1 R^T B_3 R^T B_2 \qquad (5.2.5)$$

and

$$B_2 R^V B_1 R^V B_3 \qquad (5.2.6)$$

(see Notation 5.2.14). We shall now prove that $C(E^*(H), R^N) = \emptyset$ and thereby arrive at the desired contradiction (see Lemma 5.1.20). Indeed, let $x \in B_3$. Then, by (5.2.5) and (5.2.6), $B_1 R^{T \cup V} x$. Now, $|T \cup V| = n - |S| > n - \beta(B_1) = w(B_1) - 1$ (see Lemma 5.2.11). Hence, $|T \cup V| \geqslant w(B_1)$ and $B_1 \in E^*(T \cup V)$ (see Definition 5.2.8). Similarly, let $x \in B_2$. Then $B_3 R^{S \cup T} x$ (see (5.2.4) and (5.2.5)). Now $|S \cup T| = \beta(B_1 \cup B_2) = w(A - (B_1 \cup B_2)) = w(B_3)$. Hence, $B_3 \in E^*(S \cup T)$. Finally, let $x \in B_1$. Then $B_2 R^{S \cup V} x$ (see (5.2.4) and (5.2.6)). Now, $|S \cup V| = n - |T| > n - \beta(B_2) = w(B_2) - 1$ (see Lemma 5.2.11). Hence, $|S \cup V| \geqslant w(B_2)$ and $B_2 \in E^*(S \cup V)$. Thus, we have shown that $C(E^*, R^N) = \varnothing$ (see Definition 4.1.23).

The following definition is useful.

Definition 5.2.15. Let $H: L^N \to 2^A$ be a strongly tight and anonymous SCC (see Definition 4.1.27). Assume also that H satisfies NI (see Definition 5.2.6). The *deficiency* of H is defined as

$$\text{def}(H) = \sum_{i=1}^{m} \beta(x_i) - (n+1) \tag{5.2.7}$$

where $A = \{x_1, \ldots, x_m\}$ (see Definition 5.2.8).

Theorem 5.2.16. *Let* $H: L^N \to 2^A$ *be a partially implementable and anonymous SCC* (see Definition 5.1.8). *Assume also that H satisfies NI* (see Definition 5.2.6). *Then*

$$0 \leqslant \text{def}(H) \leqslant m - 2 \tag{5.2.8}$$

where $|A| = m \geqslant 2$ (see Definition 5.2.15).

Proof: It follows from Definition 5.2.8 and Remark 5.2.12 that

$$n + 1 = \beta(A) \leqslant \sum_{i=1}^{m} \beta(x_i) \qquad (\text{where } A = \{x_1, \ldots, x_m\})$$

Hence, $\text{def}(H) \geqslant 0$. Now let $A_j = \{x_1, \ldots, x_j\}$ for $j = 1, \ldots, m-1$. Then, by Lemmata 5.2.11 and 5.2.13,

$$n + 1 = \beta(A_{m-1}) + \beta(x_m) \geqslant \beta(A_{m-2}) + \beta(x_{m-1}) - 1 + \beta(x_m)$$

$$\geqslant \cdots \geqslant \sum_{i=1}^{m} \beta(x_i) - (m-2)$$

Thus, $\text{def}(H) \leqslant m - 2$.

The following class of SCCs will play an important role in the sequel.

Definition 5.2.17. Let $H: L^N \to 2^A$ be a strongly tight and anonymous SCC (see Definition 4.1.27). Assume also that H satisfies NI (see Definition 5.2.6). We say that H is *independently blocking* if for all $B_1, B_2 \in 2^A$ such that $B_1 \cap B_2 = \varnothing$, $\beta(B_1 \cup B_2) = \beta(B_1) + \beta(B_2)$.

The following result is true.

Lemma 5.2.18. *Let $H: L^N \to 2^A$ be a partially implementable and anonymous SCC* (see Definition 5.1.8). *Assume also that H satisfies NI* (see Definition 5.2.6). *Then H is independently blocking if and only if* $\mathrm{def}(H) = 0$ (see Definitions 5.2.15 and 5.2.17).

Proof: Assume first that H is independently blocking. Let $A = \{x_1, \ldots, x_m\}$, and let $A_j = \{x_1, \ldots, x_j\}$ for $j = 1, \ldots, m-1$. Then

$$n+1 = \beta(A) = \beta(x_m) + \beta(A_{m-1}) = \beta(x_m) + \beta(x_{m-1}) + \beta(A_{m-2})$$

$$= \cdots = \sum_{i=1}^{m} \beta(x_i)$$

Thus, $\mathrm{def}(H) = \sum_{i=1}^{m} \beta(x_i) - (n+1) = 0$.

Assume now that $\mathrm{def}(H) = 0$. We have to show that H is independently blocking. Assume, on the contrary, that there exist $B_1, B_2 \in 2^A$ such that $B_1 \cap B_2 = \varnothing$ and $\beta(B_1 \cup B_2) < \beta(B_1) + \beta(B_2)$. Then

$$\beta(B_1 \cup B_2) + \sum \{\beta(x) \mid x \in A - (B_1 \cup B_2)\}$$

$$< \beta(B_1) + \beta(B_2) + \sum \{\beta(x) \mid x \in A - (B_1 \cup B_2)\} \leqslant \sum_{i=1}^{m} \beta(x_i) = n+1$$

But

$$\beta(B_1 \cup B_2) + \sum \{\beta(x) \mid x \in A - (B_1 \cup B_2)\} \geqslant \beta(B_1 \cup B_2) + \beta(A - (B_1 \cup B_2))$$

$$= \beta(B_1 \cup B_2) + w(B_1 \cup B_2) = n+1$$

(see (5.2.2)), and the desired contradiction has been obtained.

We shall now use Theorem 5.2.16 in order to prove that a partially implementable and anonymous SCC depends on every player's complete order over the alternatives. We start with the following notation.

Notation 5.2.19. Let $A = \{x_1, \ldots, x_m\}$ be a set of m alternatives, $m \geqslant 3$. For $1 \leqslant k \leqslant m-2$ and for $R \in L$ (see Definition 2.1.3), we denote $R_{(k)} = (t_1(R), \ldots, t_k(R))$ (see Notation 2.1.8). Also, if $N = \{1, \ldots, n\}$ is a society and $R^N \in L^N$ (see Notation 2.2.1), then we denote $R_{(k)}^N = (R_{(k)}^1, \ldots, R_{(k)}^n)$. Finally, $L_{(k)}^N = \{R_{(k)}^N \mid R^N \in L^N\}$.

We are now able to state the following lemma.

Lemma 5.2.20. *Let* $H: L^N \to 2^A$ *be a partially implementable anonymous SCC (see Definition 5.1.8). Assume also that* $|A| = m \geqslant 3$ *and that* H *satisfies NI (see Definition 5.2.6). If* $1 \leqslant k \leqslant m-2$ *and* $n \geqslant (m-1)/(m-k-1)$, *then there exists no function* $h: L_{(k)}^N \to 2^A$ *such that* $H(R^N) = h(R_{(k)}^N)$ *for all* $R^N \in L^N$.

Proof: Let $1 \leqslant k \leqslant m-2$ and $n \geqslant (m-1)/(m-k-1)$. We claim that there exists $R^N \in L^N$ with the following property: For each $x \in A$, the set

$$\{j \mid j \in N \text{ and } t_{k+1}(R^j) R^j x\}$$

contains at least $\beta(x)$ players (see Definition 5.2.8). Indeed, for each $x \in A$, $\beta(x) \leqslant n$. Thus, in order to show the existence of an $R^N \in L^N$ with the foregoing property, we have only to prove the inequality $n(m-k) \geqslant \sum_{x \in A} \beta(x)$. However,

$$n(m-k) = n + n(m-k-1) \geqslant n + m - 1 \geqslant \sum_{x \in A} \beta(x)$$

(see Theorem 5.2.16). Assume now, on the contrary, that there exists a function $h: L_{(k)}^N \to 2^A$ such that $H(P^N) = h(P_{(k)}^N)$ for all $P^N \in L^N$. Let $x \in H(R^N)$. By the foregoing construction, there exists $Q^N \in L^N$ such that (a) $Q_{(k)}^N = R_{(k)}^N$ and (b) $|\{j \mid j \in N \text{ and } t_m(Q^j) = x\}| = \beta(x)$ (see Notation 2.1.7). By Definition 5.2.8, $H(Q^N) \subset A - \{x\}$. On the other hand,

$$x \in H(R^N) = h(R_{(k)}^N) = h(Q_{(k)}^N) = H(Q^N)$$

and the desired contradiction has been obtained.

5.3   A characterization of the class of anonymous, exactly and strongly consistent, and independently blocking SCFs

Let $N = \{1, \ldots, n\}$ be a society, and let $A = \{x_1, \ldots, x_m\}$ be a set of m alternatives, $m \geqslant 2$. Assume that $n \geqslant m-1$. Furthermore, let $\beta_*: A \to \{1, \ldots, n\}$ satisfy $\sum_{i=1}^{m} \beta_*(x_i) = n+1$. In this section we determine all the SCFs $F: L^N \to A$ that are anonymous and exactly and strongly consistent and that satisfy, in addition, $\beta(F; x_i) = \beta_*(x_i)$ for $i = 1, \ldots, m$ (see Definitions 2.3.6 and 4.1.18 and Lemma 5.2.18). We start with the following definition.

Definition 5.3.1. *The function* $E_* = E_*(\beta_*): 2^N \to P(2^A)$ *associated with* $\beta_*(\cdot)$ *is defined by*

$$B \in E_*(S) \Leftrightarrow |S| \geqslant \beta_*(A-B) \tag{5.3.1}$$

where $\beta_*(B) = \sum_{x \in B} \beta_*(x)$ *for all* $B \in 2^A$ *(and* $\beta_*(\emptyset) = 0$*).*

Remark 5.3.2. For each $S \in 2^N$, $A \in E_*(S)$ and $\varnothing \notin E_*(S)$. Also, $E_*(N) = 2^A$. Furthermore, E_* is regular and maximal (see Definitions 5.2.1 and 5.1.16).

We are now able to show the following.

Lemma 5.3.3. *Let* $F: L^N \to A$ *be exactly and strongly consistent and anonymous, and let* $\beta(F; x_i) = \beta_*(x_i)$ *for* $i = 1, \ldots, m$. *Then* $E^*(F) = E_*$ (see Definition 4.1.21).

Proof: Let $B \in E_*(S)$. Then $\beta_*(A - B) \leq |S|$. Let $A - B = \{y_1, \ldots, y_h\}$, and let $S_1, \ldots, S_h$ be a partition of S such that $|S_i| \geq \beta_*(y_i)$ for $i = 1, \ldots, h$. Choose $R^S \in L^S$ such that $t_m(R^j) = y_i$ for all $j \in S_i$ and for $i = 1, \ldots, h$. Let $P^{N-S} \in L^{N-S}$. Then

$$y_i \notin C(E^*(F), (R^S, P^{N-S})) \quad \text{for } i = 1, \ldots, h$$

(see Definitions 4.1.23 and 5.2.8). By Lemma 4.1.25 and Corollary 4.1.29, $F(R^S, P^{N-S}) \in B$ for all $P^{N-S} \in L^{N-S}$. Thus, $B \in E_\alpha(F; S)$. Hence, by Corollary 4.1.29, $B \in E^*(F; S)$. Thus, $E^*(F; S) \supset E_*(S)$ for all $S \in 2^N$. Since E_* is maximal and $E^*(F)$ is regular, $E^*(F) = E_*$ (see Remarks 5.3.2 and 5.2.2).

Corollary 5.3.4. *Let* $F: L^N \to A$ *be exactly and strongly consistent and anonymous, and let* $\beta(F; x_i) = \beta_*(x_i)$ *for* $i = 1, \ldots, m$. *Then* F *is a selection from* $C(E_*, \cdot)$ (see Definition 4.1.23).

Proof: Lemmata 5.3.3 and 4.1.25 and Corollary 4.1.29.

We shall now prove the converse to Corollary 5.3.4. We start with the following lemmata.

Lemma 5.3.5. *Let* $R^N \in L^N$, *let* $x \in A$, *and let* $A - \{x\} = \{y_1, \ldots, y_{m-1}\}$. *Then* $x \in C(E_*, R^N)$ (see Definition 4.1.23) *if and only if there exist coalitions* $C_1, \ldots, C_{m-1}$ *such that*

$$C_i \cap C_j = \varnothing \quad \text{if } i \neq j \tag{5.3.2}$$

$$|C_i| = \beta_*(y_i) \quad \text{for } i = 1, \ldots, m-1 \tag{5.3.3}$$

$$xR^j y_i \quad \text{for all } j \in C_i \text{ and for } i = 1, \ldots, m-1 \tag{5.3.4}$$

Proof: Necessity. Let $x \in C(E_*, R^N)$. For each $y \in A - \{x\}$, let $S(y) = \{i \mid i \in N \text{ and } xR^i y\}$. Now let $B \subset A - \{x\}$. Because $x \in C(E_*, R^N)$,

$$|\{i \mid i \in N \text{ and } BR^i x\}| < \beta_*(A - B) \tag{5.3.5}$$

(see (5.3.1) and Notation 5.2.14). Now

$$\cup \{S(y) \mid y \in B\} = N - \{i \mid i \in N \text{ and } BR^i x\} \qquad (5.3.6)$$

It follows now from (5.3.5) and (5.3.6) that

$$|\cup \{S(y) \mid y \in B\}| \geqslant n + 1 - \beta_*(A - B) = \beta_*(B)$$

By a suitable generalization of the "Marriage Theorem" (see R. J. Wilson [1979, p. 118]), there exist coalitions $C_1, \ldots, C_{m-1}$, $C_i \subset S(y_i)$ for $i = 1, \ldots, m-1$, that satisfy (5.3.2) and (5.3.3).

Sufficiency. Assume that there exist coalitions $C_1, \ldots, C_{m-1}$ that satisfy (5.3.2), (5.3.3), and (5.3.4). Let $B \subset A - \{x\}$. For $y \in A - \{x\}$, denote, again, $S(y) = \{i \mid i \in N \text{ and } x R^i y\}$. Clearly, $S(y_i) \supset C_i$ for $i = 1, \ldots, m-1$. We now compute

$$|\{i \mid i \in N \text{ and } BR^i x\}| = n - |\cup \{S(y) \mid y \in B\}|$$

$$\leqslant n - |\cup \{C_i \mid y_i \in B\}| = n - \beta_*(B) < \beta_*(A - B)$$

(see Notation 5.2.14 and Definition 5.3.1). Thus,

$$B \notin E_*(\{i \mid i \in N \text{ and } BR^i x\})$$

Hence, because B is arbitrary, $x \in C(E_*, R^N)$ (see Definition 4.1.23).

Lemma 5.3.6. *If an SCF $F: L^N \to A$ is a selection from $C(E_*, \cdot)$, then F is exactly and strongly consistent.*

Proof: Let $R^N \in L^N$, let $x = F(R^N)$ and let $A - \{x\} = \{y_1, \ldots, y_{m-1}\}$. By our assumption, $x \in C(E_*, R^N)$. Hence, by Lemma 5.3.5, there exist coalitions $C_1, \ldots, C_{m-1}$ that satisfy (5.3.2), (5.3.3), and (5.3.4). Let $Q^N \in L^N$ satisfy

$$y_i = t_m(Q^j) \quad \text{for all } j \in C_i \text{ and } i = 1, \ldots, m-1 \qquad (5.3.7)$$

(see Notation 2.1.8). Then $y_i \notin C(E_*, Q^N)$ for $i = 1, \ldots, m-1$ (see Definitions 4.1.23 and 5.3.1). By our assumption, $F(Q^N) \in C(E_*, Q^N)$. Hence, $F(Q^N) = x$. We shall now prove that Q^N is a strong e.p. of $g(F, R^N)$ (see Definitions 4.1.17 and 2.5.1). Indeed, assume, on the contrary, that there exist a coalition T and $P^T \in L^T$ such that $F(Q^{N-T}, P^T) = z$, $z \neq x$, and $zR^j x$ for all $j \in T$. Then there exists $1 \leqslant h \leqslant m-1$ such that $z = y_h$. By (5.3.4), $T \cap C_h = \emptyset$. Thus, $C_h \subset N - T$ and $t_m(Q^j) = z$ for all $j \in C_h$ (see (5.3.7)). Hence, $z \notin C(E_*, (Q^{N-T}, P^T))$ (see Definitions 4.1.23 and 5.3.1). Therefore, $z \neq F(Q^{N-T}, P^T)$, and the desired contradiction has been obtained.

We are now able to prove our characterization theorem.

Theorem 5.3.7. *Let $F: L^N \to A$ be an anonymous SCF. Then F is exactly and strongly consistent, and $\beta(F; x_i) = \beta_*(x_i)$ for $i = 1, \ldots, m$, if and only if $F(R^N) \in C(E_*, R^N)$ for all $R^N \in L^N$.*

Proof: In order to complete the proof of the theorem, we have only to show that if F is a selection from $C(E_*, \cdot)$, then $\beta(F; x_i) = \beta_*(x_i)$ for $i = 1, \ldots, m$ (see Corollary 5.3.4 and Lemma 5.3.6). Thus, assume that $F(R^N) \in C(E_*, R^N)$ for all $R^N \in L^N$. By Definitions 4.1.21 and 4.1.23, $E^*(F; S) \supset E_*(S)$ for all $S \in 2^N$. Since E_* is maximal and $E^*(F)$ is regular, $E_* = E^*(F)$ (see Remarks 5.3.2 and 5.2.2). It is clear now that $\beta(F; x_i) \leqslant \beta_*(x_i)$ for $i = 1, \ldots, m$. Since F is exactly and strongly consistent (see Lemma 5.3.6), $\sum_{i=1}^{m} \beta(F; x_i) \geqslant n + 1$ (see Theorem 5.2.16). Hence, $\beta(F; x_i) = \beta_*(x_i)$ for $i = 1, \ldots, m - 1$.

We shall now prove that $C(E_*, R^N) \neq \varnothing$ for all $R^N \in L^N$. First we need the following definition.

Definition 5.3.8. Let $R^N \in L^N$. A *feasible elimination procedure* (f.e.p.), with respect to R^N and $\beta_*(\cdot)$, is a sequence $(x_{i_1}, C_1; \ldots; x_{i_{m-1}}, C_{m-1}; x_{i_m})$ (where $C_1, \ldots, C_{m-1}$ are coalitions) that satisfies the following:

If $1 \leqslant s < t \leqslant m - 1$, then $C_t \cap C_s = \varnothing$ (5.3.8)

$|C_j| = \beta_*(x_{i_j})$ for $j = 1, \ldots, m - 1$ (5.3.9)

If $1 \leqslant s < t \leqslant m$, then $x_{i_s} \neq x_{i_t}$ (5.3.10)

x_{i_j} is the worst alternative with respect to $R^s | \{x_{i_j}, \ldots, x_{i_m}\}$
for all $s \in C_j$ and for $j = 1, \ldots, m - 1$ (5.3.11)

(see Notation 2.1.5).

Lemma 5.3.9. *For each $R^N \in L^N$ there exists an f.e.p. with respect to R^N and $\beta_*(\cdot)$ (see Definition 5.3.8).*

Proof: We prove the lemma by induction on m (the number of alternatives). For $m = 2$, the lemma is obvious. We assume that the lemma is true for $m - 1 \geqslant 2$ alternatives, and prove it for m alternatives. Let $R^N \in L^N$. For $x \in A$, let

$$B(x; R^N) = \{i \mid i \in N \text{ and } t_m(R^i) = x\}$$

(see Notation 2.1.8). Since $\sum_{i=1}^{m} \beta_*(x_i) = n + 1$, there exists $x_{i_1} \in A$ such that $|B(x_{i_1}; R^N)| \geqslant \beta_*(x_{i_1})$. Let $C_1 \subset B(x_{i_1}; R^N)$ satisfy $|C_1| = \beta_*(x_{i_1})$, and let $N^* = N - C_1$. Now,

$$\sum_{i \neq i_1} \beta_*(x_i) = n + 1 - \beta_*(x_{i_1}) = n + 1 - |C_1| = n^* + 1$$

where $n^* = |N^*|$. Hence, we may apply the induction hypothesis to $A^* = A - \{x_{i_1}\}$, N^*, and $\beta_* | A^*$ (the restriction of $\beta_*(\cdot)$ to A^*) to obtain an f.e.p. $(x_{i_2}, C_2; \ldots; x_{i_{m-1}}, C_{m-1}; x_{i_m})$ with respect to $R^{N^*} | A^*$ and $\beta_* | A^*$. As the reader can easily verify, $(x_{i_1}, C_1; x_{i_2}, C_2; \ldots; x_{i_{m-1}}, C_{m-1}; x_{i_m})$ is an f.e.p. with respect to R^N and $\beta_*(\cdot)$.

The nonemptiness of $C(E_*, R^N)$ follows now as a corollary.

Corollary 5.3.10. For each $R^N \in L^N$, $C(E_*, R^N)$ is nonempty.

Proof: Let $R^N \in L^N$, and let $(x_{i_1}, C_1; \ldots; x_{i_{m-1}}, C_{m-1}; x_{i_m})$ be an f.e.p. with respect to R^N and $\beta_*(\cdot)$ (see Lemma 5.3.9). It follows now from Definition 5.3.8 and Lemma 5.3.5 that $x_{i_m} \in C(E_*, R^N)$.

Remark 5.3.11. Clearly, the SCC $C(E_*, \cdot)$ is anonymous (see Definitions 5.3.1 and 4.1.23). Hence, by Corollary 5.3.10 and Remark 2.4.7, there exists an anonymous selection from $C(E_*, \cdot)$. Thus, by Theorem 5.3.7, there exists an anonymous and exactly and strongly consistent SCF $F: L^N \to A$ that satisfies, in addition, $\beta(F; x_i) = \beta_*(x_i)$ for $i = 1, \ldots, m$.

The following simple remark guarantees the existence of monotonic selections from $C(E_*, \cdot)$.

Remark 5.3.12. Let $E: 2^N \to P(2^A)$ (see Notation 4.1.20). If the core $C(E, R^N)$ is nonempty for all $R^N \in L^N$, then $C(E, \cdot)$ is a strongly monotonic SCC (see Definitions 4.1.23 and 2.3.15).

Corollary 5.3.13. There exists an anonymous and monotonic selection from $C(E_*, \cdot)$ (see Remarks 2.4.7 and 5.3.12 and Lemma 2.4.8).

5.4   Feasible elimination procedures

Let $N = \{1, \ldots, n\}$ be a society, and let $A = \{x_1, \ldots, x_m\}$ be a set of m alternatives, $m \geq 2$. Assume that $n \geq m - 1$. Furthermore, let $\beta_*: A \to \{1, \ldots, n\}$ satisfy $\sum_{i=1}^m \beta_*(x_i) = n + 1$, and let $E_*(\beta) = E_*: 2^N \to P(2^A)$ be the function that is associated with $\beta_*(\cdot)$ (see Definition 5.3.1). If $R^N \in L^N$ and $(x_{i_1}, C_1; \ldots; x_{i_{m-1}}, C_{m-1}; x_{i_m})$ is an f.e.p. with respect to R^N and $\beta_*(\cdot)$ (see Definition 5.3.8), then $x_{i_m} \in C(E_*, R^N)$ (see the proof of Corollary 5.3.10). This section is devoted to a proof of the converse result; that is, every member of $C(E_*, R^N)$ can be "reached" by an f.e.p. We start with the following notation.

Notation 5.4.1. Let $R^N \in L^N$. If $f = (x_{i_1}, C_1; \ldots; x_{i_{m-1}}, C_{m-1}; x_{i_m})$ is an f.e.p., then we denote $x_{i_m} = t(f)$. Furthermore, we denote by $\phi(R^N) =$

$\phi(N, A, \beta_*(\cdot), R^N)$ the set of all f.e.p.'s with respect to $\beta_*(\cdot)$ and R^N. Finally,

$$M(R^N) = M(N, A, \beta_*(\cdot), R^N) = \{t(f) \mid f \in \phi(R^N)\}$$

The main result of this section is as follows.

Theorem 5.4.2. *For every* $R^N \in L^N$, $M(R^N) = C(E_*, R^N)$ (see Notation 5.4.1 and Definitions 5.3.1 and 4.1.23).

The following definition is needed in the proof of Theorem 5.4.2.

Definition 5.4.3. Let $R, Q \in L$, and let $x \in A$. R is *x-equivalent* to Q, written $R(x)Q$, if for all $y \in A$, xRy if and only if xQy. If $R^N, Q^N \in L^N$, then R^N is *x-equivalent* to Q^N, written $R^N(x)Q^N$, if $R^i(x)Q^i$ for all $i \in N$.

Remark 5.4.4. Let $R, Q \in L$ and $x \in A$. Then $R(x)Q$ if and only if

$$\{y \mid y \in A \text{ and } yRx\} = \{y \mid y \in A \text{ and } yQx\}$$

Thus, (x) is an equivalence relation.

We are now able to state the following lemma.

Lemma 5.4.5. *Let* $R^N, Q^N \in L^N$, *and let* $x \in A$. *If* $R^N(x)Q^N$ (see Definition 5.4.3) *and* $x \in M(R^N)$ (see Notation 5.4.1), *then* $x \in M(Q^N)$.

We postpone the proof of Lemma 5.4.5 and start with the proof of Theorem 5.4.2.

Proof of Theorem 5.4.2. Let $R^N \in L^N$, let $x \in C(E_*, R^N)$, and let $A - \{x\} = \{y_1, \ldots, y_{m-1}\}$. By Lemma 5.3.5, there exist coalitions $C_1, \ldots, C_{m-1}$ such that (5.3.2), (5.3.3), and (5.3.4) are satisfied. We define now a profile $Q^N \in L^N$ in the following way. Let $1 \leqslant i \leqslant m-1$ and $j \in C_i$. Q^j is determined by (a) $Q^j \mid A - \{y_i\} = R^j \mid A - \{y_i\}$ (see Notation 2.1.5) and (b) $t_m(Q^j) = y_i$ (see Notation 2.1.8). For $j \in N - \bigcup_{i=1}^{m-1} C_i$ we define $Q^j = R^j$. Clearly, $Q^N(x)R^N$. Now, $(y_1, C_1; \ldots; y_{m-1}, C_{m-1}; x)$ is an f.e.p. with respect to Q^N and $\beta_*(\cdot)$ (see Definition 5.3.8). Thus, $x \in M(Q^N)$. By Lemma 5.4.5, $x \in M(R^N)$. Thus, $C(E_*, R^N) \subset M(R^N)$. As we noted in the first paragraph of this section, $M(R^N) \subset C(E_*, R^N)$. Thus, the proof is complete.

We now return to the proof of Lemma 5.4.5.

Proof of Lemma 5.4.5. We shall prove the lemma by induction on m (the number of alternatives). If $m = 2$ and $R^N(x)Q^N$, then $R^N = Q^N$ (see Definition 5.4.3), and the lemma is true. We assume now that the lemma is true for $m-1 \geqslant 2$ alternatives and prove it for m alternatives. Thus, let $R^N, Q^N \in L^N$, let $x \in A$, and let $R^N(x)Q^N$. Assume that $x \in M(R^N)$. We have to show that $x \in M(Q^N)$. We first prove the following claim.

Claim 5.4.6. If there exists an f.e.p. $f = (x_{i_1}, C_1; \ldots; x_{i_{m-1}}, C_{m-1}; x)$ with respect to R^N and $\beta_*(\cdot)$ (see Definition 5.3.8) such that $t_m(Q^j) = x_{i_1}$ (see Notation 2.1.8) for all $j \in C_1$, then $x \in M(Q^N)$.

Proof of Claim 5.4.6. Let $N^* = N - C_1$, $A^* = A - \{x_{i_1}\}$, $R_1^{N^*} = R^{N^*} | A^*$, and $Q_1^{N^*} = Q^{N^*} | A^*$ (see Notation 2.2.4). Clearly, $R_1^{N^*}(x)Q_1^{N^*}$. Also, if $f^* = (x_{i_2}, C_2; \ldots; x_{i_{m-1}}, C_{m-1}; x)$, then $f^* \in \phi(N^*, A^*, \beta_* | A^*, R_1^{N^*})$ (see Notation 5.4.1). Hence, $x \in M(N^*, A^*, \beta_* | A^*, R_1^{N^*})$ (see, again, Notation 5.4.1). By the induction hypothesis, $x \in M(N^*, A^*, \beta_* | A^*, Q_1^{N^*})$. Thus, there exists an f.e.p. $g^* = (y_{i_2}, D_2; \ldots; y_{i_{m-1}}, D_{m-1}; x)$ with respect to $Q_1^{N^*}$ and $\beta_* | A^*$. Since $t_m(Q^j) = x_{i_1}$ for all $j \in C_1$, $g = (x_{i_1}, C_1; y_{i_2}, D_2; \ldots; y_{i_{m-1}}, D_{m-1}; x)$ is an f.e.p. with respect to Q^N and β_*. Therefore, $x \in M(Q^N)$, and the proof of our claim is complete.

Corollary 5.4.7. If $t_m(Q^j) = t_m(R^j)$ for $j = 1, \ldots, n$, then $x \in M(Q^N)$.

We now continue with the proof of the lemma. Let $y_j = t_m(R^j)$ and $z_j = t_m(Q^j)$ for $j = 1, \ldots, n$ (see Notation 2.1.8). We define now two profiles $P_0^N, P_n^N \in L^N$ in the following way. If $y_j = z_j$, then $P_0^j = P_n^j = R^j$. If $y_j \neq z_j$, then P_0^j is defined by

$$P_0^j | A - \{z_j\} = R^j | A - \{z_j\} \quad \text{and} \quad t_{m-1}(P_0^j) = z_j \tag{5.4.1}$$

and P_n^j is specified by

$$P_n^j | A - \{z_j\} = R^j | A - \{z_j\} \quad \text{and} \quad t_m(P_n^j) = z_j \tag{5.4.2}$$

(see Notation 2.1.5 and Notation 2.1.8). P_0^N and P_n^N have the following properties:

$$t_m(P_0^j) = t_m(R^j) \quad \text{for} \quad j = 1, \ldots, n \tag{5.4.3}$$

$$t_m(P_n^j) = t_m(Q^j) \quad \text{for} \quad j = 1, \ldots, n \tag{5.4.4}$$

$$P_0^j(x)R^j \quad \text{and} \quad P_n^j(x)R^j \quad \text{for} \quad j = 1, \ldots, n \tag{5.4.5}$$

(see Definition 5.4.3); (5.4.3) and (5.4.4) follow directly from (5.4.1) and (5.4.2). In order to prove (5.4.5), we distinguish the following possibilities: (a) $y_j = z_j$. In this case $R^j = P_0^j = P_n^j$. (b) $y_j \neq z_j$. Since $R^j(x)Q^j$, we must have $x \neq y_j$, $x \neq z_j$, and xR^jz_j. Hence, (5.4.5) holds.

Applying Corollary 5.4.7 to R^N and P_0^N, we conclude that $x \in M(P_0^N)$ (see (5.4.3) and (5.4.5)). Also, since $P_n^N(x)R^N$ and $R^N(x)Q^N$, we have that $P_n^N(x)Q^N$. Hence, again by Corollary 5.4.7, if $x \in M(P_n^N)$, then

$x \in M(Q^N)$ (see (5.4.4)). Thus, it remains only to prove that if $x \in M(P_0^N)$, then $x \in M(P_n^N)$. In order to prove this last claim, we consider the following sequence of profiles:

$$P_j^N = (P_n^1, \ldots, P_n^j, P_0^{j+1}, \ldots, P_0^n), \qquad j = 0, 1, \ldots, n \qquad (5.4.6)$$

Clearly, it is sufficient to prove the following.

$$\text{If } x \in M(P_j^N), \text{ then } x \in M(P_{j+1}^N), \qquad j = 0, 1, \ldots, n-1 \qquad (5.4.7)$$

Thus, let $0 \leqslant j \leqslant n-1$. By (5.4.5), $P_j^N(x)P_{j+1}^N$. Assume now that $x \in M(P_j^N)$. If $z_{j+1} = y_{j+1}$, then $P_0^{j+1} = P_n^{j+1} = R^j$ and $P_j^N = P_{j+1}^N$ (see (5.4.6)). Thus, we may assume that $z_{j+1} \neq y_{j+1}$. By our assumption, there exists an f.e.p. $f \in \phi(P_j^N)$ such that $t(f) = x$ (see Notation 5.4.1). Without loss of generality we may assume that $f = (x_1, C_1; \ldots; x_{m-1}, C_{m-1}; x)$. Now, if $j + 1 \notin C_1$, then $P_j^k = P_{j+1}^k$ for all $k \in C_1$. Hence, by Claim 5.4.6 (applied to P_j^N and P_{j+1}^N), we conclude that $x \in M(P_{j+1}^N)$. Thus, we have only to consider the possibility $j + 1 \in C_1$. We shall now prove that in this case we can find an f.e.p. $g = (x_{i_1}, D_1; \ldots; x_{i_{m-1}}, D_{m-1}; x)$ such that $g \in \phi(P_j^N)$ and $j + 1 \notin D_1$ (and thereby complete the proof). Since $y_{j+1} \neq z_{j+1}$, $x \neq z_{j+1}$. Hence, $z_{j+1} = x_{h_0}$, where $1 \leqslant h_0 \leqslant m-1$. Now, $j + 1 \in C_1$ and $t_m(P_0^{j+1}) = y_{j+1}$ (see (5.4.3)). Hence, $y_{j+1} = x_1$, and therefore $h_0 > 1$. We shall now construct two sequences of natural numbers with the following properties:

$$h_0 > h_1 > \cdots > h_{r-1} \geqslant h_r \geqslant 1 \qquad (5.4.8)$$

$$q_i \in C_{h_{i-1}}, \qquad i = 1, \ldots, r \qquad (5.4.9)$$

$$h_i = \min\{k \mid x_k = t_m(P_j^s) \text{ for some } s \in C_{h_{i-1}}\} \quad \text{and} \quad x_{h_i} = t_m(P_j^{q_i}) \qquad (5.4.10)$$

We start with the definitions of h_1 and q_1. Let

$$V_1 = \{i \mid 1 \leqslant i \leqslant m-1 \text{ and } x_i = t_m(P_j^k) \quad \text{for some } k \in C_{h_0}\}$$

and let $h_1 = \min\{i \mid i \in V_1\}$. Furthermore, let $q_1 \in C_{h_0}$ satisfy $t_m(P_j^{q_1}) = x_{h_1}$. Since $q_1 \in C_{h_0}$, we must have $h_1 \leqslant h_0$. Now, if either $h_1 = h_0$ or $h_1 = 1$, then our definition of the two sequences $h_0, h_1, \ldots, h_r$ and $q_1, \ldots, q_r$ is complete. Otherwise (i.e., if $h_0 > h_1 > 1$), we are able to define h_2 and q_2 such that (5.4.8), (5.4.9), and (5.4.10) are satisfied (with $r = 2$). Clearly, there exists a natural number r such that after r steps we shall have either $h_r = h_{r-1}$ or $h_r = 1$. First, we consider the case

$$h_{r-1} = h_r > 1 \qquad (5.4.11)$$

In this case, $x_{h_r} = x_{h_{r-1}}$ and $x_{h_r} \neq x_1$. Also, by the definition of h_r, $t_m(P_j^k) = x_{h_r}$ for all $k \in C_{h_{r-1}}$ (see (5.4.9) and (5.4.10)). Consider now the f.e.p.

$$g = (x_w, C_w; x_1, C_1; \ldots; x_{w-1}, C_{w-1}; x_{w+1}, C_{w+1}; \ldots; x_{m-1}, C_{m-1}; x)$$

where $w = h_{r-1}$. Then $g \in \phi(P_j^N)$ (see Notation 5.4.1) and $j+1 \notin C_{h_{r-1}}$ (since $j+1 \in C_1$).

Thus, it remains only to consider the case

$$h_r = 1 \qquad\qquad (5.4.12)$$

In this case, $C_1 \cap C_{h_{r-1}} = \varnothing$ (because $h_{r-1} > 1$). Since $q_r \in C_{h_{r-1}}$ and $j+1 \in C_1$, $q_r \neq j+1$. We now define $D_1 = D_{h_r} = (C_1 - \{j+1\}) \cup \{q_r\}$, $D_{h_{r-1}} = (C_{h_{r-1}} - \{q_r\}) \cup \{q_{r-1}\}, \ldots, D_{h_1} = (C_{h_1} - \{q_2\}) \cup \{q_1\}$, and $D_{h_0} = (C_{h_0} - \{q_1\}) \cup \{j+1\}$. Then $D_{h_i} \cap D_{h_k} = \varnothing$ if $k \neq i$ and $|D_{h_i}| = |C_{h_i}|$ for $i = 0, \ldots, r$. Now let $D_i = C_i$ if $i \notin \{h_0, \ldots, h_r\}$. We claim that $g = (x_1, D_1; \ldots; x_{m-1}, D_{m-1}; x)$ is an f.e.p. with respect to P_j^N (see Definition 5.3.8). Indeed, (5.3.8), (5.3.9), and (5.3.10) are (obviously) true for g; (5.3.11) follows from the following facts: (a) The order of elimination in g is the same as that of f. (b) $x_{h_i} = t_m(P_j^{q_i})$ for $i = 1, \ldots, r$ (see (5.4.10)). (c) $h_0 > 1$, $x_1 = y_{j+1} = t_m(P_j^{j+1})$, $t_{m-1}(P_j^{j+1}) = t_{m-1}(P_0^{j+1}) = z_{j+1}$, and $z_{j+1} = x_{h_0}$ (see (5.4.6) and (5.4.1)). Furthermore, $j+1 \notin D_1$.

5.5   Further results on exactly and strongly consistent anonymous SCFs

Let $N = \{1, \ldots, n\}$ be a society, and let $A = \{x_1, \ldots, x_m\}$ be a set of m alternatives, $m \geq 2$. Also, let $F: L^N \to A$ be an exactly and strongly consistent anonymous SCF (see Definition 4.1.18). If F is Paretian, then, by Theorem 5.2.16,

$$n(m-1) + 1 \leq \sum_{i=1}^{m} w(x_i) \leq (n+1)(m-1)$$

(see Definition 5.2.8 and Remarks 5.2.7 and 5.1.9). We shall now prove that for every s such that $n(m-1) + 1 \leq s \leq (n+1)(m-1)$, there exists an exactly and strongly consistent anonymous SCF $F: L^N \to A$ such that $\sum_{i=1}^{m} w(F; x_i) = s$ (see Definition 5.2.8). Indeed, we prove the following theorem.

Theorem 5.5.1. *Let* $n(m-1) + 1 \leq s \leq (n+1)(m-1)$. *Then there exists an exactly and strongly consistent, monotonic, Paretian, and anonymous SCF* $F: L^N \to A$ *such that* $\sum_{i=1}^{m} w(F; x_i) = s$.

Proof: We prove the theorem by induction on m, the number of alternatives. If $m = 2$, then $s = n+1$, and the existence of an SCF with all the aforementioned properties follows from Remark 5.3.11 and Corollary 5.3.13. Assume now that the theorem is true for $m = k \geq 2$. We shall prove that the theorem is true for $m=k+1$. Let s satisfy $nk+1\leqslant s\leqslant (n+1)k$. If $s=(n+1)k$, then, again, the theorem follows from Remark 5.3.11 and Corollary 5.3.13. Hence, we may assume that $s=nk+p$, where $0<p<k$. Let $s_1=n(k-1)+p$, and let $A^*=\{x_1,\ldots,x_k\}$. Then, $n(k-1)+1\leqslant s_1\leqslant (n+1)(k-1)$. Hence, by the induction hypothesis, there exists an exactly and strongly consistent, monotonic, Paretian, and anonymous SCF $F_*:L_*^N\to A^*$ (where $L_*=L(A^*)$; see Definition 2.1.3) such that $\sum_{i=1}^k w(F_*;x_i)=s_1$. Let $A=\{x_1,\ldots,x_k,x_{k+1}\}$, and let $L=L(A)$. We define an SCF $F:L^N\to A$ in the following way. Let $R^N\in L^N$, let $R_*^N=R^N\,|\,A^*$ (see Notation 2.2.4), and let $y=F_*(R_*^N)$. If $x_{k+1}R^iy$ for all $i\in N$, then we define $F(R^N)=x_{k+1}$. Otherwise (i.e., if there exists $j\in N$ such that yR^jx_{k+1}), we define $F(R^N)=F_*(R_*^N)=y$. As the reader can easily verify, F is monotonic, Paretian, and anonymous. We shall now prove that F is exactly and strongly consistent. Let, again, $R^N\in L^N$, let $R_*^N=R^N\,|\,A^*$, and let $y=F_*(R_*^N)$. We distinguish the following possibilities:

$$F(R^N)=x_{k+1} \tag{5.5.1}$$

Let Q_*^N be a strong e.p. of $g(F_*,R_*^N)$ (see Definitions 4.1.17 and 2.5.1) such that $F_*(Q_*^N)=y$. We define a profile $Q^N\in L^N$ by $Q^N\,|\,A^*=Q_*^N$, and $t_1(Q^i)=x_{k+1}$ for all $i\in N$ (see Notation 2.2.4 and Notation 2.1.8). Clearly, $F(Q^N)=x_{k+1}$. We claim that Q^N is a strong e.p. of $g(F,R^N)$. Indeed, assume, on the contrary, that there exist a coalition T and $P^T\in L^T$ such that $F(Q^{N-T},P^T)=x$, $x\neq x_{k+1}$, and xR^ix_{k+1} for all $i\in T$. Since $T\neq\varnothing$, $F_*(Q_*^{N-T},P_*^T)=x$, where $P_*^T=P^T\,|\,A^*$. Also, by (5.5.1), $x_{k+1}R^iy$ for all $i\in N$. Hence, xR^iy for all $i\in T$. Therefore, xR_*^iy for all $i\in T$, contradicting our assumption that Q_*^N is a strong e.p. of $g(F_*,R_*^N)$ that satisfies $F_*(Q_*^N)=y$.

$$F(R^N)=y \tag{5.5.2}$$

Let Q_*^N be a strong e.p. of $g(F_*,R_*^N)$ (see Definitions 4.1.17 and 2.5.1) such that $F_*(Q_*^N)=y$. We define a profile $Q^N\in L^N$ by $Q^N\,|\,A^*=Q_*^N$, and $t_{k+1}(Q^i)=x_{k+1}$ for all $i\in N$ (see Notation 2.2.4 and Notation 2.1.8). By the definition of F, $F(Q^N)=y$. We claim that Q^N is a strong e.p. of $g(F,R^N)$. Indeed, assume, on the contrary, that there exist a coalition T and $P^T\in L^T$ such that $F(Q^{N-T},P^T)=x$, $x\neq y$, and xR^iy for all $i\in T$. Since F_* is Paretian, $T\neq N$. Now, if $i\in N-T$, then $t_{k+1}(Q^i)=x_{k+1}$. Hence, by the definition of F, $F_*(Q_*^{N-T},P_*^T)=x$, where $P_*^T=P^T\,|\,A^*$. Thus, Q_*^N is not a strong e.p. of $g(F_*,R_*^N)$, and the desired contradiction has been obtained.

We now observe that $w(F;x_i)=w(F_*,x_i)$ for $i=1,\ldots,k$, and $w(F;x_{k+1})=n$. Hence,

$$\sum_{i=1}^{k+1} w(F; x_i) = \sum_{i=1}^{k} w(F_*; x_i) + n = s_1 + n = n(k-1) + p + n = nk + p = s$$

Remark 5.5.2. Let $n(m-1) + 1 \leqslant s \leqslant (n+1)(m-1)$, and let $h_1, \ldots, h_m$ be a partition of s (i.e., $1 \leqslant h_i \leqslant n$ for $i = 1, \ldots, m$, and $\sum_{i=1}^{m} h_i = s$). If $s = (n+1)(m-1)$, then, by Remark 5.3.11 and Corollary 5.3.13, there exists an exactly and strongly consistent, monotonic, Paretian, and anonymous SCF $F: L^N \to A$ such that $w(F; x_i) = h_i$ for $i = 1, \ldots, m$ (see Definition 5.2.8). If $m \geqslant 3$, $s < (n+1)(m-1)$, and $F: L^N \to A$ is the SCF that corresponds to m, n, and s according to the *proof* of Theorem 5.5.1, then $\max\{w(F; x_i) \mid 1 \leqslant i \leqslant m\} = n$. Thus, in particular, $G^*(F) = (n, n)$ (see Definitions 3.1.3 and 2.6.4). Very surprisingly, this is not accidental. Indeed, R. Holzman has proved the following theorem.

Theorem 5.5.3. *Let* $m \geqslant 3$. *If* $F: L^N \to A$ *is an exactly and strongly consistent, Paretian, and anonymous SCF, and if* $\sum_{i=1}^{m} w(F; x_i) < (n+1)(m-1)$, *then* $\max\{w(F; x_i) \mid 1 \leqslant i \leqslant m\} = n$.

Theorem 5.5.3 follows from Theorem 5.1 in Holzman [1982].

5.6   Concluding remarks

In this section we consider two possible applications of the theory of exactly and strongly consistent anonymous SCFs. The first application is to mass elections.

Remark 5.6.1. The problem of mass elections can be described as follows. Let $N = \{1, \ldots, n\}$ be a set of n voters, and let $A = \{x_1, \ldots, x_m\}$ be a set of m alternatives, $m \geqslant 2$. Let ANM be the family of all anonymous and monotonic SCFs from L^N to A. For $F \in$ ANM, let $k = k(F)$ be determined by the equality $G^*(F) = (n, k)$ (see Definitions 3.1.3 and 2.6.4). Our problem is as follows: *Minimize* $k = k(F)$ *subject to the conditions* (a) $F \in$ ANM *and* (b) F *is exactly and strongly consistent.*

Thus, our problem is to find an anonymous, "strongly stable," and monotonic SCF with a minimum "special majority."

Remark 5.6.2. Let $F: L^N \to A$ be an exactly and strongly consistent anonymous SCF, and let $G^*(F) = (n, k)$ (see Definitions 3.1.3 and 2.6.4). Then F is a strong representation of $G^*(F)$ (see Definition 4.1.31). Hence, by Theorem 4.1.34, $m < n/(n-k)$. Therefore,

$$k \geqslant [n(m-1)/m] + 1 \tag{5.6.1}$$

Inequality (5.6.1) constitutes a lower bound for our minimization problem. A solution to the problem of mass elections is provided by the following theorem.

Theorem 5.6.3. *Let $k(n, m) = [n(m-1)/m] + 1$. If $n \geqslant m - 1$, then there exists an exactly and strongly consistent SCF $F: L^N \to A$ such that $F \in ANM$ (see Remark 5.6.1) and $k(F) = k(n, m)$ if $n \equiv 0(m)$ or $n \equiv -1(m)$, and $k(F) = k(n, m) + 1$ otherwise.*

Proof: Let $n = qm + r$, where $q \geqslant 0$ and $0 \leqslant r \leqslant m - 1$. Let $e = m - r - 1$, and let $E \subset A$ satisfy $|E| = e$. (Notice that if $q = 0$, then $e = 0$.) Define a function $\beta_* : A \to \{1, \ldots, n\}$ by $\beta_*(x) = q$ if $x \in E$, and $\beta_*(x) = q + 1$ otherwise. Then

$$\sum_{i=1}^{m} \beta_*(x_i) = q(m - r - 1) + (q + 1)(r + 1) = qm + r + 1 = n + 1$$

By Remark 5.3.11 and Corollary 5.3.13, there exists an exactly and strongly consistent, anonymous, and monotonic SCF $F: L^N \to A$ such that $\beta(F; x_i) = \beta_*(x_i)$, $i = 1, \ldots, m$. Clearly,

$$k(F) = \max\{n + 1 - \beta_*(x_i) \mid 1 \leqslant i \leqslant m\}$$

We now distinguish the following possibilities:

(a) $n \equiv 0(m)$

In this case, $k(n, m) = q(m - 1) + 1$, and $k(F) = n + 1 - q = qm + 1 - q = q(m - 1) + 1 = k(n, m)$.

(b) $n \equiv -1(m)$

In this case, $k(n, m) = q(m - 1) + r$, and $k(F) = n + 1 - (q + 1) = qm + r - q = q(m - 1) + r = k(n, m)$.

(c) $n = qm + r$ and $1 \leqslant r \leqslant m - 2$

Again, $k(n, m) = q(m - 1) + r$. However,

$$k(F) = n + 1 - q = q(m - 1) + r + 1 = k(n, m) + 1$$

Remark 5.6.4. In Section 5.C of Holzman [1982] it is shown that Theorem 5.6.3 gives the best possible solution to the problem of mass elections. More specifically, the following claim is proved. Let $F \in ANM$ be Paretian and exactly and strongly consistent; if $n > m$, $n \not\equiv 0(m)$, and $n \not\equiv -1(m)$, then $k(F) \geqslant k(n, m) + 1$.

Remark 5.6.5. If $n=2m-1$ or $n=2m$, then $n>k(n,m)$, and if $n \geqslant 2m+1$, then $n>k(n,m)+1$. Hence, if $n \geqslant 2m-1$, then Theorem 5.6.3 yields SCFs without vetoers.

Our second application of the results of the previous sections is to strong representations of symmetric simple games.

Remark 5.6.6. Let $G=(n,k)$ be a symmetric simple game, where $n/2 < k < n$. Then, by Theorem 4.1.34, $\mu(G) \leqslant [(n-1)/(n-k)]$ (see Definitions 4.1.33 and 2.6.12). On the other hand, the following theorem is true.

Theorem 5.6.7. *Let* $G=(n,k)$ *be a symmetric simple game, where* $n/2 < k < n$, *and let* $b=n-k+1$. *Furthermore, let* $t=[(n+1)/b]$. *Then* G *has a faithful and monotonic strong representation of every order* m *such that* $2 \leqslant m \leqslant t$ (see Definitions 3.2.7 and 4.1.31).

Proof: Since $k>n/2$, we have that $t \geqslant 2$. Let $2 \leqslant m \leqslant t$, and let $A=\{x_1,\ldots,x_m\}$ be a set with m elements. There exists a function $\beta_* : A \to \{1,\ldots,n\}$ such that (a) $\beta_*(x_1)=b$, (b) $\beta_*(x_i) \geqslant b$ for $i=2,\ldots,m$, and (c) $\sum_{i=1}^{m}\beta_*(x_i)=n+1$. Hence, by Remark 5.3.11 and Corollary 5.3.13, there exists an exactly and strongly consistent, anonymous, and monotonic SCF $F: L^N \to A$ such that $\beta(F;x_i)=\beta_*(x_i)$ for $i=1,\ldots,m$. Thus, $G^*(F)=(n,k)$ (see Definition 3.1.3), and the proof is complete.

Remark 5.6.8. R. Holzman has proved that if $G=(n,k)$ and $n/2 < k < n$, then $\mu(G)=[(n+1)/b]$ (see Theorem 5.2 in Holzman [1982]). Thus, Theorem 5.6.7 cannot be improved.

CHAPTER 6

Effectivity functions and implementation

The first three sections of this chapter consist of a detailed investigation of effectivity functions. We start in Section 6.1 with a definition of effectivity function (see Definition 6.1.1). The definition is formulated so that the (set-valued) inverse, or "dual," of an effectivity function is also an effectivity function (see Remark 6.1.6). Thus, we establish a "principle of duality" for effectivity functions that is similar to the duality principle of projective geometries of the plane. We investigate the following 10 properties of effectivity functions:

(1) Monotonicity with respect to the players (see Definition 5.2.4)
(2) Monotonicity with respect to the alternatives (see Definition 6.1.7)
(3) Superadditivity (see Definition 6.1.11)
(4) Subadditivity (see Definition 6.1.24)
(5) Regularity (see Definition 5.2.1)
(6) Maximality (see Definition 5.1.16)
(7) Anonymity (see Definition 6.2.6)
(8) Neutrality (see Definition 6.2.9)
(9) Additivity (see Definition 6.2.46)
(10) Stability (see Definition 6.1.17)

A pair of properties i and j (not necessarily distinct) are *dual* if for every effectivity function E the following claim is true: E satisfies i if and only if E^d satisfies j (where E^d is the dual of E). If the pair (i, i) is dual, then i is called *self-dual*. We observe that the three pairs of properties (1)–(2), (3)–(4), and (7)–(8) are pairs of dual properties (of effectivity functions). Also, (5), (6), and (9) are self-dual properties. Unfortunately, stability is *not* a self-dual property (see Remark 6.3.17). We emphasize, however, that our usage of the foregoing duality principle is purely technical (or "formal").

Our examination of effectivity functions proceeds as follows. In Section 6.1 we consider properties (1) to (6). We observe that (3) implies (1) and (5) (see Lemma 6.1.13 and Remark 6.1.12). Hence, by duality,

(4) implies (2) and (5) (see Lemma 6.1.13.d and Remark 6.1.28). We also notice that (3) and (6) imply (2) (see Lemma 6.1.14). Hence, again by duality, (4) and (6) imply (1) (see Remark 6.1.29). Finally, we inquire which properties are satisfied by the effectivity functions $E^*(H)$, $E_\alpha(H)$, and $E_\beta(H)$, which are associated with an SCC H (see, e.g., Example 6.1.23, Remark 6.1.31, and Corollary 6.1.34).

Section 6.2 is devoted to an investigation of properties (7), (8), and (9). We define the blocking coefficients of an anonymous and monotonic effectivity function (see Definition 6.2.13). Then we find necessary and sufficient conditions, expressed as inequalities on the blocking coefficients, for an anonymous effectivity function to satisfy each of the properties (3) to (6) (see, e.g., Lemmata 6.2.20, 6.2.23.d, 6.2.26, and 6.2.28). A similar study of neutral effectivity functions is pursued using veto functions (see Definition 6.2.15 and Lemmata 6.2.20.d, 6.2.23, 6.2.26.d, and 6.2.28.d). Finally, we observe that an additive effectivity function satisfies properties (1) to (5), and we conclude with some remarks on those (additive effectivity) functions that possess one of the properties (6), (7), or (8).

Stability is investigated in Section 6.3. The main result is that additive effectivity functions are stable (see Theorem 6.3.19). We also present a characterization of the set of all effectivity functions that possess properties (1), (2), (7), (8), and (10) (see Theorem 6.3.25).

Section 6.4 is devoted to implementation theory. First we prove that the core correspondence of a stable and maximal effectivity function is implementable (see Theorem 6.4.2). Then we prove that *an SCC H is partially implementable if and only if H is stable and $E^*(H)$ is maximal* (see Theorem 6.4.4). Section 6.5 contains some remarks on implementation of SCCs. We conclude with an appendix on convex effectivity functions. The appendix relies heavily on the theory of (cooperative) games without side payments.

Section 6.2–6.5 are based mainly on Moulin and Peleg [1982], except that Theorem 6.3.25 is due to Moulin [1981].

6.1   Effectivity functions

A strong use of effectivity functions has already been made in Chapters 4 and 5. In Chapter 4 we defined the three effectivity functions that are associated with an SCC (see Definition 4.1.21) and studied, using that definition, the properties of tightness and stability of exactly and strongly consistent SCFs (see Lemma 4.1.25, Definition 4.1.27, and Corollary 4.1.29). In Chapter 5 we defined the two effectivity functions that are associated with a GF (see Definition 5.1.13). Then, by considering the appropriate effectivity functions, we proved that a partially implementable SCC is both strongly tight and stable (see Corollary 5.1.15, Definition 5.1.19, and Lemma 5.1.20). We also considered the following properties of effectivity functions: maximality, regularity, and monotonicity with respect to players (see Definitions 5.1.16, 5.2.1, and 5.2.4). In Section 5.2 we studied the foregoing properties of effectivity functions and obtained a complete characterization of the blocking coefficients of a partially implementable and anonymous SCC (see Theorem 5.2.16). Motivated by the foregoing results, we now turn to systematic investigation of effectivity functions.

Let $N = \{1, \ldots, n\}$ be a society, and let A be a finite set of m alternatives, $m \geq 2$.

Definition 6.1.1. An *effectivity function* is a function $E: 2^N \to P(2^A)$ (see Notation 4.1.20) that satisfies the following:

$$\text{For every } S \in 2^N, \quad A \in E(S) \tag{6.1.1}$$

$$\text{For every } B \in 2^A, \quad B \in E(N) \tag{6.1.2}$$

Remark 6.1.2. By Notation 4.1.13, $\varnothing \notin E(S)$ for every $S \in 2^N$.

Remark 6.1.3. Let $H: L^N \to 2^A$ be an SCC. Then $E_\alpha(H)$ and $E_\beta(H)$ satisfy (6.1.2) if and only if H satisfies NI (see Definitions 4.1.21 and 5.2.6). Also, if H is Paretian, then $E^*(H)$ satisfies (6.1.2) (see Definitions 2.3.4 and 4.1.21).

Remark 6.1.4. Let $\Gamma = (\Sigma^1, \ldots, \Sigma^n; \pi)$ be a GF (see Definition 5.1.1). Then $E_\alpha(\Gamma)$ and $E_\beta(\Gamma)$ satisfy (6.1.2) if and only if the range of π is A (i.e., $\pi(\Sigma^N) = A$) (see Definition 5.1.13).

The following definition is very helpful in the study of effectivity functions.

Definition 6.1.5. Let $E: 2^N \to P(2^A)$ be an effectivity function (see Definition 6.1.1). The *dual* function is the function $E^d: 2^A \to P(2^N)$ defined as follows:

$$\text{For all } B \in 2^A \text{ and } S \in 2^N, \quad [S \in E^d(B) \Leftrightarrow B \in E(S)] \tag{6.1.3}$$

Remark 6.1.6. Let $E: 2^N \to P(2^A)$ be an effectivity function. Then E^d is also an effectivity function (see (6.1.1), (6.1.2), and (6.1.3)). Intuitively, A is the set of "voters" and N is the set of "candidates" for E^d. Formally, E^d is the (set-valued) inverse function of E. Clearly, $(E^d)^d = E$.

We proceed now to investigate several properties of effectivity functions.

Definition 6.1.7. A function $E: 2^N \to P(2^A)$ (see Notation 4.1.20) is *monotonic with respect to the alternatives* (i.e., the members of A) if

$$[S \in 2^N, \ B \in E(S), \ B^* \in 2^A, \text{ and } B^* \supset B] \Rightarrow B^* \in E(S) \qquad (6.1.4)$$

Remark 6.1.8. Let $E: 2^N \to P(2^A)$ be an effectivity function. E is monotonic with respect to the players if and only if E^d is monotonic with respect to the alternatives (see Definitions 5.2.4, 6.1.5, and 6.1.7).

Remark 6.1.9. If $H: L^N \to 2^A$ is an SCC, then $E_\alpha(H)$ and $E_\beta(H)$ are monotonic with respect to the alternatives (see Definitions 4.1.21 and 6.1.7). Also, if Γ is a GF (see Definition 5.1.1), then $E_\alpha(\Gamma)$ and $E_\beta(\Gamma)$ (see Definition 5.1.13) are monotonic with respect to the alternatives.

Example 6.1.10. Let $n = 7$ and $m = 3$, and let $M = M(m, n)$ be the rule of choice by plurality voting (see Example 3.1.17). Let $S = \{1, 2, 3, 4\}$. If $a \in A$, then $\{a\} \in E^*(M; S) = E^*(S)$. However, if $B \subset A$ and $|B| = 2$ (see Notation 2.1.7), then $B \notin E^*(S)$ (see Definition 4.1.19). Thus, $E^*(M)$ is *not* monotonic with respect to the alternatives.

Definition 6.1.11. A function $E: 2^N \to P(2^A)$ (see Notation 4.1.20) is *superadditive* if it satisfies the following:

If $S_i \in 2^N$, $i = 1, 2$, $S_1 \cap S_2 = \varnothing$, and $B_i \in E(S_i)$, $i = 1, 2$,
then $B_1 \cap B_2 \in E(S_1 \cup S_2)$ (in particular, $B_1 \cap B_2 \neq \varnothing$).   (6.1.5)

Remark 6.1.12. Let $E: 2^N \to P(2^A)$ be a function. If E is superadditive, then E is regular (see Definitions 6.1.11 and 5.2.1).

Lemma 6.1.13. *Let $E: 2^N \to P(2^A)$ be an effectivity function* (see Definition 6.1.1). *If E is superadditive, then E is monotonic with respect to the players* (see Definitions 6.1.11 and 5.2.4).

Proof: Let $S \in 2^N$, $B \in E(S)$, and $T \supset S$, $T \in 2^N$. We have to show that $B \in E(T)$. Let $T^* = T - S$. We may assume that $T^* \neq \varnothing$. By (6.1.1), $A \in E(T^*)$. Hence, by (6.1.5), $B = A \cap B \in E(S \cup T^*) = E(T)$.

Lemma 6.1.14. *Let $E: 2^N \to P(2^A)$ be a function. If E is superadditive and maximal* (see Definitions 6.1.11 and 5.1.16), *then E is monotonic with respect to the alternatives* (see Definition 6.1.7).

Proof: Let $S \in 2^N$, $B \in E(S)$, and $B^* \supset B$, $B^* \in 2^A$. Assume, on the contrary, that $B^* \notin E(S)$. Since E is maximal, $A - B^* \in E(N - S)$. Hence, by (6.1.5), $\varnothing \in E(N)$, and the desired contradiction has been established.

Remark 6.1.15. Let $H: L^N \to 2^A$ be an SCC. Then $E_\alpha(H)$ is superadditive (see Definitions 4.1.21 and 6.1.11). Also, if Γ is a GF (see Definition 5.1.1), then $E_\alpha(\Gamma)$ is superadditive (see Definition 5.1.13).

Remark 6.1.16. Let $F: L^N \to A$ be an SCF. Then $E_\beta(F)$ may *not* be regular (see Definition 4.1.21, Remark 4.1.22, and Example 3.1.13). Thus, in particular, $E_\beta(F)$ may not be superadditive (see Remark 6.1.12).

We shall now construct an SCC H such that $E^*(H)$ is not superadditive. We start with the following definitions.

Definition 6.1.17. A function $E: 2^N \to P(2^A)$ (see Notation 4.1.20) is *stable* if for every $R^N \in L^N$ the core $C(E, R^N) \neq \varnothing$ (see Definition 4.1.23).

Definition 6.1.18. A function $E: 2^N \to P(2^A)$ (see Notation 4.1.20) is *monotonic* if it is monotonic with respect to both the players and the alternatives (see Definitions 5.2.4 and 6.1.7).

Remark 6.1.19. Let E be an effectivity function (see Definition 6.1.1). Then E is monotonic if and only if E^d is monotonic (see Definitions 6.1.18 and 6.1.5 and Remark 6.1.8).

Lemma 6.1.20. *Let* $E: 2^N \to P(2^A)$ *be a stable function* (see Definition 6.1.17), *and let* $H(R^N) = C(E, R^N)$ *for every* $R^N \in L^N$. *Then* $E^*(H)$ *is monotonic* (see Definitions 4.1.21 and 6.1.18).

Proof: We have to show that $E^* = E^*(H)$ is monotonic with respect to the alternatives (see Remark 5.2.5 and Example 6.1.10). Let $S \in 2^N$ and $B \in 2^A$. We claim that $B \in E^*(S)$ if and only if there exist sets $B_* \subset B$ and $S_* \subset S$ such that $B_* \in E(S_*)$. Assume first that there exist sets $B_* \subset B$ and $S_* \subset S$ such that $B_* \in E(S_*)$. Let $R^S \in L^S$ satisfy $B R^S(A - B)$. Then $B_* R^{S*}(A - B)$. Hence, for every $P^{N-S} \in L^{N-S}$,

$$H(R^S, P^{N-S}) = C(E, (R^S, P^{N-S})) \subset B$$

Thus, $B \in E^*(S)$ (see Definition 4.1.19). Assume now that $B \in E^*(S)$. Assume also, on the contrary, that $2^B \cap E(S_*) = \varnothing$ for every $S_* \in 2^S$. Then $B \neq A$. Let $|B| = h$ (see Notation 2.1.7), and let $y \in A - B$. Choose $R^N \in L^N$ such that $B R^S(A - B)$, $t_{h+1}(R^i) = y$ for $i \in S$, and $t_1(R^i) = y$ for $i \in N - S$ (see Notation 2.1.8). Since $B \in E^*(S)$,

$$C(E,R^N)=H(R^N)\subset B$$

(see Definition 4.1.19). On the other hand, $y\in C(E,R^N)$ and $y\notin B$. Thus, the desired contradiction has been obtained.

We are now able to prove the following interesting result.

Lemma 6.1.21. *Let $E: 2^N\to P(2^A)$ be a stable and monotonic function* (see Definitions 6.1.17 and 6.1.18). *If $H(R^N)=C(E,R^N)$ for every $R^N\in L^N$, then $E^*(H)=E$* (see Definition 4.1.21).

Proof: Let $S\in 2^N$ and $B\in 2^A$. If $B\in E(S)$, then, by the *proof* of Lemma 6.1.20, $B\in E^*(S)$. Conversely, assume that $B\in E^*(S)$. Then, again, by the *proof* of Lemma 6.1.20, there exist sets $B_*\subset B$ and $S_*\subset S$ such that $B_*\in E(S_*)$. Since E is monotonic, $B\in E(S)$.

Remark 6.1.22. Lemma 6.1.21 illustrates the importance of the first effectivity function (associated with an SCC; see Definition 4.1.21).

Example 6.1.23. Let $n=5$ and $m=4$. We define an effectivity function $E: 2^N\to P(2^A)$ by the following rule:

$$E(S)=\{A\}\quad \text{if } |S|=1$$
$$=\{B\mid B\in 2^A \text{ and } |B|\geqslant 3\}\quad \text{if } 2\leqslant |S|\leqslant 4$$
$$=2^A\quad \text{if } S=N$$

(see Notation 2.1.7). As the reader can easily verify, E is monotonic (see Definition 6.1.18). We claim that E is also stable (see Definition 6.1.17). Indeed, let $R^N\in L^N$. We shall say that $x\in A$ is blocked (with respect to R^N) if

$$|\{i\mid i\in N \text{ and } t_4(R^i)=x\}|\geqslant 2$$

(see Notation 2.1.8). If $y\in A$ is Pareto-optimal and it is not blocked, then $y\in C(E,R^N)$ (see Definitions 2.3.3 and 4.1.23). Hence, $C(E,R^N)\neq\varnothing$. Clearly, E is not superadditive (see Definition 6.1.11). If $H(R^N)=C(E,R^N)$ for every $R^N\in L^N$, then, by Lemma 6.1.21, $E^*(H)=E$. Hence, $E^*(H)$ is *not* superadditive.

The dual property of superadditivity is subadditivity.

Definition 6.1.24. A function $E: 2^N\to P(2^A)$ (see Notation 4.1.20) is *subadditive* if it satisfies the following:

If $B_i\in 2^A$, $i=1,2$, $B_1\cap B_2=\varnothing$ and $B_i\in E(S_i)$, $i=1,2$, then $B_1\cup B_2\in E(S_1\cap S_2)$ (in particular, $S_1\cap S_2\neq\varnothing$). (6.1.6)

Remark 6.1.25. Definition 6.1.24 is due to Moulin [1983].

Remark 6.1.26. Let $E: 2^N \to P(2^A)$ be an effectivity function (see Definition 6.1.1). E is superadditive if and only if E^d is subadditive (see Definitions 6.1.11, 6.1.5, and 6.1.24).

Applying the "principle of duality" for effectivity functions, we obtain the dual result of Lemma 6.1.13.

Lemma 6.1.13.d. *Let $E: 2^N \to P(2^A)$ be an effectivity function. If E is subadditive, then E is monotonic with respect to the alternatives* (see Remarks 6.1.26 and 6.1.8).

We notice now that regularity and maximality are self-dual properties. More precisely, we have the following.

Remark 6.1.27. Let $E: 2^N \to P(2^A)$ be an effectivity function. E is regular (maximal) if and only if E^d is regular (maximal) (see Definitions 6.1.1, 6.1.5, 5.1.16, and 5.2.1).

Remark 6.1.27 indicates that the following remarks should be true.

Remark 6.1.28. Let $E: 2^N \to P(2^A)$ be a function. If E is subadditive, then E is regular (see Definitions 6.1.24 and 5.2.1). (See also Remark 6.1.12.)

Remark 6.1.29. Let $E: 2^N \to P(2^A)$ be a function. If E is subadditive and maximal (see Definitions 6.1.24 and 5.1.16), then E is monotonic with respect to the players (see Definition 5.2.4). (See also Lemma 6.1.14.)

Example 6.1.30. Let $N = \{1, 2, 3\}$, and let $A = \{x_1, x_2, x_3\}$. Furthermore, let $M = M(3, 3)$ be the rule of choice by plurality voting (see Example 3.1.17). We claim that $E_\alpha = E_\alpha(M)$ is *not* subadditive. Indeed, let $B_1 = \{x_1\}$, $B_2 = \{x_2\}$, $S_1 = \{1, 2\}$, and $S_2 = \{2, 3\}$. Then, clearly, $B_1 \cap B_2 = \emptyset$ and $B_i \in E_\alpha(S_i)$ for $i = 1, 2$. However, $B_1 \cup B_2 = \{x_1, x_2\}$, $S_1 \cap S_2 = \{2\}$, and $\{x_1, x_2\} \notin E_\alpha(\{2\})$.

Remark 6.1.31. We conclude from Example 6.1.30 that subadditivity is, generally, not satisfied by the most important type of effectivity functions associated with SCCs, namely, by α-effectivity functions (see Definition 4.1.21).

We conclude this section with some observations on the tightness of SCCs that will be used in the sequel.

Lemma 6.1.32. *Let $H: L^N \to 2^A$ be an SCC. If $E_\alpha(H)$ is maximal, then $E_\alpha(H) = E_\beta(H)$* (see Definitions 4.1.21 and 5.1.16).

Proof: Let $S \in 2^N$, and let $B \in E_\beta(H; S) = E_\beta(S)$. Then $A - B \notin E_\alpha(N - S)$ (see Definition 4.1.19). Since E_α is maximal, $B \in E_\alpha(S)$. Hence, $E_\alpha(S) = E_\beta(S)$.

Lemma 6.1.33. *Let* $E_1: 2^N \to P(2^A)$ *be a maximal function* (see Definition 5.1.16). *If* $E_2: 2^N \to P(2^A)$ *is a regular function* (see Definition 5.2.1) *and* $E_2(S) \supset E_1(S)$ *for every* $S \in 2^N$, *then* $E_1 = E_2$.

Proof: Let $S \in 2^N$ and $B \in E_2(S)$. Since E_2 is regular, $A - B \notin E_2(N - S)$. Because $E_2(N - S) \supset E_1(N - S)$, $A - B \notin E_1(N - S)$. Since E_1 is maximal, $B \in E_1(S)$. Thus, $E_1(S) = E_2(S)$.

Corollary 6.1.34. Let $H: L^N \to 2^A$ be an SCC. If $E^*(H)$ is maximal, then H is strongly tight (see Definitions 4.1.21, 5.1.16, and 4.1.27).

Proof: $E_\alpha(H)$ is regular (see Remark 5.2.2). Hence, by Lemma 6.1.33, $E^*(H) = E_\alpha(H)$. It follows now from Lemma 6.1.32 that $E_\alpha(H) = E_\beta(H)$. Thus, $E^*(H) = E_\beta(H)$, and H is strongly tight.

The converse of Corollary 6.1.34 is not true. This is shown by the following example.

Example 6.1.35. Let $n \geqslant 2$, and let $m \geqslant 2$. Furthermore, let $H: L^N \to 2^A$ be the Pareto correspondence (i.e., $H(R^N) = \text{PAR}(R^N)$ for every $R^N \in L^N$) (see Definition 2.3.3). Then, as the reader can easily verify, $E^*(H) = E_\alpha(H) = E_\beta(H)$; that is, H is strongly tight (see Definition 4.1.27). Since $n \geqslant 2$ and $m \geqslant 2$, $E^*(H)$ is not maximal (see Definition 5.1.16).

6.2   Families of effectivity functions

In this section we continue our study of effectivity functions. Specifically, we define and investigate anonymous, neutral, and additive effectivity functions. We start with the following definition. Let A be a finite set of m alternatives, $m \geqslant 2$, and let $N = \{1, \ldots, n\}$ be a society.

Definition 6.2.1. Let $G = (N, W)$ be a simple game (see Definition 2.6.1). Assume that G is non-null (i.e., $N \in W$). The *standard* effectivity function associated with G, $E = E(G)$, is given by $E(S) = 2^A$ if $S \in W$, and $E(S) = \{A\}$ otherwise (see Notation 2.3.1).

Remark 6.2.2. Definition 6.2.1 is (partially) motivated by Remark 4.1.22 (notice, however, (4.1.4)).

Remark 6.2.3. Let $G = (N, W)$ be a non-null simple game, and let $E = E(G)$ (see Definition 6.2.1). Because $N \in W$, $E(N) = 2^A$. Thus, E is, indeed, an effectivity function (see Definition 6.1.1). Clearly, E is monotonic (see Definitions 2.6.1 and 6.1.18). E is regular if and only if G is proper (see Definitions 5.2.1 and 2.6.4). (If G is proper, then E is, actually, superadditive (see Definition 6.1.11).) E is maximal if and only if G is strong (see Definitions 5.1.16 and 2.6.4). Finally, E is stable if and only if $C(N, W, A, R^N) \neq \varnothing$ for every $R^N \in L^N$ (see Definitions 6.1.17 and 2.6.8).

Remark 6.2.4. It follows from Remark 6.2.3 that if G is proper but *not* strong, then we can associate with G many "reasonable" effectivity functions (see, again, Remark 4.1.22).

Remark 6.2.5. Let $G = (N, W)$ be a non-null simple game, and let $E = E(G)$ (see Definition 6.2.1). The dual function $E^d : 2^A \rightarrow P(2^N)$ is given by $E^d(B) = W$ if $B \neq A$, and $E^d(A) = 2^N$ (see Definition 6.1.5). We observe that E is stable if and only if E^d is stable (see Remark 6.2.3 and Theorem 2.6.14).

Definition 6.2.6. A function $E : 2^N \rightarrow P(2^A)$ (see Notation 4.1.20) is *anonymous* if for every $S \in 2^N$ and every $B \in 2^A$

$$[B \in E(S), \ T \in 2^N, \ \text{and} \ |T| = |S|] \Rightarrow B \in E(T) \tag{6.2.1}$$

(see Notation 4.1.13 and Notation 2.1.7).

Thus, an anonymous function does not discriminate among voters.

Remark 6.2.7. Let $H : L^N \rightarrow 2^A$ be an SCC. If H is anonymous, then $E^*(H)$, $E_\alpha(H)$, and $E_\beta(H)$ are anonymous (see Definitions 2.3.6, 4.1.21, and 6.2.6).

Remark 6.2.8. Let $G = (N, W)$ be a non-null simple game, and let $E = E(G)$ (see Definition 6.2.1). Then E is anonymous if and only if G is symmetric (see Definitions 6.2.6 and 2.6.4).

Definition 6.2.9. A function $E : 2^N \rightarrow P(2^A)$ (see Notation 4.1.20) is *neutral* if for every $S \in 2^N$ and every $B \in 2^A$,

$$[B \in E(S), \ B^* \in 2^A, \ \text{and} \ |B^*| = |B|] \Rightarrow B^* \in E(S) \tag{6.2.2}$$

(see Notation 2.3.1 and Notation 2.1.7).

Thus, a neutral function does not discriminate among alternatives.

Remark 6.2.10. Let $H: L^N \rightarrow 2^A$ be an SCC. If H is neutral, then $E^*(H)$, $E_\alpha(H)$, and $E_\beta(H)$ are neutral (see Definitions 2.3.8, 4.1.21, and 6.2.9).

Remark 6.2.11. Let $G = (N, W)$ be a non-null simple game, and let $E = E(G)$ (see Definition 6.2.1). Then E is neutral.

Neutrality is the dual property of anonymity. More precisely, we have the following.

Remark 6.2.12. Let E be an effectivity function. Then E is anonymous if and only if E^d is neutral (see Definitions 6.1.5, 6.2.6, and 6.2.9).

Following Definition 5.2.8, we may now define the winning and blocking coefficients of an anonymous effectivity function. Some interesting properties of anonymous effectivity functions are discovered by the study of their coefficients.

Definition 6.2.13. Let $E: 2^N \rightarrow P(2^A)$ be an effectivity function (see Definition 6.1.1). Assume that E is anonymous and monotonic with respect to the players (see Definitions 6.2.6 and 5.2.4). Let $B \subset A$, $B \neq \varnothing, A$. The *winning coefficient* of B is defined by

$$w(E; B) = w(B) = \min\{|S| \mid B \in E(S)\} \tag{6.2.3}$$

We also define $w(A) = 1$ and $w(\varnothing) = n + 1$. Let, again, $B \subset A$. The *blocking coefficient* of B is defined by $\beta(B) = w(A - B)$.

Remark 6.2.14. Notice that under the assumptions of Definition 6.2.13, $w(\cdot)$ is well defined. Moreover, $w(\cdot)$ determines E completely.

Let E be an effectivity function. The "veto power" of a coalition S (relative to E) is the maximum number of alternatives that S can block. A measure of the veto power is called a veto function. Veto functions provide a useful tool mainly for studying *neutral* effectivity functions. The formal definition is as follows.

Definition 6.2.15. Let $E: 2^N \rightarrow P(2^A)$ be an effectivity function (see Definition 6.1.1). Assume that E is neutral and monotonic with respect to the alternatives (see Definitions 6.2.9 and 6.1.7). For every $S \in 2^N$, let

$$e(E; S) = e(S) = \min\{|B| \mid B \in E(S)\} \tag{6.2.4}$$

Also, we define $e(\varnothing) = m + 1$. The *veto function* of E is defined by $v(S) = m - e(S)$ for every $S \in 2^N$. Also, we define $v(\varnothing) = -1$.

Remark 6.2.16. Notice that under the assumptions of Definition 6.2.15, $v(\cdot)$ completely determines E.

Remark 6.2.17. Definition 6.2.15 is due to Moulin [1982a].

Remark 6.2.18. Let $E: 2^N \to P(2^A)$ be an effectivity function (see Definition 6.1.1). Assume that E is neutral and monotonic with respect to the alternatives (see Definitions 6.2.9 and 6.1.7). Then, for every $S \in 2^N$, $0 \leqslant v(S) \leqslant m - 1$, and $v(N) = m - 1$. Also, for every $S \in 2^N$,

$$e(E; S) = \min\{|B| \mid B \in E(S)\} = \min\{|B| \mid S \in E^d(B)\} = w(E^d; S)$$

(see Definitions 6.2.15 and 6.2.13).

Remark 6.2.19. Let $E: 2^N \to P(2^A)$ be an effectivity function (see Definition 6.1.1). Assume that E is anonymous and monotonic with respect to the players (see Definitions 6.2.6 and 5.2.4). Then $w(\cdot)$ is *monotonic* (nonincreasing); that is,

$$[B, B^* \in 2^A \text{ and } B^* \supset B] \Rightarrow w(B^*) \leqslant w(B)$$

if and only if E is monotonic with respect to the alternatives (see Definitions 6.2.13 and 6.1.7).

The dual result of Remark 6.2.19 is as follows.

Remark 6.2.19.d. Let $E: 2^N \to P(2^A)$ be an effectivity function (see Definition 6.1.1). Assume that E is neutral and monotonic with respect to the alternatives (see Definitions 6.2.9 and 6.1.7). Then $e(\cdot)$ is *monotonic* (nonincreasing); that is,

$$[S, T \in 2^N \text{ and } T \supset S] \Rightarrow e(T) \leqslant e(S)$$

if and only if E is monotonic with respect to the players (see Definitions 6.2.15 and 5.2.4 and Remark 6.1.8).

Lemma 6.2.20. *Let $E: 2^N \to P(2^A)$ be an effectivity function* (see Definition 6.1.1). *Assume that E is anonymous and monotonic with respect to the players* (see Definitions 6.2.6 and 5.2.4). *Then E is superadditive if and only if for all $B_1, B_2 \in 2^A$,*

$$w(B_1 \cap B_2) \leqslant w(B_1) + w(B_2) \tag{6.2.5}$$

(see Definitions 6.1.11 and 6.2.13).

Proof: Necessity. Let $B_1, B_2 \in 2^A$. If $w(B_1) + w(B_2) \geqslant n + 1$, then (6.2.5) is true. Therefore, we may assume that $w(B_1) + w(B_2) \leqslant n$. Thus, there exist $S_1, S_2 \in 2^N$ such that (a) $|S_i| = w(B_i)$, $i = 1, 2$, and (b) $S_1 \cap S_2 = \varnothing$. By the superadditivity of E, $B_1 \cap B_2 \in E(S_1 \cup S_2)$. Hence, $w(B_1 \cap B_2) \leqslant |S_1 \cup S_2| = w(B_1) + w(B_2)$.

Sufficiency. Assume that $S_1, S_2 \in 2^N$, $S_1 \cap S_2 = \emptyset$, and $B_i \in E(S_i)$, $i = 1, 2$. Then

$$w(B_1 \cap B_2) \le w(B_1) + w(B_2) \le |S_1| + |S_2| = |S_1 \cup S_2|$$

Hence, $B_1 \cap B_2 \in E(S_1 \cup S_2)$.

The dual result of Lemma 6.2.20 is as follows.

Lemma 6.2.20.d. *Let $E: 2^N \to P(2^A)$ be an effectivity function* (see Definition 6.1.1). *Assume that E is neutral and monotonic with respect to the alternatives* (see Definitions 6.2.9 and 6.1.7). *Then E is subadditive if and only if for all $S_1, S_2 \in 2^N$,*

$$e(S_1 \cap S_2) \le e(S_1) + e(S_2) \tag{6.2.6}$$

(see Definitions 6.1.24 and 6.2.15 and Remark 6.1.26).

Corollary 6.2.21. Under the assumptions of Lemma 6.2.20, E is superadditive if and only if $\beta(\cdot)$ is subadditive, that is, if for all $B_1, B_2 \in 2^A$,

$$\beta(B_1 \cup B_2) \le \beta(B_1) + \beta(B_2) \tag{6.2.7}$$

(see Definition 6.2.13).

Corollary 6.2.22. Under the assumptions of Lemma 6.2.20.d, E is subadditive if and only if for all $S_1, S_2 \in 2^N$,

$$v(S_1 \cap S_2) \ge v(S_1) + v(S_2) - m \tag{6.2.8}$$

(see Definition 6.2.15).

Lemma 6.2.23. *Let $E: 2^N \to P(2^A)$ be an effectivity function* (see Definition 6.1.1). *Assume that E is neutral and monotonic with respect to the alternatives* (see Definitions 6.2.9 and 6.1.7). *Then E is superadditive if and only if for all $S_1, S_2 \in 2^N$ such that $S_1 \cap S_2 = \emptyset$,*

$$e(S_1 \cup S_2) \le e(S_1) + e(S_2) - m \tag{6.2.9}$$

(see Definitions 6.1.11 and 6.2.15).

Proof: Necessity. Let $S_1, S_2 \in 2^N$ satisfy $S_1 \cap S_2 = \emptyset$. There exist $B_1, B_2 \in 2^A$ such that (a) $|B_i| = e(S_i)$, $i = 1, 2$, and (b) $|B_1 \cap B_2| = |B_1| - (m - |B_2|)$. Since E is superadditive, $B_1 \cap B_2 \in E(S_1 \cup S_2)$. Hence,

$$e(S_1 \cup S_2) \le |B_1 \cap B_2| = |B_1| + |B_2| - m = e(S_1) + e(S_2) - m$$

Sufficiency. Let, again, $S_1, S_2 \in 2^N$ satisfy $S_1 \cap S_2 = \emptyset$. If $B_i \in E(S_i)$, $i = 1, 2$, then $|B_i| \ge e(S_i)$, $i = 1, 2$. Hence,

$$|B_1 \cap B_2| \geqslant |B_1| - (m - |B_2|) \geqslant e(S_1) + e(S_2) - m$$

Thus, by (6.2.9), $|B_1 \cap B_2| \geqslant e(S_1 \cup S_2)$. Hence, $B_1 \cap B_2 \in E(S_1 \cup S_2)$, and E is superadditive.

The dual result of Lemma 6.2.23 is as follows.

Lemma 6.2.23.d. Let $E: 2^N \to P(2^A)$ be an effectivity function (see Definition 6.1.1). Assume that E is anonymous and monotonic with respect to the players (see Definitions 6.2.6 and 5.2.4). Then E is subadditive if and only if for all $B_1, B_2 \in 2^A$ such that $B_1 \cap B_2 = \varnothing$,

$$w(B_1 \cup B_2) \leqslant w(B_1) + w(B_2) - n \qquad (6.2.10)$$

(see Definitions 6.1.24 and 6.2.13 and Remark 6.1.26).

Corollary 6.2.24. Under the assumptions of Lemma 6.2.23, E is superadditive if and only if $v(\cdot)$ is superadditive, that is, if

$$[S_1, S_2 \in 2^N \text{ and } S_1 \cap S_2 = \varnothing] \Rightarrow v(S_1 \cup S_2) \geqslant v(S_1) + v(S_2) \qquad (6.2.11)$$

(see Definition 6.2.15).

Corollary 6.2.25. Under the assumptions of Lemma 6.2.23.d, E is subadditive if and only if for all $B_1, B_2 \in 2^A$ such that $B_1 \cup B_2 = A$,

$$\beta(B_1 \cap B_2) \leqslant \beta(B_1) + \beta(B_2) - n \qquad (6.2.12)$$

(see Definition 6.2.13).

Lemma 6.2.26. Let $E: 2^N \to P(2^A)$ be an effectivity function (see Definition 6.1.1). Assume that E is anonymous and monotonic with respect to the players (see Definitions 6.2.6 and 5.2.4). Then E is regular if and only if for every $B \in 2^A$,

$$w(B) + w(A - B) \geqslant n + 1 \qquad (6.2.13)$$

(see Definitions 5.2.1 and 6.2.13).

Proof: Necessity. Let $B \in 2^A$. Assume, on the contrary, that

$$w(B) + w(A - B) \leqslant n$$

Then, $B \neq A$. Let $S \in 2^N$ satisfy $w(B) = |S|$. Clearly, $B \in E(S)$. Also,

$$|N - S| = n - |S| = n - w(B) \geqslant w(A - B)$$

Hence, $A - B \in E(N - S)$, and the desired contradiction has been established.

Sufficiency. Let $S \in 2^N$, and let $B \in E(S)$. Then $|S| \geqslant w(B)$. Hence,

$$w(A-B) \geqslant n+1-w(B) \geqslant n+1-|S| > n-|S| = |N-S|$$

Thus, $A-B \notin E(N-S)$.

The dual result of Lemma 6.2.26 is as follows.

Lemma 6.2.26.d. *Let* $E: 2^N \to P(2^A)$ *be an effectivity function* (see Definition 6.1.1). *Assume that* E *is neutral and monotonic with respect to the alternatives* (see Definitions 6.2.9 and 6.1.7). *Then* E *is regular if and only if for every* $S \in 2^N$,

$$e(S) + e(N-S) \geqslant m+1 \qquad (6.2.14)$$

(see Definitions 5.2.1 and 6.2.15).

Remark 6.2.27. Inequality (6.2.13) is equivalent to

$$\beta(B) + \beta(A-B) \geqslant n+1 \quad \text{for every } B \in 2^A \qquad (6.2.15)$$

and (6.2.14) is equivalent to

$$v(S) + v(N-S) \leqslant m-1 \quad \text{for every } S \in 2^N \qquad (6.2.16)$$

Lemma 6.2.28. *Let* $E: 2^N \to P(2^A)$ *be an effectivity function* (see Definition 6.1.1). *Assume that* E *is anonymous and monotonic with respect to the players* (see Definitions 6.2.6 and 5.2.4). *Then* E *is maximal if and only if for every* $B \in 2^A$, $B \neq A$,

$$w(B) + w(A-B) \leqslant n+1 \qquad (6.2.17)$$

(see Definitions 5.1.16 and 6.2.13).

Proof: Sufficiency. Let $S \in 2^N$, and let $B \in 2^A$. If $B \notin E(S)$, then $|S| < w(B)$. Hence,

$$|N-S| = n-|S| \geqslant n+1-w(B) \geqslant w(A-B)$$

Therefore, $A-B \in E(N-S)$. Thus, E is maximal.

Necessity. Assume that E is maximal. Let $B \in 2^A$, $B \neq A$. If $w(A-B) \leqslant 1$, then (6.2.17) is true. Thus, we may assume that $w(A-B) > 1$. Let $S \in 2^N$ satisfy $|S| = w(A-B)-1$. Then $A-B \notin E(S)$. Since E is maximal, $B \in E(N-S)$. Hence, $|N-S| \geqslant w(B)$. Thus,

$$n+1 = |S|+1+|N-S| \geqslant w(A-B)+w(B)$$

The dual result of Lemma 6.2.28 is as follows.

Lemma 6.2.28.d. *Let* $E: 2^N \to P(2^A)$ *be an effectivity function* (see Definition 6.1.1). *Assume that* E *is neutral and monotonic with respect to the* *alternatives* (see Definitions 6.2.9 and 6.1.7). *Then E is maximal if and only if for every $S \in 2^N$, $S \neq N$,*

$$e(S) + e(N - S) \leqslant m + 1 \tag{6.2.18}$$

(see Definitions 5.1.16 and 6.2.15).

Remark 6.2.29. Inequality (6.2.17) is equivalent to

$$\beta(B) + \beta(A - B) \leqslant n + 1 \tag{6.2.19}$$

and (6.2.18) is equivalent to

$$v(S) + v(N - S) \geqslant m - 1 \tag{6.2.20}$$

Remark 6.2.30. Let $E: 2^N \to P(2^A)$ be an effectivity function (see Definition 6.1.1). Assume that E is anonymous and monotonic with respect to the players (see Definitions 6.2.6 and 5.2.4). Then E is both regular and maximal if and only if for every $B \in 2^A$, $B \neq A$,

$$\beta(B) + \beta(A - B) = n + 1 \tag{6.2.21}$$

(see Remarks 6.2.27 and 6.2.29). Furthermore, if E satisfies (6.2.21), then E is subadditive if and only if for all $B_1, B_2 \in 2^A$ such that $B_1 \cap B_2 = \varnothing$,

$$\beta(B_1 \cup B_2) \geqslant \beta(B_1) + \beta(B_2) - 1 \tag{6.2.22}$$

(see Lemma 6.2.23.d).

Remark 6.2.31. Let $E: 2^N \to P(2^A)$ be an effectivity function (see Definition 6.1.1). Assume that E is neutral and monotonic with respect to the alternatives (see Definitions 6.2.9 and 6.1.7). Then E is both regular and maximal if and only if for every $S \in 2^N$, $S \neq N$,

$$v(S) + v(N - S) = m - 1 \tag{6.2.23}$$

(see Remarks 6.2.27 and 6.2.29). Furthermore, if E is monotnoic with respect to the players and satisfies (6.2.23), then E is subadditive if and only if for all $S_1, S_2 \in 2^N$,

$$v(S_1 \cup S_2) \leqslant v(S_1) + v(S_2) + 1 \tag{6.2.24}$$

(see Corollary 6.2.22).

Unfortunately, the veto function is *not* the dual concept of the blocking function. Indeed, the following remark is true.

Remark 6.2.32. Let $E: 2^N \to P(2^A)$ be an effectivity function (see Definition 6.1.1). Assume that E is anonymous, monotonic with respect to the players, regular, and maximal (see Definitions 6.2.6, 5.2.4, 5.2.1, and 5.1.16). Then, for every $B \in 2^A$, $B \neq A$,

$$v(E^d; B) = \beta(E; B) - 1 \tag{6.2.25}$$

(see Definitions 6.1.5, 6.2.13, and 6.2.15). Indeed,

$$v(E^d; B) = n - e(E^d; B) = n - w(E; B) = n - (n + 1 - \beta(E; B))$$
$$= \beta(E; B) - 1$$

(see Remarks 6.2.18 and 6.2.30).

Following the discussion in Section 5.2, we shall consider now independently blocking anonymous effectivity functions.

Definition 6.2.33. Let $E: 2^N \to P(2^A)$ be an effectivity function (see Definition 6.1.1). Assume that E is anonymous and monotonic with respect to the players (see Definitions 6.2.6 and 5.2.4). E is *independently blocking* if the following condition is satisfied:

If $B_1, B_2 \in 2^A$ and $B_1 \cap B_2 = \varnothing$, then $\beta(B_1 \cup B_2) = \beta(B_1) + \beta(B_2)$
$$\tag{6.2.26}$$

(see Definition 6.2.13).

Remark 6.2.34. Let E be an independently blocking effectivity function (see Definition 6.2.33). Then (6.2.26) implies (6.2.7), (6.2.21), and (6.2.22). Hence, E is superadditive, regular, maximal, and subadditive (see Corollary 6.2.21 and Remark 6.2.30). It follows now from Lemma 6.1.13.d that E is also monotonic with respect to the alternatives.

Remark 6.2.35. Let $E: 2^N \to P(2^A)$ be an effectivity function (see Definition 6.1.1). Assume that E is anonymous, monotonic with respect to the players, and independently blocking (see Definition 6.2.33). Then, for every $B \in 2^A$ and every $S \in 2^N$,

$$B \in E(S) \Leftrightarrow |S| \geq n + 1 - \sum_{x \in B} \beta(x) \tag{6.2.27}$$

(see Definition 6.2.13 and Remark 6.2.30). Since $\sum_{x \in A} \beta(x) = \beta(A) = n + 1$, E is stable (see Definitions 5.3.1 and 6.1.17 and Corollary 5.3.10).

We now turn to review neutral effectivity functions whose veto functions are additive.

Definition 6.2.36. Let $E: 2^N \to P(2^A)$ be an effectivity function (see Definition 6.1.1). Assume that E is neutral and monotonic with respect to the alternatives (see Definitions 6.2.9 and 6.1.7). E is *additively blocking* if $v(E; \cdot)$ is additive, that is, if

$$[S_1, S_2 \in 2^N \text{ and } S_1 \cap S_2 = \varnothing] \Rightarrow v(S_1 \cup S_2) = v(S_1) + v(S_2) \qquad (6.2.28)$$

(see Definition 6.2.15).

Remark 6.2.37. Let E be an additively blocking effectivity function (see Definition 6.2.36). Then (6.2.28) implies (6.2.11), (6.2.23), and (6.2.24). Hence, E is superadditive, regular, maximal, and subadditive (see Corollary 6.2.24 and Remark 6.2.31). It follows now from Lemma 6.1.13 that E is also monotonic with respect to the players.

Remark 6.2.38. Let E be an additively blocking effectivity function (see Definition 6.2.36). Then, as will be shown in the next section, E is stable (see Definition 6.1.17).

Example 6.2.39. Let $\mu: N \to \{1, \ldots, m-1\}$ satisfy $\sum_{i=1}^{n} \mu(i) = m-1$. Consider the following game form $\Gamma = \Gamma(\mu)$ (see Definition 5.1.1). A strategy of player 1 is a subset $x^1 \subset A$ such that $|x^1| = \mu(1)$. Let Σ^1 be the set of all strategies of player 1. A strategy of player 2 is a function $x^2: \Sigma^1 \to 2^A$ that satisfies (a) $x^2(x^1) \subset A - x^1$ for every $x^1 \in \Sigma^1$ and (b) $|x^2(x^1)| = \mu(2)$ for every $x^1 \in \Sigma^1$. Let Σ^2 be the set of all strategies of player 2. The definition of the strategy sets $\Sigma^1, \ldots, \Sigma^n$ is now completed by repeating the foregoing procedure. More precisely, if $\Sigma^1, \ldots, \Sigma^k$ are defined for $2 \leqslant k < n$, then a strategy of player $k+1$ is a function

$$x^{k+1}: \Sigma^1 \times \cdots \times \Sigma^k \to 2^A$$

such that

(a) $\quad x^{k+1}(x^1, \ldots, x^k) \subset A - \bigcup_{i=1}^{k} x^i(x^1, \ldots, x^{i-1}) \quad$ for all $x^1 \in \Sigma^1, \ldots, x^k \in \Sigma^k$

and

(b) $\quad |x^{k+1}(x^1, \ldots, x^k)| = \mu(k+1) \quad$ for all $x^1 \in \Sigma^1, \ldots, x^k \in \Sigma^k$

For all $x^1 \in \Sigma^1, \ldots, x^n \in \Sigma^n$, let $\pi(x^1, \ldots, x^n)$ be defined by

$$\{\pi(x^1, \ldots, x^n)\} = A - \bigcup_{i=1}^{n} x^i(x^1, \ldots, x^{i-1})$$

Because $\sum_{i=1}^{n} \mu(i) = m-1$, π is well defined. Let $\Gamma = (\Sigma^1, \ldots, \Sigma^n; \pi)$. Then $E_\alpha(\Gamma)$ is neutral and monotonic with respect to the alternatives (see Definitions 5.1.13, 6.2.9, and 6.1.7 and Remark 6.1.9). Furthermore, $E_\alpha(\Gamma)$ is additively blocking, and $v(E_\alpha(\Gamma); S) = \sum_{i \in S} \mu(i)$ for every $S \in 2^N$ (see Definitions 6.2.36 and 6.2.15).

Remark 6.2.40. Let $\mu: N \to \{1, \ldots, m-1\}$ satisfy $\sum_{i=1}^{n} \mu(i) = m-1$. Then the game form $\Gamma = \Gamma(\mu)$ is called a "voting by (integer) veto" procedure (see Example 6.2.39). Indeed, the outcome of a play of Γ is determined in the following way. First player 1 eliminates (or "vetoes") $\mu(1)$ alternatives. Then player 2 eliminates $\mu(2)$ of the remaining alternatives, and so on. There is exactly one alternative that is not eliminated during all the n moves of the play, and it is defined as the outcome of the play.

Remark 6.2.41. Chapter V of Moulin [1983] contains a comprehensive study of voting by veto procedures. In particular, it contains important modifications of Example 6.2.39.

The computation of the coefficients of the Borda SCC is interesting enough to be reported.

Example 6.2.42. Let $B = B(m, n)$ be the Borda SCC (see Example 3.1.18), and let $E = E_\alpha(B)$ (see Definition 4.1.21). Then E is monotonic, anonymous, and neutral (see Definition 6.1.18 and Remarks 6.1.9, 5.2.5, 2.3.14, 6.2.7, and 6.2.10). Let $B \in 2^A$ such that $|B| = r < m$, and let $S \in 2^N$ such that $|S| = k \geqslant 2$. By Lemma 3.1.21, $B \in E(S)$ if and only if

$$k(m-1) > (n-k)(m-1) + k(m-r-1)/2 + 1/2$$

Hence,

$$w(B) = [(2(m-1)n+1)/(3(m-1)+r)] + 1 \tag{6.2.29}$$

and

$$v(S) = \max(0, \min(m-1, \lceil (2(m-1)(2k-n)-1)/k \rceil)) \tag{6.2.30}$$

where for a real number x, $\lceil x \rceil = -[-x]$ (see Definitions 6.2.13 and 6.2.15).

Remark 6.2.43. Formula (6.2.30) is due to Moulin [1982a].

We now begin our investigation of additive effectivity functions. As we shall show, independently blocking and additively blocking effectivity functions are additive. We start with the following notation.

Notation 6.2.44. Let B be a finite set, and let q be a real function on B. If $B_* \in 2^B$, then we denote $q(B_*) = \sum_{x \in B_*} q(x)$ (see Notation 4.1.13). Also, $q(\emptyset) = 0$.

Clearly, Notation 6.2.44 generalizes Notation 3.3.16.

Remark 6.2.45. Let B be a finite set, and let q be a real function on B; q is a probability measure on B if $q(x) \geqslant 0$ for all $x \in B$ and $q(B) = 1$ (see Notation 6.2.44).

We are now able to state the following important definition.

Definition 6.2.46. A function $E: 2^N \to P(2^A)$ is an *additive effectivity function* (AEF) if there exist *positive* probability measures, p on A and q on N, such that for every $B \in 2^A$ and every $S \in 2^N$,

$$B \in E(S) \Leftrightarrow q(S) > 1 - p(B) \tag{6.2.31}$$

(see Notation 6.2.44 and Remark 6.2.45).

Formula (6.2.31) tells us that S is effective for B if it has enough weight to "block" $A - B$.

Notation 6.2.47. Let E be an AEF (see Definition 6.2.46). If p and q are positive probability measures on A and N, respectively, such that (6.2.31) is satisfied, then we write $E = E(p, q)$.

Remark 6.2.48. Let $E = E(p, q)$ be an AEF (see Notation 6.2.47). Since p and q are positive, E is, indeed, an effectivity function (see Definition 6.1.1). Also, as the reader can easily verify, E is monotonic (see Definition 6.1.18). Finally, E^d is also an AEF (see Definition 6.1.5). Indeed, $E^d = E^d(q, p)$.

Lemma 6.2.49. *An AEF is superadditive* (see Definitions 6.2.46 and 6.1.11).

Proof: Let $E = E(p, q)$ be an AEF. If $S_1, S_2 \in 2^N$, $S_1 \cap S_2 = \varnothing$, and $B_i \in E(S_i)$, $i = 1, 2$, then

$$q(S_1 \cup S_2) = q(S_1) + q(S_2) > 1 - P(B_1) + 1 - p(B_2)$$
$$\geqslant p((A - B_1) \cup (A - B_2)) = 1 - p(B_1 \cap B_2)$$

Hence, $B_1 \cap B_2 \in E(S_1 \cup S_2)$, and E is superadditive.

Corollary 6.2.50. An AEF is subadditive (see Lemma 6.2.49 and Remarks 6.2.48 and 6.1.26). Also, an AEF is regular (see Lemma 6.2.49 and Remark 6.1.12).

Lemma 6.2.51. *Let $E = E(p, q)$ be an AEF* (see Notation 6.2.47). *Then E is maximal* (see Definition 5.1.16) *if and only if*

$$[B \in 2^A, \ B \neq A, \ and \ S \in 2^N, \ S \neq N] \Rightarrow p(B) \neq q(S) \tag{6.2.32}$$

Proof: Necessity. Let E be maximal. Assume, on the contrary, that there exist $B \in 2^A$, $B \neq A$, and $S \in 2^N$, $S \neq N$, such that $p(B) = q(S)$. Then $A - B \notin E(S)$. Also, $q(N - S) = 1 - q(S) = 1 - p(B)$. Hence, $B \notin E(N - S)$, and the desired contradiction has been obtained.

Sufficiency. Let $S \in 2^N$, and let $B \in 2^A$. If $B \notin E(S)$, then $B \neq A$ and $q(S) \leqslant 1 - p(B)$. Hence, by (6.2.32), $q(S) < 1 - p(B)$. Therefore, $A - B \in E(N - S)$, and E is maximal.

Remark 6.2.52. Let $E = E(p, q)$ be an AEF (see Notation 6.2.47). If E is anonymous (see Definition 6.2.6), then we may assume that $q(i) = 1/n$ for all $i \in N$. Let $S \in 2^N$ and $B \in 2^A$. Then

$$B \in E(S) \Leftrightarrow |S|/n > 1 - p(B) \qquad (6.2.33)$$

(see (6.2.31)). Therefore, the blocking function β of E is given by $\beta(B) = [np(B)] + 1$ for all $B \in 2^A$ (see Definition 6.2.13). Furthermore, E is maximal if and only if for every $B \in 2^A$, $B \neq A$, $p(B) \neq i/n$ for $i = 1, \ldots, n-1$ (see Lemma 6.2.51).

The following notation will be used in the sequel.

Notation 6.2.53. If x is a real number, then we denote by $\lceil x \rceil$ the smallest integer z that satisfies $z \geq x$.

Remark 6.2.54. Let $E = E(p, q)$ be an AEF (see Notation 6.2.47). If E is neutral (see Definition 6.2.9), then we may assume that $p(a) = 1/m$ for all $a \in A$. Let $S \in 2^N$ and $B \in 2^A$. Then

$$B \in E(S) \Leftrightarrow q(S) > 1 - |B|/m \qquad (6.2.34)$$

(see (6.2.31)). Therefore, the veto function of E is given by $v(S) = \lceil mq(S) \rceil - 1$ for all $S \in 2^N$ (see Definition 6.2.15 and Notation 6.2.53). Furthermore, E is maximal if and only if for every $S \in 2^N$, $S \neq N$, $q(S) \neq i/m$ for $i = 1, \ldots, m-1$ (see Lemma 6.2.51).

We shall now prove that every (anonymous) independently blocking effectivity function is additive.

Lemma 6.2.55. *Let $E: 2^N \to P(2^A)$ be an effectivity function* (see Definition 6.1.1). *Assume that E is anonymous, monotonic with respect to the players, and independently blocking* (see Definition 6.2.33). *Then E is additive* (see Definition 6.2.46).

Proof: For $a \in A$, let $p(a) = \beta(a)/(n+1)$, where $\beta(a) = \beta(E; a)$ is the blocking coefficient of a (see Definition 6.2.13). We shall prove that $E = E(p, q^*)$, where $q^* = (1/n, \ldots, 1/n)$ (see Notation 6.2.47). By (6.2.27) and (6.2.33), we have to show that for $S \in 2^N$ and $B \in 2^A$,

$$|S|/n > 1 - p(B) \Leftrightarrow |S| \geq n + 1 - \sum_{x \in B} \beta(x)$$

Assume first that $|S|/n > 1 - p(B)$. Then

$$|S| > n - n \sum_{x \in B} \beta(x)/(n+1) > n - \sum_{x \in B} \beta(x)$$

Hence, $|S| \geq n + 1 - \sum_{x \in B} \beta(x)$. Assume now that $|S| \geq n + 1 - \sum_{x \in B} \beta(x)$. We may assume that $B \neq A$. Then

$$|S|/n \geq (n+1)/n - \sum_{x \in B} \beta(x)/n > 1 - \sum_{x \in B} \beta(x)/(n+1) = 1 - p(B)$$

Similarly, one can show that every (neutral) additively blocking effectivity function is additive.

Lemma 6.2.56. *Let* $E: 2^N \to P(2^A)$ *be an effectivity function* (see Definition 6.1.1). *Assume that E is neutral, monotonic with respect to the alternatives, and additively blocking* (see Definition 6.2.36). *Then E is additive* (see Definition 6.2.46).

The proof of Lemma 6.2.56 is similar to that of Lemma 6.2.55. Hence, it is left to the reader.

The anonymous and neutral AEFs are completely determined by the following remark.

Remark 6.2.57. There is only one neutral and anonymous AEF (for fixed m and n), namely, $E = E(p^*, q^*)$, where $p^* = (1/m, \ldots, 1/m)$ and $q^* = (1/n, \ldots, 1/n)$. It is characterized by the *proportional veto function*

$$v_{m,n}^*(S) = v^*(S) = \lceil m|S|/n \rceil - 1 \tag{6.2.35}$$

(see Remarks 6.2.52 and 6.2.54). Clearly, $v^*(\cdot)$ is maximal if and only if m and n are relatively prime (see Lemma 6.2.51).

Remark 6.2.58. A detailed investigation of the proportional veto function is contained in Moulin [1981].

Remark 6.2.59. If E is an effectivity function (see Definition 6.1.1), then it is possible to define the winning coefficients of E by (6.2.3). However, unless E is anonymous and monotonic with respect to the players (see Definitions 6.2.6 and 5.2.4), the function $w(\cdot) = w(E; \cdot)$ carries very little information on E. A similar remark holds with regard to veto functions (see Definition 6.2.15).

6.3 Stability of effectivity functions

This section is devoted to an investigation of cores of effectivity functions. First we find some necessary conditions for stability. Then we prove that every AEF is stable (see Theorem 6.3.19). Finally, we formulate and verify a necessary and sufficient condition for stability of a neutral and anonymous effectivity function (see Theorem 6.3.25).

Let A be a finite set of m alternatives, $m \geq 2$, and let $N = \{1, \ldots, n\}$ be a society.

Lemma 6.3.1. *Let* $E: 2^N \to P(2^A)$ *be a function* (see Notation 4.1.20). *If E is stable, then E is regular* (see Definitions 6.1.17 and 5.2.1).

Proof: Let $E: 2^N \to P(2^A)$ be stable. Assume, on the contrary, that there exist $B \in 2^A$ and $S \in 2^N$ such that $B \in E(S)$ and $A - B \in E(N - S)$. Let $R^N \in L^N$ satisfy $BR^S(A - B)$ and $(A - B)R^{N-S}B$ (see Notation 5.2.14). Then, obviously, $C(E, R^N) = \varnothing$, and the desired contradiction has been obtained.

The following example shows that stability (of an effectivity function) does not imply any additional property besides regularity.

Example 6.3.2. Let $m = 3$, and let $G = (7, 5)$ (see Definition 2.6.4). Then $E = E(G)$ is stable (see Remark 6.2.3). Now let $B \subset A$ satisfy $|B| = 2$. We define an effectivity function E_* by $E_*(S) = E(S)$ if $S \neq \{1, 2, 3, 4, 5, 6\}$, and $E_*(\{1, 2, 3, 4, 5, 6\}) = 2^A - \{B\}$. Then, obviously, E_* is stable. However, E_* violates every known property (of effectivity functions) except regularity.

The stability of an effectivity function E implies the stability of the "monotonic cover" of E. This will be now stated in detail.

Definition 6.3.3. Let $E: 2^N \to P(2^A)$ be an effectivity function (see Definition 6.1.1). The *monotonic cover* E^m of E is defined by the following rule. Let $B \in 2^A$ and $S \in 2^N$. Then $B \in E^m(S)$ if and only if there exist $B_* \subset B$ and $S_* \subset S$ such that $B_* \in E(S_*)$.

Lemma 6.3.4. *The monotonic cover E^m of an effectivity function E is a monotonic effectivity function* (see Definitions 6.3.3 and 6.1.18). *Furthermore, $C(E, R^N) = C(E^m, R^N)$ for every $R^N \in L^N$* (see Definition 4.1.23).

The proof of Lemma 6.3.4 is left to the reader.
We now observe that a stable effectivity function has well-behaved superadditive and subadditive covers. We start with the following definition.

Definition 6.3.5. Let $E: 2^N \to P(2^A)$ be an effectivity function (see Definition 6.1.1). The *superadditive cover* E^p of E is defined by the following rule. Let $S \in 2^N$, and let $B \subset A$. Then $B \in E^p(S)$ if and only if there exist a partition $S_1, \ldots, S_k$ of S, $k \geqslant 1$, and sets $B_1, \ldots, B_k \in 2^A$ such that $B_i \in E(S_i)$, $i = 1, \ldots, k$, and $B = \bigcap_{i=1}^k B_i$. E^p is *well-behaved* if $\varnothing \notin E^p(S)$ for all $S \in 2^N$.

Lemma 6.3.6. *Let $E: 2^N \to P(2^A)$ be a stable effectivity function* (see Definition 6.1.17). *Then the superadditive cover of E is well-behaved* (see Definition 6.3.5).

Proof: Assume, on the contrary, that there exist $S_1, \ldots, S_k \in 2^N$ and $B_1, \ldots, B_k \in 2^A$ such that (a) if $i \neq j$, then $S_i \cap S_j = \varnothing$, (b) $B_i \in E(S_i)$, $i = 1, \ldots, k$, and (c) $\bigcap_{i=1}^{k} B_i = \varnothing$. Let $R^N \in L^N$ satisfy $B_i R^{S_i}(A - B_i)$ for $i = 1, \ldots, k$ (see Notation 5.2.14). If $1 \leqslant i \leqslant k$ and $x \notin B_i$, then $B_i \, \mathrm{Dom}(R^N, S_i) x$ (see Definition 4.1.23). By (c), $\bigcup_{i=1}^{k} (A - B_i) = A$. Hence, $C(E, R^N) = \varnothing$, and the desired contradiction has been obtained.

We shall now show that the superadditive cover of a stable effectivity function may be unstable.

Example 6.3.7. Let $A = \{a, b, c, d\}$ and $N = \{1, 2, 3, 4\}$. We consider an effectivity function that is defined by

$$E(\{4\}) = \{A, \{a, b, d\}, \{a, c, d\}, \{b, c, d\}\}$$

$E(\{1, 2\}) = \{A, \{a, b\}\}$, $E(\{1, 3\}) = \{A, \{a, c\}\}$, $E(\{2, 3\}) = \{A, \{b, c\}\}$, $E(\{1, 2, 3\}) = \{A, \{d\}\}$, $E(N) = 2^A$, and $E(S) = \{A\}$ otherwise. We claim that E is stable (see Definition 6.1.17). Indeed, let $R^N \in L^N$. Without loss of generality, $a R^4 \{b, c\}$ (see Notation 5.2.14). If $a \notin C(E, R^N)$, then we distinguish the following possibilities: (1) $d \, \mathrm{Dom}(R^N, \{1, 2, 3\}) a$. Now, if d is also dominated, then $\{b, c\} R^{\{2, 3\}} d$, or $b R^N d$ or $c R^N d$. In each case, $\{b, c\} \cap C(E, R^N) \neq \varnothing$. (2) $\{b, c\} \, \mathrm{Dom}(R^N, \{2, 3\}) a$. Without loss of generality, $b R^4 c$. If $b \notin C(E, R^N)$, then $d \, \mathrm{Dom}(R^N, \{1, 2, 3\}) b$. Hence, either $d \in C(E, R^N)$ or $c R^N d$ and $c \in C(E, R^N)$.

We now observe that $\{a\} \in E^p(\{1, 2, 4\})$, $\{b\} \in E^p(\{2, 3, 4\})$, and $\{c\} \in E^p(\{1, 3, 4\})$. Consider now the following situation:

R^1	R^2	R^3	R^4
d	b	c	a
a	d	b	c
c	a	d	b
b	c	a	d

$d \, \mathrm{Dom}(R^N, \{1, 2, 3\}) a$, $a \, \mathrm{Dom}(R^N, \{1, 2, 4\}) c$, $c \, \mathrm{Dom}(R^N, \{1, 3, 4\}) b$, and $b \, \mathrm{Dom}(R^N, \{2, 3, 4\}) d$. Hence, $C(E^p, R^N) = \varnothing$.

Remark 6.3.8. Let $E: 2^N \to P(2^A)$ be an effectivity function, and let E^m be the monotonic cover of E (see Definition 6.3.3). If E is superadditive, then, as the reader can easily verify, E^m is superadditive.

Remark 6.3.9. Let $E: 2^N \to P(2^A)$ be an effectivity function, and let E^p be the superadditive cover of E (see Definition 6.3.5). If E is monotonic and E^p is well-behaved, then E^p is monotonic. (Indeed, E^p is superadditive. Hence, E^p is monotonic with respect to the players (see Lemma 6.1.13). We shall now prove that E^p is monotonic with respect to the alternatives. Let $S \in 2^N$, $B \in E^p(S)$, and $B^* \supset B$. There exist a partition $S_1, \ldots, S_k$ of S and sets $B_i \in E(S_i)$, $i = 1, \ldots, k$, such that $B = \bigcap_{i=1}^k B_i$. Let $B_i^* = B_i \cup (B^* - B)$, $i = 1, \ldots, k$. Since E is monotonic, $B_i^* \in E(S_i)$, $i = 1, \ldots, k$. Hence, $B^* = \bigcap_{i=1}^k B_i^* \in E^p(S)$.)

We now turn to consider the subadditive cover of an effectivity function.

Definition 6.3.10. Let $E: 2^N \to P(2^A)$ be an effectivity function (see Definition 6.1.1). The *subadditive cover* E^b of E is defined by the following rule. Let $S \subset N$, and let $B \in 2^A$. Then $B \in E^b(S)$ if and only if $S \in (E^d)^p(B)$ (see Definitions 6.1.5 and 6.3.5). E^b is *well-behaved* if $(E^d)^p$ is well-behaved (see, again, Definition 6.3.5).

Remark 6.3.11. Let E be an effectivity function (see Definition 6.1.1). If E^b is well-behaved, then $E^b = ((E^d)^p)^d$ (see Definition 6.3.10).

Lemma 6.3.12. *Let $E: 2^N \to P(2^A)$ be a stable effectivity function* (see Definition 6.1.17). *Then the subadditive cover of E is well-behaved* (see Definition 6.3.10).

Proof: Assume, on the contrary, that E^b is not well-behaved. Then there exist $B_1, \ldots, B_k \in 2^A$ and $S_1, \ldots, S_k \in 2^N$ such that (a) if $i \neq j$, then $B_i \cap B_j = \varnothing$, (b) $B_i \in E(S_i)$, $i = 1, \ldots, k$, and (c) $\bigcap_{i=1}^k S_i = \varnothing$. We define a profile $R^N \in L^N$ in the following way. Let $i \in N$. Then there exists $h = h(i)$ such that $i \notin S_h$ (see (c)). We choose $R^i \in L$ that satisfies

$$B_{h+1} R^i B_{h+2}, \ldots, B_k R^i B_1, B_1 R^i B_2, \ldots, B_{h-1} R^i B_h, B_h R^i B^*$$

where $B^* = A - \bigcup_{i=1}^k B_i$. We shall now prove that $C(E, R^N) = \varnothing$ (and thereby obtain the desired contradiction). Indeed, let $x \in A$. If $x \in B^*$, then $B_1 \, \mathrm{Dom}(R^N, S_1)x$ (see Definition 4.1.23). If $x \in B_h$, $h > 1$, then $B_{h-1} \, \mathrm{Dom}(R^N, S_{h-1})x$, and if $x \in B_1$, then $B_k \, \mathrm{Dom}(R^N, S_k)x$.

Corollary 6.3.13. Let E be a maximal and stable effectivity function (see Definitions 5.1.16 and 6.1.17). Then E is both superadditive and subadditive (see Definitions 6.1.11 and 6.1.24).

Proof: Because E is stable, E^p is well-behaved; that is, E^p is an effectivity function (see Lemma 6.3.6). Clearly, E^p is superadditive (see Definition 6.3.5). Hence, E^p is regular (see Remark 6.1.12). Since E is maximal and $E^p(S) \supset E(S)$ for every $S \in 2^N$, we conclude from Lemma

6.1.33 that $E = E^p$. Similarly, it can be proved that $E = E^b$. Thus, E is both superadditive and subadditive.

Remark 6.3.14. Corollary 6.3.13 is due to Abdou [1981] (see Moulin [1983]).

We shall now show that the subadditive cover of a stable effectivity function may be unstable. First we need the following notation.

Notation 6.3.15. Let K be a finite set, and let $M \in 2^K$ (see Notation 4.1.13). We denote

$$M^+ = \{M_1 \mid M_1 \in 2^K \text{ and } M_1 \supset M\}$$

Example 6.3.16. Let $A = \{a, b, c, d\}$ and $N = \{1, 2, 3, 4\}$. We consider an effectivity function that is defined by $E(\{1, 2, 3\}) = \{a\}^+$, $E(\{1, 4\}) = \{b, c\}^+$, $E(\{2, 4\}) = \{b, d\}^+$, $E(\{3, 4\}) = \{c, d\}^+$, $E(\{1, 2, 4\}) = E(\{1, 4\}) \cup E(\{2, 4\})$, $E(\{1, 3, 4\}) = E(\{1, 4\}) \cup E(\{3, 4\})$, $E(\{2, 3, 4\}) = E(\{2, 4\}) \cup E(\{3, 4\})$, $E(N) = 2^A$, and $E(S) = \{A\}$ otherwise (see Notation 6.3.15). We claim that E is stable (see Definition 6.1.17). Indeed, let $R^N \in L^N$. Without loss of generality, we may assume that $dR^4\{b, c\}$ (see Notation 5.2.14). If $d \notin C(E, R^N)$, then $a \operatorname{Dom}(R^N, \{1, 2, 3\})d$ (see Definition 4.1.23). Hence, $aR^i d$, $i = 1, 2, 3$. If, also, a is not in the core, then we distinguish the following possibilities: (1) $\{b, c\} \operatorname{Dom}(R^N, \{1, 4\})a$. Now, $t_2(R^4) \in \{b, c\}$ (see Notation 2.1.8). Hence, $t_2(R^4) \in C(E, R^N)$. (2) $c \operatorname{Dom}(R^N, N)a$. If c is not in the core, then $b \operatorname{Dom}(R^N, N)c$, and $b \in C(E, R^N)$. (3) $b \operatorname{Dom}(R^N, N)a$. Again, as in the previous case, $\{b, c\} \cap C(E, R^N) \neq \varnothing$. Thus, E is stable.

Consider now the subadditive cover E^b of E (see Definition 6.3.10). We have $\{a, b, c\} \in E^b(\{1\})$, $\{a, b, d\} \in E^b(\{2\})$, and $\{a, c, d\} \in E^b(\{3\})$. Hence, the core $C(E^b, R^N)$ of the following profile is empty:

R^1	R^2	R^3	R^4
b	d	c	b
c	b	d	c
a	a	a	d
d	c	b	a

Using Example 6.3.16, we shall now show that stability is *not* a self-dual property.

Remark 6.3.17. Let E be the effectivity function of Example 6.3.16. The dual effectivity function E^d (see Definition 6.1.5) satisfies $\{1, 2, 3\} \in E^d(\{a\})$, $\{1, 4\} \in E^d(\{b, c\})$, $\{2, 4\} \in E^d(\{b, d\})$, and $\{3, 4\} \in E^d(\{c, d\})$.

Let L_* be the set of all *linear orders of N* (i.e., $L_* = L(N)$) (see Definition 2.1.3). Also, let L_*^A be the set of all functions from A to L_*. Consider now the following profile $Q^A \in L_*^A$:

Q^a	Q^b	Q^c	Q^d
1	4	4	4
2	1	3	2
3	2	1	3
4	3	2	1

Now,

$$\{1,2,3\}\,\mathrm{Dom}(Q^A,\{a\})4, \quad \{1,4\}\,\mathrm{Dom}(Q^A,\{b,c\})2,$$

$$\{2,4\}\,\mathrm{Dom}(Q^A,\{b,d\})3, \quad \text{and} \quad \{3,4\}\,\mathrm{Dom}(Q^A,\{c,d\})1$$

Thus, $C(E^d, Q^A) = \varnothing$. (We observe that E is superadditive.)

We conclude our discussion of the superadditive cover of an effectivity function with the following remarks, which are derived from the duality principle for effectivity functions.

Remark 6.3.18. Let $E: 2^N \to P(2^A)$ be an effectivity function. Then $E^m = ((E^d)^m)^d$ (see Definitions 6.1.5 and 6.3.3).

The dual result of Remark 6.3.8 is as follows.

Remark 6.3.8.d. Let $E: 2^N \to P(2^A)$ be an effectivity function, and let E^m be the monotonic cover of E (see Definition 6.3.3). If E is subadditive, then E^m is subadditive (see Remark 6.3.18).

Finally, the dual result of Remark 6.3.9 is as follows.

Remark 6.3.9.d. Let $E: 2^N \to P(2^A)$ be an effectivity function, and let E^b be the subadditive cover of E (see Definition 6.3.10). If E is monotonic and E^b is well-behaved, then E^b is monotonic (see Remarks 6.1.9 and 6.3.11).

We now prove that additivity implies stability.

Theorem 6.3.19. *Every AEF is stable* (see Definitions 6.2.46 and 6.1.17).

The following two lemmata will enable us to deduce the stability of AEFs from Remark 6.2.35.

Lemma 6.3.20. *Let $E = E(p,q)$ be an AEF* (see Notation 6.2.47). *Then there exist two vectors of positive integers $\mu = (\mu(i))_{i \in N}$ and $\lambda = (\lambda(a))_{a \in A}$ such that the following conditions are satisfied:*

$$\lambda(A) = \mu(N) + 1 \tag{6.3.1}$$

For all $B \in 2^A$ and $S \in 2^N$,

$$[q(S) + p(B) > 1] \Rightarrow [\mu(S) + \lambda(B) \geqslant \lambda(A)] \tag{6.3.2}$$

(see Notation 6.2.44).

Proof: We denote

$$U = \{(S, B) \mid S \in 2^N, \ B \in 2^A, \text{ and } q(S) + p(B) > 1\}$$

and define

$$\epsilon = \min\{q(S) + p(B) - 1 \mid (S, B) \in U\}$$

We now choose positive integers $\mu(i)$, $i \in N$, and $\lambda(a)$, $a \in A$, such that (6.3.1) is satisfied, and, furthermore,

$$|p(a) - \lambda(a)/\lambda(A)| < \epsilon/2m \quad \text{for every } a \in A \tag{6.3.3}$$

and

$$|q(i) - \mu(i)/\lambda(A)| < \epsilon/2n \quad \text{for every } i \in N \tag{6.3.4}$$

(6.3.3) and (6.3.4) entail, respectively,

$$|p(B) - \lambda(B)/\lambda(A)| < \epsilon/2 \quad \text{for every } B \in 2^A \tag{6.3.5}$$

and

$$|q(S) - \mu(S)/\lambda(A)| < \epsilon/2 \quad \text{for every } S \in 2^N \tag{6.3.6}$$

Clearly, (6.3.5) and (6.3.6) imply (6.3.2).

In order to state our second lemma, we need the following notation. Let $E = E(p, q)$ be an AEF, and let λ and μ be vectors of positive integers that satisfy (6.3.1) and (6.3.2) (see Lemma 6.3.20). We denote

$$A^* = A^*(\lambda) = \{(a, z) \mid a \in A, \ z \in Z_+, \ 1 \leqslant z \leqslant \lambda(a)\} \tag{6.3.7}$$

where Z_+ is the set of positive integers. Intuitively, we replicate each $a \in A$ $\lambda(a)$ times, in order to obtain $A^*(\lambda)$ from A. Similarly, we denote

$$N^* = N^*(\mu) = \{(i, t) \mid i \in N, \ t \in Z_+, \ 1 \leqslant t \leqslant \mu(i)\} \tag{6.3.8}$$

Note that $|N^*(\mu)| = \mu(N)$ and $|A^*(\lambda)| = \lambda(A)$ (see Notation 2.1.7 and Notation 6.2.44). We define now an effectivity function $E_* = E_*(\lambda, \mu)$, relative to $A^*(\lambda)$ and $N^*(\mu)$, as follows. Let $\beta_*(x) = 1$ for all $x \in A^*(\lambda)$. Then E_* is defined by (5.3.1). More explicitly, let $B \in 2^{A^*}$ and $S \in 2^{N^*}$ (see (6.3.7) and (6.3.8)). Then

$$B \in E_*(S) \Leftrightarrow |S| \geqslant \mu(N) + 1 - |B| \tag{6.3.9}$$

By Corollary 5.3.10, E_* is stable (see also Remark 6.2.35). It remains now to prove that the stability of E_* implies that of E. This will be done by the next lemma. First, we need further notation. Let $L_* = L_*(\lambda)$ be the set of all linear orders of $A^*(\lambda)$ (see Definition 2.1.3). With each $R \in L$ we associate a member $R_* \in L_*(\lambda)$ in the following way. Let (a, y) and (b, z) be two distinct members of $A^*(\lambda)$ (see (6.3.7)). Then

$$(a, y) R_*(b, z) \Leftrightarrow [a \neq b \text{ and } aRb, \text{ or } a = b \text{ and } y < z] \qquad (6.3.10)$$

Let now $R^N \in L^N$. We associate with R^N a profile $R_*^{N^*}$ in $L_*^{N^*}$ as follows:

$$R_*^{(i, t)} = R_*^i, \qquad t = 1, \ldots, \mu(i), \quad i = 1, \ldots, n \qquad (6.3.11)$$

(see (6.3.10) and (6.3.8)). We are now able to state the following.

Lemma 6.3.21. *Let $E = E(p, q)$ be an AEF, and let λ and μ be vectors of positive integers that satisfy (6.3.1) and (6.3.2) (see Lemma 6.3.20). Furthermore, let $E_* = E_*(\lambda, \mu)$ be defined by (6.3.9), let $R^N \in L^N$, and let $R_*^{N^*}$ be given by (6.3.11). Then, for every $a \in A$,*

$$(a, 1) \in C(E_*, R_*^{N^*}) \Rightarrow a \in C(E, R^N) \qquad (6.3.12)$$

Proof: Let $a \notin C(E, R^N)$. Then there exist $S \in 2^N$ and $B \subset A - \{a\}$ such that BR^Sa and $q(S) > 1 - p(B)$ (see Definition 4.1.23 and Notation 5.2.14). Now let

$$S^* = \{(i, t) \mid i \in S \text{ and } 1 \leq t \leq \mu(i)\}$$

and

$$B^* = \{(b, z) \mid b \in B \text{ and } 1 \leq z \leq \lambda(b)\}$$

If $(i, t) \in S^*$ and $(b, z) \in B^*$, then $(b, z) R_*^{(i, t)}(a, 1)$ (see (6.3.10) and (6.3.11)). Also, $|S^*| = \mu(S)$ and $|B^*| = \lambda(B)$. Because $q(S) + p(B) > 1$, $\mu(S) + \lambda(B) \geq \lambda(A)$ (see (6.3.2)). Hence, $|S^*| \geq \mu(N) + 1 - |B^*|$, and $B^* E_*(S^*)$ (see (6.3.9)). Thus, $(a, 1) \notin C(E_*, R_*^{N^*})$, and the proof is complete.

Proof of Theorem 6.3.19. Let E be an AEF, and let $R^N \in L^N$. By Lemma 6.3.20, there exist vectors $(\mu(i))_{i \in N}$ and $(\lambda(a))_{a \in A}$ of positive integers that satisfy (6.3.1) and (6.3.2). Let $E_* = E_*(\lambda, \mu)$ be defined by (6.3.9), and let $R_*^{N^*}$ be given by (6.3.11). Then, as we have already noticed, $C(E_*, R_*^{N^*}) \neq \emptyset$. Because $C(E_*, R_*^{N^*}) \subset \{(a, 1) \mid a \in A\}$ (see (6.3.10) and (6.3.11)), it follows now from Lemma 6.3.21 that $C(E, R^N) \neq \emptyset$.

Remark 6.3.22. It follows now from Lemma 6.2.56 and Theorem 6.3.19 that an additively blocking effectivity function is stable (see Remark 6.2.38).

For the sake of completeness, we show now that a stable and maximal effectivity function may *not* be additive.

Example 6.3.23. Let $G = (N, W)$ be a weak game (see Definition 2.6.4) that is *not* a weighted majority game (see Definition 3.3.25), and let A be a finite set of m alternatives, $m \geqslant 2$. By Theorem 4.2.1, there exists an SCF $F: L^N \to A$ that is a strong representation of G. By Corollary 4.1.29, F is strongly tight. Hence, by Lemma 5.1.17, $E = E_\alpha(F)$ is maximal. Also, by Lemma 4.1.25, E is stable (see Definition 6.1.17). We claim that E is not additive. Assume, on the contrary, that there exist positive probability vectors, p on A and q on N, such that $E = E(p, q)$ (see Notation 6.2.47). Let $a \in A$ satisfy $p(a) \leqslant p(b)$ for all $b \in A$, and let $r = 1 - p(a)$. If $S \in W$, then, since F is a representation of G, $q(S) > r$ (see Definition 6.2.46). Also, if $S \notin W$, then $\{a\} \notin E(S)$, and therefore $q(S) \leqslant r$. Clearly, there exists $e > 0$ such that if $r^* = r + e$, then $[r^*; q(1), \ldots, q(n)]$ is a representation of G (see, again, Definition 3.3.25). Since G is *not* a weighted majority game, the desired contradiction has been obtained.

Using Remark 6.2.57, we shall now characterize the class of all monotonic, anonymous, neutral, and stable effectivity functions. We start with the following remark.

Remark 6.3.24. Let $E: 2^N \to P(2^A)$ be an effectivity function (see Definition 6.1.1). If E is monotonic, anonymous, and neutral (see Definitions 6.1.18, 6.2.6, and 6.2.9), then the veto function of E, $v(\cdot)$, is actually a function from $\{1, \ldots, n\}$ into $\{0, 1, \ldots, m - 1\}$ (see Definition 6.2.15).

Theorem 6.3.25. *Let $E: 2^N \to P(2^A)$ be an effectivity function* (see Definition 6.1.1). *Assume that E is monotonic, anonymous, and neutral* (see Definitions 6.1.18, 6.2.6, and 6.2.9). *Then E is stable if and only if $v(t) \leqslant v^*(t)$ for $t = 1, \ldots, n$, where v is the veto function of E and v^* is the proportional veto function* (see Definition 6.2.15 and Remarks 6.2.57 and 6.3.24).

Proof: Sufficiency. By Theorem 6.3.19, v^* is stable. By Definition 6.2.15, if $v^*(t) \geqslant v(t)$ for $t = 1, \ldots, n$, then $E_*(S) \supset E(S)$ for every $S \in 2^N$, where E_* is the effectivity function of the proportional veto function. Hence, E is stable.

In order to prove the necessity part, we need the following lemmata. Let $n = dm + s$, where $0 \leqslant s < m$ and $d \geqslant 0$ are integers. We define

$$\theta_k = kd + [ks/m], \qquad k = 0, 1, \ldots, m \qquad (6.3.13)$$

Lemma 6.3.26. $v^*(t) = k - 1$ for $\theta_{k-1} < t \leqslant \theta_k$, $k = 1, 2, \ldots, m$.

Proof: First we show that $v^*(\theta_k) \leqslant k - 1$. Indeed, $\theta_k \leqslant kd + ks/m$. Hence,

$$v^*(\theta_k) = \lceil m\theta_k/n \rceil - 1 \leqslant \lceil m(kd + ks/m)/n \rceil - 1 = k - 1$$

(see Remark 6.2.57). Next we show that if $t > \theta_{k-1}$, then $v^*(t) \geqslant k - 1$. Indeed,

$$\theta_{k-1} + 1 = (k-1)d + [(k-1)s/m] + 1 > (k-1)d + (k-1)s/m$$

Hence, if $t > \theta_{k-1}$, then

$$k - 1 = m((k-1)d + (k-1)s/m)/n < m(\theta_{k-1} + 1)/n \leqslant mt/n$$
$$\leqslant \lceil mt/n \rceil = v^*(t) + 1$$

Hence, $v^*(t) \geqslant k - 1$, and the proof is complete (see Notation 6.2.53).

Corollary 6.3.27. $v(t) \leqslant v^*(t)$ for $t = 1, \ldots, n$ if and only if $v(\theta_k) \leqslant k - 1$ for $k = 1, \ldots, m$.

Proof: Lemma 6.3.26 and the monotonicity of v (as a function of t).

In order to state our second lemma, we need the following terminology. A subset I of $\{1, \ldots, m\}$ is called a *circular interval starting at a* if it is of the form $\{a, a+1, \ldots, b\}$, where $b \geqslant a$, or of the form $\{1, \ldots, b-1, b\} \cup \{a, a+1, \ldots, m\}$, where $a > b$. The *length* of I is respectively $b - a$ or $m + b - a$.

Lemma 6.3.28. Let $0 \leqslant r \leqslant s$ and $1 \leqslant k \leqslant m$ such that $rm \leqslant ks$. Then there exists a set $\Omega \subset \{1, \ldots, m\}$ such that (a) $|\Omega| = s$ (see Notation 2.1.7) and (b) if I is a circular interval of length at least $k - 1$, then $|I \cap \Omega| \geqslant r$.

Proof: Let $m = es + f$, where $e \geqslant 1$ and $0 \leqslant f < s$ are integers. For $h = 1, \ldots, s$, let $j_h = he + [hf/s]$, and let $\Omega = \{j_1, \ldots, j_s\}$. Since $e \geqslant 1$, $|\Omega| = s$. Notice also that $j_s = m$. Now let I be a circular interval starting at j. Assume also that the length of I is at least $k - 1$. We distinguish the following possibilities:

(a) $j + k \leqslant m$. Let $v^*(t) = v^*_{s,m}(t) = \lceil ts/m \rceil - 1$ (see Remark 6.2.57). Then

$$v^*(j+k) \geqslant v^*(j + \lceil rm/s \rceil) \geqslant \lceil (j + rm/s)s/m \rceil - 1$$
$$= \lceil js/m \rceil - 1 + r = v^*(j) + r$$

By Lemma 6.3.26, $|I \cap \Omega| \geqslant r$.

(b) $j+k>m$. Then $j+k-m \geqslant j+\lceil rm/s \rceil -m \geqslant j-m(s-r)/s$. Hence, $v^*(j+k-m) \geqslant \lceil (j-m(s-r)/s)s/m \rceil -1 = v^*(j)-(s-r)$. Now $m=j_s \in \Omega$. Hence, $|\Omega \cap \{j,j+1,\ldots,m\}| \geqslant s-v^*(j)$. Thus,

$$|I \cap \Omega| \geqslant s-v^*(j)+v^*(j)-(s-r)=r$$

and the proof is complete.

We now complete the proof of the necessity part of Theorem 6.3.25.

Necessity. Let E be stable. Assume, on the contrary, that there exists $1 \leqslant t < n$ such that $v(t) > v^*(t)$. By Corollary 6.3.27, there exists k, $1 \leqslant k < m$, such that $v(\theta_k) \geqslant k$ (see 6.3.13). Consider the following m linear orders of $A = \{x_1,\ldots,x_m\}$:

$$R_1=(x_1,x_2,\ldots,x_m), R_2=(x_m,x_1,\ldots,x_{m-1}),\ldots,R_m=(x_2,x_3,\ldots,x_m,x_1)$$

Let $r=[sk/m]$. By Lemma 6.3.28, there exists a set $\Omega \subset \{1,\ldots,m\}$ such that (a) $|\Omega|=s$ and (b) if I is a circular interval of length at least $k-1$, then $|I \cap \Omega| \geqslant r$. Let τ be a bijection from $\{md+1, md+2,\ldots,n\}$ onto Ω. We define now a profile $R^N \in L^N$ by the following rules. $R^i = R_j$ for $(j-1)d+1 \leqslant i \leqslant jd$, $j=1,\ldots,m$, and $R^i = R_{\tau(i)}$ for $md+1 \leqslant i \leqslant n$. We shall now prove that $C(E,R^N)=\varnothing$ (and thereby obtain the desired contradiction). Indeed, let $a \in A$. Then $a=x_j$ for some $1 \leqslant j \leqslant m$. Let

$$I=\{h \mid x_j=t_f(R_h) \text{ and } f \geqslant m-k+1\}$$

(see Notation 2.1.8). Then I is a circular interval of length $k-1$. Hence, $|I \cap \Omega| \geqslant r$. Furthermore, if

$$T=\{i \mid R^i=R_h \text{ for some } h \in I\}$$

then T contains at least $kd+r$ voters. Now let

$$B=\{x_{j-1},x_{j-2},\ldots,x_1,x_m,\ldots,x_{k+j}\} \quad \text{if } j \leqslant m-k$$

and

$$B=\{x_{j-1},\ldots,x_{j+k-m}\} \quad \text{if } j \geqslant m-k+1$$

Then $|B|=m-k$, and BR^Tx_j (see Notation 5.2.14). Now

$$v(T) \geqslant v(\theta_k) \geqslant k=m-|B|$$

Hence, $B \in E(T)$. Thus, $a \notin C(E,R^N)$. Because a is arbitrary, $C(E,R^N)=\varnothing$.

Theorem 6.3.25 is due to Moulin [1981].

We are now able to characterize those anonymous and neutral effectivity functions that are also stable and maximal.

Theorem 6.3.29. *Let $E: 2^N \to P(2^A)$ be a stable, monotonic, anonymous, and neutral effectivity function (see Definitions 6.1.18, 6.2.6, 6.2.9, and 6.1.17). If m and n are not relatively prime, then E is not maximal (see Definition 5.1.16). If m and n are relatively prime and E is maximal, then E is given by (6.2.35).*

Proof: Let v be the veto function of E (see Remark 6.3.24). Now, since E is stable, $v(t) \leqslant v^*(t)$ for $t = 1, \ldots, n$, where v^* is given by (6.2.35) (see Theorem 6.3.25). Hence, v is maximal if and only if $v = v^*$ and v^* is maximal (see Lemma 6.3.1 and Remark 6.2.31). Now, v^* is maximal if and only if m and n are relatively prime (see Remark 6.2.57). Thus, the proof is complete.

6.4   A characterization of the class of partially implementable SCCs

In this section we provide a necessary and sufficient condition for an SCC to be partially implementable (see Theorem 6.4.4). We start by proving the following result on implementability of the core of a stable effectivity function.

Let A be a finite set of m alternatives, $m \geqslant 2$, and let $N = \{1, \ldots, n\}$ be a society. First, we need the following generalization of Lemma 4.1.25.

Lemma 6.4.1. *Let $\Gamma = (\Sigma^1, \ldots, \Sigma^n; \pi)$ be a GF (see Definition 5.1.1), and let $R^N \in L^N$. If $\sigma^N \in \Sigma^N$ is a strong e.p. of $g(\Gamma, R^N)$, then $\pi(\sigma^N) \in C(E_\beta(\Gamma), R^N)$ (see Definitions 5.1.4, 5.1.13, and 4.1.23 and Remark 5.1.7).*

Proof: Let $x = \pi(\sigma^N)$. Assume, on the contrary, that $x \notin C(E_\beta(\Gamma), R^N)$. Then there exist $S \in 2^N$ and $B \subset A - \{x\}$ such that BR^Sx and $B \in E_\beta(\Gamma; S)$ (see Notation 5.2.14). Since $B \in E_\beta(\Gamma; S)$, there exists $\mu^S \in \Sigma^S$ such that $\pi(\sigma^{N-S}, \mu^S) \in B$. Let $y = \pi(\sigma^{N-S}, \mu^S)$. Then $y \neq x$, and yR^ix for all $i \in S$. Thus, σ^N is not a strong e.p. of $g(\Gamma, R^N)$, and the desired contradiction has been obtained.

We are now able to prove the following theorem.

Theorem 6.4.2. *Let $E: 2^N \to P(2^A)$ be a stable and monotonic effectivity function (see Definitions 6.1.17, 6.1.18, and 6.1.1). Then the core $C(E, R^N)$ is implementable if and only if E is maximal (see Definitions 5.1.8 and 5.1.16).*

Proof: Necessity. Assume that $H(R^N) = C(E, R^N)$ is implementable. By Corollary 5.1.18, $E^*(H)$ is maximal. By Lemma 6.1.21, $E^*(H) = E$. Hence, E is maximal.

Sufficiency. Assume that E is maximal. We shall define now a GF $\Gamma = (\Sigma^1, \ldots, \Sigma^n; \pi)$ that implements $C(E, R^N)$ (see Definitions 5.1.1 and 5.1.8). For $i \in N$, we denote

$$\tau^i = \{T \mid T \in 2^N \text{ and } i \in T\} \tag{6.4.1}$$

The set of strategies of player i, Σ^i, is now defined by

$$\Sigma^i = \{\sigma^i \mid \sigma^i : \tau^i \to 2^A, \ \sigma^i(T) \in E(T) \text{ for all } T \in \tau^i\} \tag{6.4.2}$$

(see Notation 2.3.1 and (6.4.1)). Thus, a strategy σ^i of player i is a function that assigns for every coalition T containing i a set of alternatives $\sigma^i(T)$ for which T is effective (according to the effectivity function E). We now define the outcome function π of Γ as follows. Let $\sigma^N \in \Sigma^N$. We associate with σ^N a sequence of partitions of N in the following way. First, let $T \in 2^N$. Then we denote by $Q(T, \sigma^N)$ the partition of T into equivalence classes with respect to the following equivalence relation:

$$i \sim j \Leftrightarrow \sigma^i(T) = \sigma^j(T) \qquad (i, j \in T)$$

Now let the first partition be $P_0(\sigma^N) = \{N\}$. We continue inductively: If $P_k(\sigma^N) = \{T_1^k, \ldots, T_{r_k}^k\}$, then

$$P_{k+1}(\sigma^N) = \{Q(T_1^k, \sigma^N), \ldots, Q(T_{r_k}^k, \sigma^N)\} \tag{6.4.3}$$

Because N is finite, there exists a first partition $P_h(\sigma^N)$ such that $P_h(\sigma^N) = P_{h+1}(\sigma^N)$. $P_h(\sigma^N)$ is called the *partition associated with* σ^N. Clearly, if $P_h(\sigma^N) = \{T_1, \ldots, T_r\}$ and $i, j \in T_s$, where $1 \leqslant s \leqslant r$, then $\sigma^i(T_s) = \sigma^j(T_s)$. Hence, we may define $\sigma^N(T_s)$ by $\sigma^N(T_s) = \sigma^i(T_s)$ for some $i \in T_s$. Now let $\rho : 2^A \to A$ satisfy $\rho(B) \in B$ for all $B \in 2^A$. Further, let $\sigma^N \in \Sigma^N$ and $P_h(\sigma^N) = \{T_1, \ldots, T_r\}$ be the partition associated with σ^N. Since E is stable and maximal, E is also superadditive (see Corollary 6.3.13). Also, $\sigma^N(T_i) \in E(T_i)$ for $i = 1, \ldots, r$. Hence, $B = \bigcap_{i=1}^r \sigma^N(T_i) \neq \varnothing$. We define $\pi(\sigma^N) = \rho(B)$.

Let $\Gamma = (\Sigma^1, \ldots, \Sigma^n; \pi)$ be the GF defined earlier. First we show that $C(E, R^N)$ is partially implemented by Γ. Indeed, let $R^N \in L^N$, and let $a \in C(E, R^N)$. For $T \in 2^N$, we denote

$$\Pr(T, a, R^N) = \{b \mid b \neq a \text{ and } bR^ia \text{ for all } i \in T\}$$

Since $a \in C(E, R^N)$, it follows that

$$\Pr(T, a, R^N) \notin E(T) \quad \text{for every } T \in 2^N \tag{6.4.4}$$

Hence, by maximality,

$$A - \Pr(N-T, a, R^N) \in E(T) \quad \text{for every } T \in 2^N \tag{6.4.5}$$

Define now, for $i \in N$ and $T \in \tau^i$, $\sigma^i(T) = A - \Pr(N-T, a, R^N)$ if $T \neq N$, and $\sigma^i(N) = \{a\}$. Clearly, $P_0(\sigma^N) = \{N\}$ is the partition associated with σ^N. Hence, $\pi(\sigma^N) = a$. We now prove that σ^N is a strong e.p. of $g(\Gamma, R^N)$ (see Definition 5.1.4 and Remark 5.1.7). Indeed, let $T \in 2^N$ and $\mu^T \in \Sigma^T$. We shall prove that

$$\pi(\sigma^{N-T}, \mu^T) \notin \Pr(T, a, R^N) \tag{6.4.6}$$

If $T = N$, then (6.4.6) follows from the fact that a, as a member of $C(E, R^N)$, is Pareto-optimal. Thus, let $T \neq N$. Let $P_h(\sigma^{N-T}, \mu^T) = \{T_1, \ldots, T_r\}$ be the partition associated with (σ^{N-T}, μ^T). By the definition of σ^N and (6.4.3), there exists $1 \leqslant j \leqslant r$ such that $T_j \supset N-T$ and $(\sigma^{N-T}, \mu^T)(T_j) = A - \Pr(N-T_j, a, R^N)$. Thus, $\pi(\sigma^{N-T}, \mu^T) \in A - \Pr(N-T_j, a, R^N)$. Now, $T \supset N - T_j$. Hence, $\Pr(N-T_j, a, R^N) \supset \Pr(T, a, R^N)$. Therefore, $\pi(\sigma^{N-T}, \mu^T) \notin \Pr(T, a, R^N)$. Thus, σ^N is a strong e.p. of $g(F, R^N)$.

We have proved that Γ partially implements $C(E, R^N)$. By Lemmata 5.1.14 and 6.1.21, $E = E_\beta(\Gamma)$. By Lemma 6.4.1,

$$\pi(\text{s.e.p.}(\Gamma, R^N)) \subset C(E_\beta(\Gamma), R^N) \quad \text{for every } R^N \in L^N$$

(see Remark 5.1.7). Thus, Γ implements $C(E, R^N)$ (see Definition 5.1.8).

Remark 6.4.3. The proof of Theorem 6.4.2 supplies a finite algorithm for the implementation of the core of a stable and maximal effectivity function. More precisely, given a stable and maximal effectivity function E, one can construct from E, in a finite number of steps (i.e., examinations of the effectivity relation represented by E), a GF that implements the core $C(E, \cdot)$ (see the proof of the sufficiency part of Theorem 6.4.2). Furthermore, the aforementioned construction lends itself to an almost obvious description (see, again, the proof of the sufficiency part).

We are now ready for our characterization theorem.

Theorem 6.4.4. *Let $H: L^N \to 2^A$ be an SCC, and let $E = E^*(H)$ (see Definition 4.1.21). Assume that H satisfies NI (see Definition 5.2.6). Then H is partially implementable if and only if E is maximal and H is stable (see Definitions 5.1.8, 5.1.16, and 5.1.19).*

Proof: Necessity. Assume that H is partially implementable. Then, by Corollary 5.1.18, E is maximal, and, by Lemma 5.1.20, H is stable.

Sufficiency. Assume that E is maximal and H is stable. By Definitions 5.1.19 and 6.1.17, E is stable. Because H satisfies NI, E is an effectivity function (see Definition 6.1.1). Hence, by Theorem 6.4.2, $C(E, R^N)$ is implementable. Hence, H is partially implementable (see Definitions 5.1.19 and 5.1.8).

Remark 6.4.5. Let $H: L^N \to 2^A$ be an SCC, and let $E = E^*(H)$. It is possible to decide in a finite number of steps whether or not H is stable and E is maximal. Thus, by Theorem 6.4.4, there is a finite algorithm that enables us to decide whether or not H is partially implementable. The existence of such an algorithm is very far from being apparent. Indeed, according to Definition 5.1.8, the class of all possible implementations of H is infinite.

6.5 Some remarks on implementation of SCCs

Let $N = \{1, \ldots, n\}$ be a society, and let A be a finite set of m alternatives, $m \geqslant 2$.

Lemma 6.5.1. *Let $H: L^N \to 2^A$ be an SCC, and let $M \subset 2^N$, $M \neq \varnothing$. If H is M-implementable, then H has the SPA property* (see Definitions 5.1.8 and 2.3.24).

Proof: Let $R^N \in L^N$ and $x \in H(R^N)$. If $R_1^N \in L^N$ and for all $i \in N$ and $y \in A$, $xR^i y$ implies $xR_1^i y$, then we have to show that $x \in H(R_1^N)$. By our assumption, there exists a GF $\Gamma = (\Sigma^1, \ldots, \Sigma^n; \pi)$ that M-implements H. Thus,

$$H(R^N) = \pi(\text{e.p.}(M, \Gamma, R^N))$$

(see Definition 5.1.6). In particular, there exists an M-e.p. σ^N of $g(\Gamma, R^N)$ (see Definition 5.1.4) such that $\pi(\sigma^N) = x$. We claim that σ^N is an M-e.p. of $g(\Gamma, R_1^N)$. Indeed, let $S \in M$, and let $\mu^S \in \Sigma^S$. Then there exists $i \in S$ such that

$$\pi(\sigma^N) R^i \pi(\sigma^{N-S}, \mu^S)$$

Clearly, $\pi(\sigma^N) R_1^i \pi(\sigma^{N-S}, \mu^S)$. Hence, σ^N is, indeed, an M-e.p. of $g(\Gamma, R_1^N)$. Since

$$H(R_1^N) = \pi(\text{e.p.}(M, \Gamma, R_1^N))$$

$x = \pi(\sigma^N) \in H(R_1^N)$.

Remark 6.5.2. Lemma 6.5.1 consists of a straightforward generalization of Theorem 1 of Maskin [1979].

Corollary 6.5.3. Let $F: L^N \to A$ be an SCF, and let $M \subset 2^N$, $M \neq \varnothing$. If F is M-implementable and $|R(F)| \geq 3$, then F is dictatorial (see Definitions 5.1.8 and 2.4.10 and Notation 2.4.9).

Proof: Lemma 6.5.1 and Corollary 2.4.20.

Corollary 6.5.4. Let $H: L^N \to 2^A$ be an SCC. If H is implementable, then H is strongly monotonic (see Definitions 5.1.8 and 2.3.15).

Proof: Lemmata 6.5.1 and 2.3.25.

Remark 6.5.5. Let $H: L^N \to 2^A$ be an SCC. If H is implementable, then H is strongly monotonic and stable (see Corollary 6.5.4 and Theorem 6.4.4). It is worthwhile to notice that strong monotonicity implies stability. Indeed, the following generalization of Lemma 3.2.12 is true.

Lemma 6.5.6. *Let $H: L^N \to 2^A$ be an SCC. If H is strongly monotonic, then H is stable* (see Definitions 2.3.15 and 5.1.19).

Proof: Let $R^N \in L^N$, and let $x \in A$. If $x \notin C(E^*, R^N)$, where $E^* = E^*(H)$, then there exist $S \in 2^N$ and $B \subset A - \{x\}$ such that $BR^S x$ and $B \in E^*(S)$ (see Definitions 4.1.21 and 4.1.23). Let $B^* = B \cup \{x\}$, and let $Q^N = R^N(B^*)$ (see Notation 2.4.12). Because $B \in E^*(S)$ and $BQ^S x$, $x \notin H(Q^N)$ (see Definition 4.1.19). By Lemma 2.4.13, $x \notin H(R^N)$. Thus, $H(R^N) \subset C(E^*, R^N)$, and the proof is complete.

We shall now show that Theorem 6.4.2 does *not* consist of a complete solution of the implementation problem. Indeed, we shall give an example of an implementable SCC that is *not* the core correspondence of any effectivity function.

Example 6.5.7. Let $N = \{1, 2, 3, 4\}$, and let $A = \{a, b, c\}$. We define an SCC $H: L^N \to 2^A$ by the following rules. Let $\beta(a) = 1$ and $\beta(b) = \beta(c) = 2$, and let $R^N \in L^N$. If there exists $x \in A$ such that

$$|\{i \mid i \in N \text{ and } t_1(R^i) = x\}| \geq 3 \qquad (6.5.1)$$

(see Notation 2.1.8), then $H(R^N) = x$. If there exists no $x \in A$ that satisfies (6.5.1), then $H(R^N) = C(E_*, R^N)$, where $E_* = E_*(\beta)$ is defined by (5.3.1). $H(R^N)$ is well defined (see Corollary 5.3.10). As the reader can easily verify, $E^*(H)$ is given by $E^*(S) = 2^A$ if $|S| \geq 3$, $E^*(S) = \{B \mid B \in 2^A$ and $|B| \geq 2\}$ if $|S| = 2$, and $E^*(S) = \{A\}$ if $|S| = 1$. Let $F: L^N \to A$ be a selection from H (see Definition 2.4.4). Clearly, $E^*(F) = E^*(H)$. We claim that for every $R^N \in L^N$, the game $g(F, R^N)$ has a strong e.p. (see Definitions 2.5.1 and 4.1.17). In order to prove the foregoing claim, we distinguish the following possibilities:

There exist $x \in A$ and distinct players $i, j, k \in N$ such that
$$t_1(R^i) = t_1(R^j) = x \text{ and } x \neq t_3(R^k). \tag{6.5.2}$$

If $x = t_1(R^k)$, then R^N itself is a strong e.p. of $g(F, R^N)$. If $x = t_2(R^k)$, let $y = t_1(R^k)$. Furthermore, let $Q^N \in L^N$ satisfy $t_1(Q^h) = x$ and $t_3(Q^h) = y$ for $h = i, j, k$. Then, as the reader can easily verify, Q^N is a strong e.p. of $g(F, R^N)$.

R^N has the following form:

R^1	R^2	R^3	R^4
x	x	y	y
z	z	z	z
y	y	x	x

$$\tag{6.5.3}$$

Let $Q^1 = Q^2 = (z, x, y)$ and $Q^3 = Q^4 = (z, y, x)$. Then Q^N is a strong e.p. of $g(F, R^N)$.

R^N has the following form:

R^1	R^2	R^3	R^4
x	x	y	z
y	y	z	y
z	z	x	x

$$\tag{6.5.4}$$

Let $Q^1 = Q^2 = (y, x, z)$ and $Q^3 = Q^4 = (y, z, x)$. Then Q^N is a strong e.p. of $g(F, R^N)$.

R^N has the following form:

R^1	R^2	R^3	R^4
x	x	y	z
y	z	z	y
z	y	x	x

$$\tag{6.5.5}$$

Without loss of generality, $y \neq a$. Let $Q^1 = (y, x, z)$ and $Q^4 = (y, z, x)$. We now distinguish the following subcases:

$x = a$. Let $Q^3 = (y, x, z)$, and let $Q^2 \in L$. Then, as the reader can verify, Q^N is a strong e.p. of $g(F, R^N)$. $\tag{6.5.5.1}$

$z = a$. Let $Q^3 = R^3$, and let $Q^2 \in L$. Then, again, it can be verified that Q^N is a strong e.p. of $g(F, R^N)$. $\tag{6.5.5.2}$

Now let $\Gamma = (L, \ldots, L; F)$ be the GF that is determined by F (see Remark 5.1.3), and let

$$H^*(R^N) = F(\text{s.e.p.}(\Gamma, R^N)) \quad \text{for all } R^N \in L^N$$

(see Remark 5.1.7). Then, by definition, H^* is implemented by F (see Definition 5.1.8). By Lemma 5.1.14, $E^*(H^*) = E^*(F)$, and by Lemma 5.1.20, H^* is stable. Consider now the following profile:

R^1	R^2	R^3	R^4
c	c	a	b
a	b	b	a
b	a	c	c

$C(E^*(H^*), R^N) = \{a, b\}$. However, we claim that $a \notin H^*(R^N)$. Indeed, assume, on the contrary, that there exists a strong e.p. $Q^N \in L^N$ of $g(F, R^N)$ such that $F(Q^N) = a$. We distinguish the following possibilities:

$$t_3(Q^3) = c \tag{6.5.6}$$

Then $F(Q^{\{1,3\}}, R^{\{2,4\}}) = b$. Since $bR^i a$ for $i = 2, 4$, the desired contradiction has been obtained.

$$t_3(Q^3) = b \tag{6.5.7}$$

Then $F(R^{\{1,2\}}, Q^{\{3,4\}}) = c$. Since $cR^i a$ for $i = 1, 2$, the desired contradiction has been obtained.

$$t_3(Q^3) = a \tag{6.5.8}$$

Let $P^1 = P^2 = R^1$. Then $F(P^{\{1,2\}}, Q^{\{3,4\}}) = c$, and, again, a contradiction is obtained.

We conclude that $H^*(\cdot) \neq C(E^*(H^*), \cdot)$. By Lemmata 6.1.21 and 6.3.4, there exists no effectivity function $E_1: 2^N \to P(2^A)$ such that $H^*(R^N) = C(E_1, R^N)$ for every $R^N \in L^N$.

We conclude with the following observation. Consider the profile

R^1	R^2	R^3	R^4
a	a	c	b
b	b	a	c
c	c	b	a

Then $H(R^N) = b$, and $C(E^*(H), R^N) = a$. Thus, H is not stable. Furthermore, every selection from H is not stable. Hence, every selection from H is *not* exactly and strongly consistent (see Lemma 4.1.25). Thus, in spite of the fact that H^* is implementable by a selection F from H, H^* may not be considered "reasonable" because F violates exact and strong consistency (and therefore F itself is not reasonable; see Remarks 4.1.2 and 5.1.11).

Appendix: Convex effectivity functions

This appendix consists of a continuation of the study of the stability of effectivity functions. We prove that convex effectivity functions are stable (see Theorem 6.A.7). As a corollary, we obtain a complete characterization of the class of maximal and stable effectivity functions: A maximal effectivity function is stable if and only if it is convex. Finally, we deduce a "duality theorem" for maximal effectivity functions: A maximal effectivity function is stable if and only if its dual is stable (see Theorem 6.A.11). The proof of the main result (Theorem 6.A.7) relies heavily on the theory of (ordinal) convex games without side payments (which we shall immediately review). Hence, we have decided to relegate the investigation of convex effectivity functions to an appendix.

Let N be a society, and let Ω_+ be the set of all non-negative real numbers. If S is a coalition, then we denote by Ω_+^S the set of all functions from S to Ω_+. If $x \in \Omega_+^N$ and S is a coalition, then we denote by x^S the restriction of x to S. Let S be a coalition, and let $x^S, y^S \in \Omega_+^S$. We write $x^S \geqslant y^S$ if $x^i \geqslant y^i$ for all $i \in S$, and $x^S \gg y^S$ if $x^i > y^i$ for all $i \in S$. Finally, Ω_+^S is considered as a (topological) subspace of the Euclidean space Ω^S (of all real functions on S).

Definition 6.A.1. An *n-person cooperative game without side payments* is a pair (N, v), where N is a society and v is a function that assigns to every subset S of N a subset $v(S)$ of Ω_+^N such that

$$v(\varnothing) = \varnothing \tag{6.A.1}$$

$$\text{If } S \neq \varnothing, \text{ then } v(S) \neq \varnothing, \tag{6.A.2}$$

$$v(S) \text{ is closed.} \tag{6.A.3}$$

$$\text{If } x \in v(S), y \in \Omega_+^N, \text{ and } x^S \geqslant y^S, \text{ then } y \in v(S). \tag{6.A.4}$$

$$v_p(S) = \{x^S \mid x \in v(S)\} \text{ is bounded.} \tag{6.A.5}$$

Definition 6.A.2. Let (N, v) be an n-person cooperative game without side payments (see Definition 6.A.1), and let $x, y \in v(N)$; x *dominates* y *via a coalition* S, written $x \operatorname{Dom}(S) y$, if $x^S \gg y^S$ and $x \in v(S)$; x *dominates* y, written $x \operatorname{Dom} y$, if there exists $T \in 2^N$ such that $x \operatorname{Dom}(T) y$. The *core* of (N, v) is the set of all undominated vectors in $v(N)$ and it is denoted by $C(N, v)$.

Definition 6.A.3. Let (N, v) be an n-person cooperative game without side payments (see Definition 6.A.1). (N, v) is an *ordinal convex* game if for all $S, T \subset N$,

$$v(S) \cap v(T) \subset v(S \cap T) \cup v(S \cup T) \qquad (6.A.6)$$

Theorem 6.A.4. *If (N, v) is an ordinal convex game, then $C(N, v) \neq \varnothing$* (see Definitions 6.A.2 and 6.A.3).

A short proof of Theorem 6.A.4 is given by Greenberg [1982].

Now let A be a finite set of m alternatives, $m \geqslant 2$, and let N be a society.

Definition 6.A.5. A function $E: 2^N \to P(2^A)$ (see Notation 4.1.20) is *convex* if it satisfies the following:

> If $S_i \in 2^N$ and $B_i \in E(S_i)$, $i = 1, 2$, then
> $B_1 \cap B_2 \in E(S_1 \cup S_2)$ or $B_1 \cup B_2 \in E(S_1 \cap S_2)$. $\qquad (6.A.7)$

Remark 6.A.6. A convex function is both superadditive and subadditive (see Definitions 6.A.5, 6.1.11, and 6.1.24). Also, as the reader can easily verify, every AEF is convex (see Definition 6.2.46).

The main result of this appendix is as follows.

Theorem 6.A.7. *Every convex function is stable* (see Definitions 6.A.5 and 6.1.17).

Proof: Let $E: 2^N \to P(2^A)$ be a convex function, and let $R^N \in L^N$. For each $i \in N$, we choose a function $u_i: A \to \Omega_+$ such that for all $x, y \in A$,

$$u_i(x) \geqslant u_i(y) \Leftrightarrow x R^i y \qquad (6.A.8)$$

We now define n functions $w_i: 2^A \to \Omega_+$, $i = 1, \ldots, n$, by the following rule:

$$w_i(B) = \min\{u_i(x) \mid x \in B\} \quad \text{for all } B \in 2^A \qquad (6.A.9)$$

Let $S \in 2^N$ and $B \in 2^A$. We associate with S and B a vector $t^S = t^S(B)$ in Ω_+^S in the following way:

$$t^i(B) = w_i(B) \quad \text{for every } i \in S \qquad (6.A.10)$$

Let, again, $S \in 2^N$. We define

$$v(S) = \{r \in \Omega_+^N \mid \text{there exists } B \in E(S) \text{ such that } r^S \leqslant t^S(B)\} \qquad (6.A.11)$$

(see (6.A.10)). Because $E(S) \neq \varnothing$, $v(S)$ is well defined. We also define $v(\varnothing) = \varnothing$. As the reader can easily verify, (N, v) is a cooperative game without side payments (see Definition 6.A.1). We now show the following.

Claim a: If $C(N, v) \neq \emptyset$, then $C(E, R^N) \neq \emptyset$ (see Definitions 6.A.2 and 4.1.23).

Indeed, let $r \in C(N, v)$. Then there exists $B \in 2^A$ such that $r = r^N \leqslant t^N(B)$. Let $x \in B$. We claim that $x \in C(E, R^N)$. Assume, on the contrary, that $x \notin C(E, R^N)$. Then there exists $B_1 \in 2^A$ and $S \in 2^N$ such that $B_1 \in E(S)$ and $w_i(B_1) > u_i(x)$ for all $i \in S$ (see Definition 4.1.23 and (6.A.8) and (6.A.9)). Let $q \in v(S)$ satisfy $q^S = t^S(B_1)$ (see (6.A.10) and (6.A.11)). Then $q \operatorname{Dom}(S) r$ (see Definition 6.A.2), which is the desired contradiction.

Next we prove another claim.

Claim b: (N, v) is an ordinal convex game (see Definition 6.A.3).

Indeed, let $S_1, S_2 \in 2^N$, and let $r \in v(S_1) \cap v(S_2)$. Then there exist $B_1, B_2 \in 2^A$ such that $B_i \in E(S_i)$, $i = 1, 2$, and $r^{S_i} \leqslant t^{S_i}(B_i)$, $i = 1, 2$. Since E is convex, $B_1 \cap B_2 \in E(S_1 \cup S_2)$ or $B_1 \cup B_2 \in E(S_1 \cap S_2)$ (see Definition 6.A.5). Thus, we have to distinguish the following possibilities:

(b.1) $\quad B_1 \cap B_2 \in E(S_1 \cup S_2)$

Denote $B = B_1 \cap B_2$ and $S = S_1 \cup S_2$. Then $t^{S_i}(B) \geqslant t^{S_i}(B_i)$ for $i = 1, 2$ (see (6.A.9) and (6.A.10)). Hence, $t^S(B) \geqslant r^S$, and $r \in v(S) = v(S_1 \cup S_2)$ (see (6.A.11)).

(b.2) $\quad B_1 \cup B_2 \in E(S_1 \cap S_2)$

If $i \in S_1 \cap S_2$, then $r^i \leqslant \min(w_i(B_1), w_i(B_2)) = w_i(B_1 \cup B_2)$ (see (6.A.9)). Thus, $r \in v(S_1 \cap S_2)$ (see (6.A.10) and (6.A.11)).

Now, it follows from claim b and Theorem 6.A.4 that $C(N, v) \neq \emptyset$. Thus, by claim a, $C(E, R^N) \neq \emptyset$.

Remark 6.A.8. Theorem 6.3.19 is a corollary of Theorem 6.A.7 (see Remark 6.A.6). However, the *proof* of Theorem 6.3.19 supplies an explicit voting procedure that yields alternatives in the core of a given AEF (for a given profile), whereas the proof of Theorem 6.A.7 tells us nothing about such voting procedures. Thus, we have decided to keep Theorem 6.3.19 and its proof.

Clearly, stability (of effectivity functions) does not imply convexity (see Example 6.3.2). However, stability and maximality entail convexity, as is shown by the next theorem.

Theorem 6.A.9. *A stable and maximal effectivity function is convex* (see Definitions 6.1.17, 5.1.16, 6.1.1, and 6.A.5).

Proof: Let $E: 2^N \to P(2^A)$ (see Notation 4.1.20) be a stable and maximal effectivity function. Further, let $S_i \in 2^N$ and $B_i \in E(S_i)$, $i = 1, 2$. Assume that $B_1 \cap B_2 \notin E(S_1 \cup S_2)$. We have to show that $B_1 \cup B_2 \in E(S_1 \cap S_2)$. By Corollary 6.3.13, E is subadditive. Hence, if $B_1 \cap B_2 = \varnothing$, then $B_1 \cup B_2 \in E(S_1 \cap S_2)$ (see Definition 6.1.24). Thus, we may assume that $B_1 \cap B_2 \neq \varnothing$. Let $B = A - (B_1 \cap B_2)$ and $S = N - (S_1 \cup S_2)$. Since E is maximal, $B \in E(S)$ (see Definition 5.1.16). By Corollary 6.3.13, E is also superadditive. Furthermore, $S \cap S_1 = \varnothing$. Hence, $B \cap B_1 = B_1 - B_2$ is in $E(S \cup S_1)$. Using, again, the subadditivity of E, we obtain

$$(B_1 - B_2) \cup B_2 = B_1 \cup B_2 \in E((S \cup S_1) \cap S_2) = E(S_1 \cap S_2)$$

Remark 6.A.10. Let $E: 2^N \to P(2^A)$ be an effectivity function, and let E^d be the dual function (see Definition 6.1.5). Then E is convex if and only if E^d is convex (see Definition 6.A.5).

We are now able to formulate a "duality theorem" for maximal effectivity functions.

Theorem 6.A.11. *Let $E: 2^N \to P(2^A)$ be a maximal effectivity function* (see Definitions 5.1.16 and 6.1.1). *Then E is stable if and only if E^d is stable* (see Definitions 6.1.17 and 6.1.5).

Proof: by Theorems 6.A.7 and 6.A.9, E is stable if and only if it is convex. By Remark 6.A.10, E is convex if and only if E^d is convex. Since E is maximal, E^d is also maximal (see Remark 6.1.27). Hence, E^d is stable if and only if E^d is convex. Thus, E is stable if and only if E^d is stable.

Remark 6.A.12. We remark that a superadditive and subadditive effectivity function may *not* be stable. Thus, in particular, convexity is stronger than the conjunction of superadditivity and subadditivity.

CHAPTER 7

Concluding remarks

In this chapter we make a few remarks on the relationship between the existing theory and our work, and on possible generalizations of our results. First, in Section 7.1, we observe that all known restrictions on individual preferences guarantee that cores of voting games are nonempty. Thus, we may have a richer theory of representation (of committees) under the (usual) assumptions of restricted preferences. Next, we remark that restriction of preferences does *not* eliminate manipulability. Then we argue that there is a need to generalize the notion of exact and strong consistency to allow restricted preferences, and we notice that Dutta [1980*b*] contains such a generalization (see Section 7.2).

In Section 7.3 we discuss the problem of the existence of faithful and neutral representations of committees. We show how that problem can be resolved by the use of even-chance lotteries on alternatives. Section 7.4 is devoted to a systematic generalization of our results to weak orders. Finally, we discuss possible extensions of our results to infinite sets of alternatives (see Section 7.5).

7.1 Restricted preferences and the core

Let $G = (N, W)$ be a proper simple game without veto players (see Definition 2.6.4). Further, let A be a finite set of m alternatives. If $m \geqslant \nu(G)$, then there exists $R^N \in L^N$ such that the core $C(N, W, A, R^N) = \varnothing$ (see Theorem 2.6.14). Thus, if $m \geqslant \nu(G)$, then the following problems arise naturally. Let

$$\rho = \{ R^N \mid R^N \in L^N \text{ and } C(N, W, A, R^N) \neq \varnothing \}$$

Is it possible to characterize the set ρ in a suitable way? Does the set ρ contain all "reasonable" profiles of preferences?

The answer to the first problem is, quite obviously, negative. Indeed,

151

$R^N \in \rho$ if and only if there exists a maximal alternative with respect to (the binary relation) $\mathrm{Dom}(R^N)$ (see Definition 2.6.8). Now, R^N may be quite "pathological" and still $\mathrm{Dom}(R^N)$ may have a maximal alternative. For example, $\mathrm{Dom}(R^N)$ may contain cycles while $C(N, W, A, R^N) \neq \varnothing$.

Our answer to the second problem depends on the following simple observation: If $R^N \in L^N$ and $\mathrm{Dom}(R^N)$ is transitive, then the core $C(N, W, A, R^N) \neq \varnothing$. Now, if G is the simple majority game, that is, $G = (n, [n/2]+1)$ (see Definition 2.6.4), then $\mathrm{Dom}(R^N)$ is the strict preference that is derived from the method of majority decision (see Sen [1970, p. 71]). Thus, Theorems 10*1, 10*2, and 10*4 of Sen [1970] provide sufficient conditions for the transitivity of $\mathrm{Dom}(R^N)$. (Notice that the transitivity of $\mathrm{Dom}(R^N)$ is equivalent to the quasi transitivity of the method of majority decision.) In particular, Sen's well-known condition of value restriction is a sufficient condition for the transitivity of $\mathrm{Dom}(R^N)$. (We also recall that Sen's value restriction is implied by single-peakedness (see Sen [1970, p. 168]).) Thus, we may conclude that all known customary restrictions on individual preferences imply the nonemptiness of the core $C(N, W, A, R^N)$, when $(N, W) = G = (n, [n/2]+1)$. In the general case, Kaneko provides a necessary and sufficient condition for the transitivity of $\mathrm{Dom}(R^N)$ when $G = (N, W)$ is a proper simple game (see Kaneko [1975]). Again, Kaneko's condition is implied by Sen's value restriction. Hence, we may conclude that, in general, all customary restrictions on individual preferences entail the nonemptiness of the core.

7.2   Restricted preferences and nonmanipulability

Let $N = \{1, \ldots, n\}$ be a society, and let A be a finite set of m alternatives, $m \geqslant 3$. Further, let $F: L^N \to A$ be an SCF (see Definition 2.4.1). If $|R(F)| \geqslant 3$ and F is not dictatorial, then F is manipulable (see Theorem 2.5.5). Thus, there exists $R^N \in L^N$ such that R^N is not an e.p. of $g(F, R^N)$ (see Definition 2.5.4). Let

$$\rho = \{R^N \mid R^N \in L^N \text{ and } R^N \text{ is an e.p. of } g(F, R^N)\}$$

That is, ρ is the set of profiles that are nonmanipulable with respect to F. Then, as in the previous section, the following problems arise naturally. Is it possible to characterize the set ρ in a suitable way? Does the set ρ contain all "reasonable" profiles of preferences?

For a survey of papers that pertain to the first problem, the reader is referred to Pattanaik [1978, pp. 135-51]. We should also mention Dutta [1980a], who investigated necessary and sufficient conditions for (strict) nonmanipulability of a class of voting procedures.

The answer to the second problem is negative. Indeed, Blin and Satterthwaite [1977] show, for example, that single-peakedness is not sufficient to prevent the manipulability of majority rule with Borda completion. Additional negative results may be found in Pattanaik [1978, Section 7.3]. Thus, we conclude that customary restrictions on preferences do not eliminate manipulation.

As a result of the foregoing discussion, we conclude that it would be desirable to generalize the notion of exact and strong consistency (see Definition 4.1.18) to include restricted preferences. This would enable us to obtain voting procedures that are not distorted by manipulation when preferences are "reasonably" restricted (see Remark 4.1.30). Now, it turns out that Dutta has already taken such a line of investigation. Indeed, Dutta has proved that value restriction is a necessary and sufficient condition for the strong consistency of a class of voting procedures (see Dutta [1980b, Theorem 5]). It seems to us that Dutta's results can be considerably generalized.

7.3 Symmetry, neutrality, and lotteries on alternatives

In this section we address ourselves to the following problem. Is it necessary, from the point of view of the theory of representation of committees, to introduce lotteries on alternatives? In order to render the foregoing problem precise, we consider the following situation. Let $G = (N, W)$ be a committee (see Remark 2.6.3), and let A be a finite set of m alternatives, $m \geqslant 2$. Also, let an SCF $F: L^N \to A$ be a representation of G (see Definition 3.2.1). It seems to us that F may be considered as a "completely" nice representation of G only if it satisfies (at least) the following three conditions: (a) F is Paretian (see Definition 2.3.4); (b) F is faithful (see Definition 3.2.7); (c) F is neutral (see Definition 2.3.8). Indeed, condition a is widely acceptable and hardly needs justification. Condition b is also easily understandable; it says that F and G have the same (group of) symmetries. The justification of condition c is indirect and runs as follows. Because A (the set of alternatives) has no "structure" (i.e., no alternative, or set of alternatives, is singled out a priori), F should treat all the alternatives equally. Thus, F has to be neutral. Now, by Remark 3.3.14, G may have no Paretian, faithful, and neutral representation of order m. Thus, we may not be able to meet conditions a, b, and c simultaneously.

In order to resolve the difficulty described earlier, we suggest the following procedure. Let, again, $G = (N, W)$ be a committee, and let A be a finite set of m alternatives, $m \geqslant 2$. By Examples 3.2.14, 3.2.20, and 3.2.22, there exist "completely" nice representations of G by SCCs. Let

$H: L^N \to 2^A$ be a Paretian, faithful, and neutral representation of G. We now suggest the following two-stage procedure for choosing *one* alternative out of A. Let $R^N \in L^N$. In the first stage, the set of alternatives $H(R^N)$ is chosen. Then, in the second stage, one alternative is chosen from $H(R^N)$ by an even-chance lottery on $H(R^N)$. We shall denote the foregoing two-stage procedure by H^*. Thus, for each $R^N \in L^N$, $H^*(R^N)$ assigns an even-chance lottery on $H(R^N)$. Clearly, H^* is, in an obviously generalized sense, a Paretian, faithful, and neutral representation of G. However, the application of H^* raises the following problem. In order to evaluate possible outcomes of H^*, the voters must be able to compare even-chance lotteries on nonempty subsets of A. Equivalently, for each $i \in N$ and each $R^i \in L$, it must be possible to extend R^i to a preference relation R_*^i on 2^A, when it is understood that for each $B \in 2^A$ the final outcome is determined by an even-chance lottery on B. Fortunately, this last problem has been completely solved by Fishburn [1972]. For a comprehensive study of extension of preferences from A to 2^A, the reader is referred to Gärdenfors [1979].

7.4   Weak orders

In this section we extend the results of Chapters 2–6 to allow weak orders. We start with the following definition. Let A be a set of alternatives.

Definition 7.4.1. A binary relation R on A is a *weak order* if it is complete and transitive (see Definition 2.1.1). The set of all weak orders on A is denoted by $K = K(A)$.

If R is a weak order on A and $x, y \in A$, then we denote

$$xPy \text{ if } xRy \text{ and not } yRx \tag{7.4.1}$$

and

$$xIy \text{ if } xRy \text{ and } yRx \tag{7.4.2}$$

We notice that P is asymmetric and transitive, and I is an equivalence relation (i.e., it is reflexive, symmetric, and transitive).

Let $N = \{1, \ldots, n\}$ be a society, and let S be a coalition. We denote by K^S the set of all functions from S to K. We shall now formulate Arrow's Impossibility Theorem for weak orders. First, the following definitions are needed.

Definition 7.4.2. A *social welfare function* (SWF) is a function $F: K^N \to K$.

Definition 7.4.3. Let F be an SWF. F is *Paretian* if it satisfies the following condition: For all $R^N \in K^N$ and for all $x, y \in A$, $x \neq y$,

$$[xP^i y \text{ for all } i \in N] \Rightarrow xPy$$

where P is derived from $R = F(R^N)$ by (7.4.1).

Notation 7.4.4. Let $R \in K$, and let $B \subset A$. We denote by $R \mid B$ the restriction of R to B.

Notation 7.4.5. Let S be a coalition, and let $B \subset A$. For $R^S \in K^S$, we denote by $R^S \mid B$ the $|S|$-tuple whose ith component is $R^i \mid B$ for $i \in S$ (see Notation 2.1.7 and Notation 7.4.4).

Definition 7.4.6. An SWF F satisfies the condition of *independence of irrelevant alternatives* if for all $R^N, Q^N \in K^N$ and for all $x, y \in A$,

$$[R^N \mid \{x, y\} = Q^N \mid \{x, y\}] \Rightarrow F(R^N) \mid \{x, y\} = F(Q^N) \mid \{x, y\}$$

(see Notation 7.4.5).

Definition 7.4.7. Let F be an SWF. A player $j \in N$ is a *dictator* (with respect to F) if for all $R^N \in K^N$ and for all $x, y \in A$, $x \neq y$, $xP^j y$ implies that xPy, where P is derived from $R = F(R^N)$ by (7.4.1). F is *dictatorial* if there exists a dictator with respect to F.

Theorem 7.4.8. *Let $F: K^N \to K$ be an SWF. If F is Paretian and satisfies the condition of independence of irrelevant alternatives* (see Definitions 7.4.3 and 7.4.6), *and if A contains at least three members, then F is dictatorial* (see Definition 7.4.7).

The proof of Theorem 7.4.8 is essentially the same as that of Theorem 2.2.7.

We now generalize part of the results of Section 2.3. Assume that $|A| = m$, where $2 \leqslant m < \infty$.

Definition 7.4.9. A *social choice correspondence* (SCC) is a function H from K^N to 2^A.

Definition 7.4.10. Let $R^N \in K^N$ and $x \in A$; x is *Pareto-optimal* if there exists no $y \in A$, $y \neq x$, such that $yP^i x$ for all $i \in N$. The set of all Pareto-optimal alternatives is denoted by $\mathrm{PAR}(R^N)$.

Since A is finite, $\mathrm{PAR}(R^N) \neq \varnothing$ for all $R^N \in K^N$. Hence, $\mathrm{PAR}(\cdot)$ is an SCC.

Definition 7.4.11. An SCC H is *Paretian* if for all $R^N \in K^N$, $H(R^N) \subset$ PAR(R^N).

Definition 7.4.12. Let H be an SCC. A permutation π of N is a *symmetry* of H if for all $R^N = (R^1, \ldots, R^n)$ in K^N, $H(R^N) = H(R^{\pi(1)}, \ldots, R^{\pi(n)})$. The group of all symmetries of H will be denoted by SYM(H).

Definition 7.4.13. An SCC H is *anonymous* if SYM$(H) = S_n$, the group of all permutations of N.

Remark 7.4.14. PAR$(\cdot)$ (see Definition 7.4.10) is anonymous.

Let σ be a permutation of A, and let $R \in K$ (see Definition 7.4.1). We denote by $\sigma(R)$ the weak order defined by the following condition: For all $x, y \in A$, $\sigma(x) \sigma(R) \sigma(y)$ if and only if xRy.

Definition 7.4.15. An SCC H is *neutral* if for every permutation σ of A, and for every $R^N = (R^1, \ldots, R^n)$ in K^N, $H(\sigma(R^1), \ldots, \sigma(R^n)) = \sigma(H(R^n))$.

Remark 7.4.16. PAR$(\cdot)$ is neutral.

The generalization of monotonicity properties is somewhat elaborate.

Definition 7.4.17. Let $R^N \in K^N$, and let $x \in A$. $R_1^N \in K^N$ is *obtained from R^N by an improvement of the position of x*, written $R^N(x) \uparrow R_1^N$, if

$$\text{for all } a, b \in A - \{x\} \text{ and for all } i \in N, \; aR^i b \Leftrightarrow aR_1^i b \qquad (7.4.3)$$

$$\text{for all } a \in A \text{ and for all } i \in N, \; xP^i a \Rightarrow xP_1^i a \text{ and } xI^i a \Rightarrow xR_1^i a \qquad (7.4.4)$$

Definition 7.4.18. An SCC H is *monotonic* if it satisfies the following:

$$\text{If } R^N \in K^N, \; x \in H(R^N), \text{ and } R^N(x) \uparrow R_1^N, \text{ then}$$
$$x \in H(R_1^N) \text{ and } H(R_1^N) \subset H(R^N). \qquad (7.4.5)$$

Definition 7.4.19. An SCC H is *strongly monotonic* if it satisfies the following:

$$\text{If } R^N \in K^N, \; x \in A, \text{ and } R^N(x) \uparrow R_1^N, \text{ then}$$
$$H(R_1^N) \subset \{x\} \cup H(R^N). \qquad (7.4.6)$$

Lemma 7.4.20. *A strongly monotonic SCC is monotonic.*

The proof of Lemma 7.4.20, which is similar to that of Lemma 2.3.16, is omitted.

Definition 7.4.21. An SCC H has the *strong positive association* (SPA) property if it satisfies the following:

Let $R^N \in K^N$ and $x \in H(R^N)$. If $R_1^N \in K^N$ and for all $i \in N$ and $y \in A$, $xP^iy \Rightarrow xP_1^iy$, and $xI^iy \Rightarrow xR_1^iy$, then $x \in H(R_1^N)$. (7.4.7)

Lemma 7.4.22. *An SCC is strongly monotonic if and only if it has the SPA property.*

The proof of Lemma 7.4.22, which is similar to that of Lemma 2.3.25, is omitted.

We proceed now to generalize Theorem 2.4.11.

Definition 7.4.23. A *social choice function* (SCF) is a single-valued SCC (see Definition 7.4.9).

Remark 7.4.24. An SCF F may also be considered as a function $F: K^N \to A$.

Let $F: K^N \to A$ be an SCF. The range of F is denoted by $R(F)$.

Definition 7.4.25. An SCF $F: K^N \to A$ is *dictatorial* if there exists a player $j \in N$ (a *dictator*) such that for every $R^N \in K^N$ and for every $x \in R(F)$, $F(R^N)R^jx$.

Theorem 7.4.26. *Let $F: K^N \to A$ be a strongly monotonic SCF. If $|R(F)| \geqslant 3$, then F is dictatorial.*

Proof: Let F_* be the restriction of F to L^N (i.e., $F_*(R^N) = F(R^N)$ for all $R^N \in L^N$), and let $R^N \in K^N$. Since F has the SPA property (see Lemma 7.4.22), there exists a profile $R_*^N \in L^N$ such that $F(R_*^N) = F(R^N)$. Hence, $R(F_*) = R(F)$ (where $R(F_*)$ is the range of F_*). We conclude now from Theorem 2.4.11 that F_* is dictatorial. Let j be a dictator for F_*. We shall prove that j is a dictator for F. Let $R^N \in K^N$, and let $x = F(R^N)$. There exists a profile $R_*^N \in L^N$ with the following property:

For all $i \in N$ and all $y \in A$, $xR^iy \Leftrightarrow xR_*^iy$.

Invoking, again, the SPA property of F, we conclude that $F_*(R_*^N) = F(R_*^N) = x$. Now, xR_*^jy for all $y \in R(F_*)$. Hence, xR^jy for all $y \in R(F)$.

We shall now formulate and prove the Gibbard–Satterthwaite Theorem (Theorem 2.5.5) for weak orders. We start with the following definitions.

Let $\Gamma = (\Sigma^1, \ldots, \Sigma^n; \pi)$ be a GF (see Definition 5.1.1), and let $R^N \in K^N$. *The game associated with Γ and R^N,*

$$g(\Gamma, R^N) = (\Sigma^1, \ldots, \Sigma^n; \pi; R^1, \ldots, R^n)$$

is defined in exactly the same way as in Definition 5.1.4. Further, let $M \subset 2^N$, $M \neq \varnothing$. The set of all M-e.p.'s of $g(\Gamma, R^N)$, e.p.(M, Γ, R^N), is defined in the same way as in Definition 5.1.6.

Remark 7.4.27. Let $\Gamma = (\Sigma^1, \ldots, \Sigma^n; \pi)$ be a GF, and let $R^N \in K^N$. If $M_1 = \{\{i\} \mid i \in N\}$, then an M_1-e.p. of $g(\Gamma, R^N)$ is called, simply, an e.p. (or a *Nash* e.p.).

Now let $F: K^N \to A$ be an SCF. We associate with F the following GF:

$$\Gamma(F) = (K, \ldots, K; F)$$

Definition 7.4.28. Let $F: K^N \to A$ be an SCF. F is *nonmanipulable* if for each $R^N \in L^N$, R^N itself is an e.p. of $g(\Gamma(F), R^N)$ (see Remark 7.4.27). (See also Definition 2.5.4.)

Theorem 7.4.29. *Let $F: K^N \to A$ be an SCF. If F is nonmanipulable and $|R(F)| \geqslant 3$, then F is dictatorial* (see Definitions 7.4.28 and 7.4.25).

Proof: Let F_* be the restriction of F to L^N (i.e., $F_*(R^N) = F(R^N)$ for every $R^N \in L^N$). Then F_* is nonmanipulable (in the sense of Definition 2.5.4). We claim also that $R(F_*) = R(F)$. Indeed, let $x \in R(F)$. Then there exists $R_1^N \in K^N$ such that $x = F(R_1^N)$. Let $R^N \in L^N$ satisfy $t_1(R^i) = x$ for every $i \in N$ (see Notation 2.1.8). We shall prove that $x = F(R^N)$. Indeed, assume, on the contrary, that $F(R^N) = y$ and $y \neq x$. Let

$$z_j = F(R_1^1, \ldots, R_1^j, R^{j+1}, \ldots, R^n), \qquad j = 0, \ldots, n$$

Clearly, $z_0 = F(R^N) \neq x$, and $z_n = F(R_1^N) = x$. Hence, there exists t, $1 \leqslant t \leqslant n$, such that $z_{t-1} \neq x$ and $z_t = x$. Let $R_*^N = (R_1^1, \ldots, R_1^{t-1}, R', \ldots, R^n)$. Since $x = t_1(R')$, $xR'z_{t-1}$. Hence, R_*^N is not an e.p. of $g(\Gamma(F), R_*^N)$, and the desired contradiction has been obtained.

It follows now from Theorem 2.5.5 that F_* is dictatorial. Let j be a dictator of F_* (see Definition 2.4.10). We claim that j is a dictator for F (see Definition 7.4.25). Indeed, let $R^N \in K^N$, let $z = F(R^N)$, and let

$$B = \{x \mid x \in R(F) \text{ and } xR^j y \text{ for all } y \in R(F)\}$$

We have to show that $z \in B$. Assume, on the contrary, that $z \notin B$. Let $R_1^N \in L^N$ satisfy $BR_1^j(A-B)$, and $(A-B)R_1^i B$ for all $i \neq j$ (see Notation (5.2.14)). Because j is a dictator of F_*, $F(R_1^N) \in B$. Let

$$w_k = F(R_1^1, \ldots, R_1^k, R^{k+1}, \ldots, R^n), \qquad k = 0, \ldots, n$$

Clearly, $w_0 = F(R^N) = z \notin B$, and $w_n = F(R_1^N) \in B$. Hence, there exists t, $1 \leq t \leq n$, such that $w_{t-1} \notin B$ and $w_t \in B$. Let $R_k^N = (R_1^1, \ldots, R_1^k, R^{k+1}, \ldots, R^n)$, $k = 0, \ldots, n$. If $t = j$, then R_{t-1}^N is not an e.p. of $g(\Gamma(F), R_{t-1}^N)$. (Notice that $xP^j y$ for every $x \in B$ and $y \in R(F) - B$.) If $t \neq j$, then R_t^N is not an e.p. of $g(\Gamma(F), R_t^N)$. (Recall that $(A - B)R_1^j B$.) Thus, the desired contradiction has been obtained, and the proof is complete.

Remark 7.4.30. Our proof of Theorem 7.4.29 follows the discussion of Schmeidler and Sonnenschein [1978, p. 230].

We now proceed to investigate stability theory with weak orders. We start with the following definition.

Definition 7.4.31. Let $E: 2^N \to P(2^A)$ be a function; let $R^N \in K^N$, $x \in A$, and $B \subset A - \{x\}$. B *dominates* x *via a coalition* S, written $B \, \mathrm{Dom}(R^N, S)x$, if (a) $B \in E(S)$ and (b) $bP^i x$ for all $b \in B$ and all $i \in S$. B *dominates* x, written $B \, \mathrm{Dom}(R^N)x$, if there exists $T \in 2^N$ such that $B \, \mathrm{Dom}(R^N, T)x$. The *core* of A (*with respect to E and* R^N) is the set of undominated alternatives in A and is denoted by $C(E, R^N)$.

The following simple observation is true.

Lemma 7.4.32. Let $E: 2^N \to P(2^A)$ be a function. Then $C(E, R^N) \neq \emptyset$ for every $R^N \in K^N$ if and only if E is stable (see Definition 6.1.17).

Proof: We have only to prove that if E is stable and $R^N \in K^N$, then $C(E, R^N) \neq \emptyset$. Let $Q^N \in L^N$ satisfy

$$xP^i y \Rightarrow xQ^i y \quad \text{for all } x, y \in A \text{ and all } i \in N$$

Since E is stable, $C(E, Q^N) \neq \emptyset$. Now, $C(E, R^N) \supset C(E, Q^N)$. Hence, $C(E, R^N) \neq \emptyset$.

Lemma 7.4.32 says, essentially, that the stability of effectivity functions is not affected by the introduction of weak orders. It has many (straightforward) corollaries. For example, Theorems 2.6.14 (see Remark 6.2.3) and 6.3.19 hold for weak orders.

We shall now discuss representations of simple games by SCCs that are defined on K^N (see Definition 7.4.9). Only a few modifications are needed in order to generalize the results of Sections 3.1 and 3.2.

Definition 7.4.33. Let $H: K^N \to 2^A$ be an SCC, and let $x \in A$. A coalition S is *winning for* x if

$$[R^N \in K^N \text{ and } xP^i y \text{ for all } i \in S \text{ and all } y \in A - \{x\}] \Rightarrow H(R^N) = x$$

The set of all winning coalitions for x is denoted by $W^*(H, x)$ or $W^*(x)$.

Remark 7.4.34. Let $H: K^N \to 2^A$ be an SCC. The first simple game associated with H, $G^*(H) = (N, W^*)$, is given now by Definition 3.1.3. The second and the third games, $G_\alpha(H)$ and $G_\beta(H)$, are given by Definitions 3.1.7 and 3.1.11, respectively (when L^N is replaced by K^N in the appropriate places (see Definitions 3.1.5 and 3.1.9)).

Remark 7.4.35. Remark 3.1.16, Definition 3.1.25, and Theorem 3.1.28 apply to SCCs defined on K^N, provided that L^N is replaced throughout by K^N.

Remark 7.4.36. All the results of Section 3.2, except Example 3.2.25 and Remark 3.2.26, generalize, in a straightforward way, to SCCs defined on K^N (see Definition 7.4.31, Lemma 7.4.32, and Remark 6.2.3). Thus, we obtain a theory of representations of simple games by SCCs that are defined for profiles of weak orders.

The existence of representations of simple games by SCFs that are defined on K^N is guaranteed by the following lemma (see Remark 3.3.10).

Lemma 7.4.37. *Let $G = (N, W)$ be a proper simple game, and let $F: L^N \to A$ be a representation of G. Then there exists an SCF $F^*: K^N \to A$ that is a representation of G (see Definition 3.2.1 and Remark 7.4.36). Furthermore, if F is tight (respectively Paretian, faithful, monotonic), then F^* is tight (respectively Paretian, faithful, monotonic). Finally, if F satisfies the Condorcet condition, so does F^*.*

Proof: Let $S \in L$ be fixed. We define a mapping $g: K \to L$ by the following rule. If $R \in K$, then $R_1 = g(R)$ is given by

$$xPy \Rightarrow xR_1 y \tag{7.4.8}$$

$$xIy \Rightarrow [xR_1 y \Leftrightarrow xSy] \tag{7.4.9}$$

We now associate with every $R^N \in K^N$ a profile $R_1^N = g_*(R^N)$ in L^N that is defined by

$$g_*(R^1, \ldots, R^n) = (g(R^1), \ldots, g(R^n)) \tag{7.4.10}$$

Finally, we define $F^*(R^N) = F(g_*(R^N))$ for every $R^N \in K^N$. As the reader can easily verify, F^* has all the desirable properties.

Let G be a proper simple game. Then G has no neutral representations by SCFs that are defined on K^N. Indeed, the following observation is true.

Remark 7.4.38. There exists no neutral SCF $F: K^N \to A$. Indeed, let $I \in K$ be given by xIy for all $x, y \in A$, and let $R_0^i = I$ for $i = 1, \ldots, n$. Now let $F: K^N \to A$. Then there is no way of defining $F(R_0^N)$ that is compatible with the neutrality of F.

Remark 7.4.39. Remark 7.4.38 may be considered as a (partial) justification for special investigations of SCFs that are defined on L^N (see Section 3.3).

The extension of our existence theorems for strong representations of committees (see Theorems 4.2.1 and 5.6.7) depends on the following definition and observation.

Definition 7.4.40. Let $F: K^N \to A$ be an SCF. F is *exactly and strongly consistent* if for every $R^N \in K^N$ the game

$$g(\Gamma(F), R^N) = (K, \ldots, K; F; R^N)$$

has a 2^N-e.p. Q^N such that $F(Q^N) = F(R^N)$.

Lemma 7.4.41. *Let* $G = (N, W)$ *be a proper simple game, and let* $F: L^N \to A$ *be a strong representation of* G *(see Definition 4.1.31). Then there exists an SCF* $F^*: K^N \to A$ *that is also a strong representation of* G *(i.e.,* $G^*(F^*) = G$ *(see Remark 7.4.34), and* F^* *is exactly and strongly consistent (see Definition 7.4.40)).*

Proof: Let $F^*(R^N) = F(g_*(R^N))$ for every $R^N \in K^N$ (see (7.4.10)). By Lemma 7.4.37, F^* is a representation of G (i.e., $G^*(F^*) = G$). We claim that F^* is also exactly and strongly consistent. Let $R^N \in K^N$, and let $R_1^N = g_*(R^N)$. Then $R_1^N \in L^N$. Let $Q^N \in L^N$ be a strong e.p. of $g(F, R_1^N)$ such that $F(Q^N) = F(R_1^N)$. Then

$$F^*(Q^N) = F(g_*(Q^N)) = F(Q^N) = F(R_1^N) = F(g_*(R^N)) = F^*(R^N)$$

We shall prove now that Q^N is a strong e.p. of $g(\Gamma(F^*), R^N)$. Indeed, let $S \in 2^N$, and let $T^S \in K^S$. Further, let $T_1^S = (g(T^i))_{i \in S}$. Since Q^N is a strong e.p. of $g(F, R_1^N)$, there exists $j \in S$ such that $F(Q^N) R_1^j F(Q^{N-S}, T_1^S)$. Now, $R_1^j = g(R^j)$ (see (7.4.8) and (7.4.9)) and $(Q^{N-S}, T_1^S) \in L^N$. Hence, $F^*(Q^N) R^j F^*(Q^{N-S}, T_1^S)$. Finally, by definition, $F^*(Q^{N-S}, T^S) = F(Q^{N-S}, T_1^S) = F^*(Q^{N-S}, T_1^S)$. Thus, $F^*(Q^N) R^j F^*(Q^{N-S}, T^S)$, and Q^N is, indeed, a strong e.p. of the game $(K, \ldots, K; F^*; R^N)$.

7.5 Some remarks on the number of alternatives

Remark 7.5.1. We recall that Arrow's Impossibility Theorem (Theorem 2.2.7) was proved for arbitrary sets of alternatives. The Gibbard-

Satterthwaite Theorem also holds true without any restriction on the number of alternatives. In order to show this, it is sufficient to prove Theorem 2.4.11 for infinite A. This can be achieved by proving Lemma 2.4.13 by transfinite induction.

Remark 7.5.2. Almost all our definitions carry over to the case in which A, the set of alternatives, is infinite. This is not true for our results, as is explained by the next remark.

Remark 7.5.3. Let $N = \{1, \ldots, n\}$ be a society, and let A be an infinite set. If $E: 2^N \to P(2^A)$ is an effectivity function (see Definition 6.1.1 and Remark 7.5.2), then, obviously, there exists a profile $R^N \in L^N$ such that $C(E, R^N) = \varnothing$ (see Definition 4.1.23). Thus, all our results on representations of committees, which depend on the existence of cores (or core extensions), do *not* hold when A is infinite.

Remark 7.5.4. One possible way to extend our results to infinite A is to assume that A is a *compact topological space* and restrict the investigation to *continuous* linear orderings of A. For an existence theorem for cores of simple games under these assumptions, see Nakamura [1979]. Such extension is beyond the scope of this book.

Addendum

R. Holzman, in a brilliant (unpublished) manuscript, has recently solved the problem of existence of strong representations for committees (see (3*) on p. 6). However, the problem of finding *all* strong representations of a given committee is, in the general case, still completely open.

References

Abdou, J. (1981). "Stabilité et maximalité des fonctions veto," Thesis, CEREMADE, University of Paris IX.

Arrow, K. J. (1963). *Social Choice and Individual Values*, 2nd ed. New York: Wiley.

Aumann, R. J. (1961). "The Core of a Cooperative Game without Side Payments," *Transactions of the American Mathematical Society*, 98, 539-52.

Aumann, R. J., and B. Peleg (1960). "von Neumann–Morgenstern Solutions to Cooperative Games without Side Payments," *Bulletin of the American Mathematical Society*, 66, 173-9.

Biggs, N. L., and A. T. White (1979). *Permutation Groups and Combinatorial Structures*. Cambridge University Press.

Black, D. (1958). *The Theory of Committees and Elections*. Cambridge University Press.

Blin, J.-M., and M. A. Satterthwaite (1977). "Strategy-Proofness and Single-Peakedness," *Public Choice*, 26, 51-8.

(1978). "Individual Decisions and Group Decisions: The Fundamental Differences," *Journal of Public Economics*, 10, 247-67.

Bloomfield, S. (1971). "An Axiomatic Formulation of Constitutional Games," Operations Research House, Stanford University.

Borda, J. C. (1781). "Mémoire sur les elections au scrutin," *Mémoire de l'Académie Royale des Sciences*. (English translation by A. de Grazia, *Isis*, 44, 1953.)

Campbell, D. E. (1976). "Democratic Preference Functions," *Journal of Economic Theory*, 12, 259-72.

Condorcet, Marquis de (1785). *Essai sur l'application de l'analyse à la probabilité des décisions rendues à la pluralité des voix*. Paris.

Dasgupta, P., Hammond, P., and E. Maskin (1979). "The Implementation of Social Choice Rules: Some General Results on Incentive Compatibility," *Review of Economic Studies*, 46, 185-216.

Dummett, M., and R. Farquharson (1961). "Stability in Voting," *Econometrica*, 29, 33-43.

Dutta, B. (1980a). "Restricted Preferences and Strategy-proofness of Single-valued Social Decision Functions," *Mathematical Social Sciences*, 1, 39-49.

(1980b). "On the Possibility of Consistent Voting Procedures," *Review of Economic Studies*, 47, 603-16.

Dutta, B., and P. K. Pattanaik (1978). "On Nicely Consistent Voting Systems," *Econometrica*, 46, 163-70.

Farquharson, R. (1969). *Theory of Voting.* New Haven: Yale University Press.

Ferejohn, J. A., and D. Grether (1977). "Weak Path Independence," *Journal of Economic Theory*, 14, 19-31.

Fishburn, P. C. (1972). "Even-Chance Lotteries in Social Choice Theory," *Theory and Decision*, 3, 18-40.

Gärdenfors, P. (1979). "On Definitions of Manipulation of Social Choice Functions." In *Aggregation and Revelation of Preferences*, J.-J. Laffont, Ed., pp. 29-36. Amsterdam: North Holland.

Gardner, R. (1977). "The Borda Game," *Public Choice*, 30, 43-50.

Gibbard, A. (1973). "Manipulation of Voting Schemes: A General Result," *Econometrica*, 41, 587-601.

(1978). "Social Decision, Strategic Behavior, and Best Outcomes." In *Decision Theory and Social Ethics: Issues in Social Choice*, H. W. Gottinger and W. Leinfellner, Eds., pp. 153-68. Dordrecht: D. Reidel.

Gillies, D. B. (1959). "Solutions to General Non-Zero-Sum Games." In *Contributions to the Theory of Games IV*, A. W. Tucker and R. D. Luce, Eds., pp. 47-85. *Annals of Mathematics Studies, 40.* Princeton University Press.

Greenberg, J. (1982). "Cores of Convex Games without Side Payments." Department of Economics, University of Haifa, Israel.

Holzman, R. (1982). "On Strong Representations of Games by Social Choice Functions," The Institute of Mathematics, Hebrew University of Jerusalem.

Hurwicz, L., and D. Schmeidler (1978). "Construction of Outcome Functions Guaranteeing Existence and Pareto Optimality of Nash Equilibria," *Econometrica*, 46, 1447-74.

Isbell, J. R. (1957). "Homogeneous Games," *The Mathematics Student*, 25, 123-8.

Kaneko, M. (1975). "Necessary and Sufficient Conditions for Transitivity in Voting Theory," *Journal of Economic Theory*, 11, 385-93.

Laffont, J.-J., and E. Maskin (1981). "The Theory of Incentives: An Overview," Department of Economics, University of Toulouse.

Luce, R. D., and H. Raiffa (1957). *Games and Decisions.* New York: Wiley.

Maskin, E. (in press). "Nash Equilibrium and Welfare Optimality," *Mathematics of Operations Research*.

(1979). "Implementation and Strong Nash Equilibrium." In *Aggregation and Revelation of Preferences*, J.-J. Laffont, Ed., pp. 433-9. Amsterdam: North Holland.

McKelvey, R. D., and P. C. Ordeshook (1979). "An Experimental Test of Several Theories of Committee Decision Making Under Majority Rule." In *Applied Game Theory*, S. J. Brams, A. Schotter, and G. Schwödiauer, Eds., pp. 152-67. Würzburg: Physica-Verlag.

Moulin, H. (1979). "Dominance-Solvable Voting Schemes," *Econometrica*, 47, 1337-51.

(1980). "Implementing Efficient, Anonymous and Neutral Social Choice Functions," *Journal of Mathematical Economics*, 7, 249-69.

(1981). "The Proportional Veto Principle," *Review of Economic Studies*, 48, 407-16.

(1982a). "Voting with Proportional Veto Power," *Econometrica*, 50, 145-62.

(1982*b*). "Non Cooperative Implementation: A Survey of Recent Results," *Mathematical Social Sciences*, 3, 243–57.

(1983). *The Strategy of Social Choice*. Amsterdam: North Holland.

Moulin, H., and B. Peleg (1982). "Cores of Effectivity Functions and Implementation Theory," *Journal of Mathematical Economics*, 10, 115–145.

Muller, E., and M. A. Satterthwaite (1977). "The Equivalence of Strong Positive Association and Strategy-Proofness," *Journal of Economic Theory*, 14, 412–18.

Nakamura, K. (1975). "The Core of a Simple Game with Ordinal Preferences," *International Journal of Game Theory*, 4, 95–104.

(1979). "The Vetoers in a Simple Game with Ordinal Preferences," *International Journal of Game Theory*, 8, 55–61.

Nanson, E. J. (1882). "Methods of Elections," *Transactions and Proceedings of the Royal Society of Victoria*, 18.

Oren, I. (1981). "The Structure of Exactly Strongly Consistent Social Choice Functions," *Journal of Mathematical Economics*, 8, 207–20.

Pattanaik, P. K. (1973). "On the Stability of Sincere Voting Situations," *Journal of Economic Theory*, 6, 558–74.

(1978). *Strategy and Group Choice*. Amsterdam: North Holland.

Peleg, B. (1978*a*). "Consistent Voting Systems," *Econometrica*, 46, 153–61.

(1978*b*). "Representations of Simple Games by Social Choice Functions," *International Journal of Game Theory*, 7, 81–94.

(1979). "Game Theoretic Analysis of Voting Schemes." In *Game Theory and Related Topics*, O. Moeschlin and D. Pallaschke, Eds., pp. 83–9. Amsterdam: North Holland.

(1980). "A Theory of Coalition Formation in Committees," *Journal of Mathemathical Economics*, 7, 115–34.

(1981). "Monotonicity Properties of Social Choice Correspondences." In *Game Theory and Mathematical Economics*, O. Moeschlin and D. Pallaschke, Eds., pp. 97–101. Amsterdam: North Holland.

(1983). "On Simple Games and Social Choice Correspondences." In *Social Choice and Welfare*, P. K. Pattanaik and M. Salles, Eds., pp. 251–68. Amsterdam: North Holland.

Plott, C. R. (1973). "Path Independence, Rationality and Social Choice," *Econometrica*, 41, 1075–91.

(1976). "Axiomatic Social Choice Theory: An Overview and Interpretation," *American Journal of Political Science*, 20, 511–96.

Polishchuk, I. (1978). "Monotonicity and Uniqueness of Consistent Voting Systems," Center for Research in Mathematical Economics and Game Theory, Hebrew University of Jerusalem.

Satterthwaite, M. A. (1975). "Strategy-Proofness and Arrow's Conditions: Existence and Correspondence Theorems for Voting Procedures and Social Welfare functions," *Journal of Economic Theory*, 10, 187–217.

Schmeidler, D., and H. Sonnenschein (1978). "Two Proofs of the Gibbard-Satterthwaite Theorem on the Possibility of a Strategy-Proof Social Choice Function." In *Decision Theory and Social Ethics: Issues in Social Choice*, H. W. Gottinger and W. Leinfellner, Eds., pp. 227–34. Dordrecht: D. Reidel.

Sen, A. K. (1970). *Collective Choice and Social Welfare*. San Francisco: Holden-Day.

(1977). "Social Choice Theory: A Re-Examination," *Econometrica*, 45, 53–89.

(1983). "Social Choice Theory." In *Handbook of Mathematical Economics,* K. J. Arrow and M. Intriligator, Eds. Amsterdam: North Holland.

Sengupta, M. (1983). "Implementable Social Choice Rules: Characterization and Correspondence Theorems under Strong Nash Equilibrium," *Journal of Mathematical Economics,* 11, 1–24.

Shapley, L. S. (1962). "Simple Games: An Outline of the Descriptive Theory," *Behavioral Science,* 7, 59–66.

(1967). "Compound Simple Games, III: On Committees," The Rand Corporation, RM-5438-PR.

Vickrey, W. (1960). "Utility, Strategy and Social Decision Rules," *Quarterly Journal of Economics,* 74, 507–35.

von Neumann, J., and O. Morgenstern (1944). *Theory of Games and Economic Behavior.* Princeton University Press.

Wilson, R. B. (1972). "The Game-Theoretic Structure of Arrow's General Possibility Theorem," *Journal of Economic Theory,* 5, 14–20.

Wilson, R. J. (1979). *Introduction to Graph Theory,* 2nd ed., London: Longman.

Young, H. P. (1974). "An Axiomatization of Borda's Rule," *Journal of Economic Theory,* 9, 43–52.

Author index

167

Subject index

Arrow's Impossibility Theorem, 2, 22, 76, 155

binary relation
acyclic, defined, 20
antisymmetric, defined, 20
asymmetric, defined, 20
complete, defined, 20
irreflexive, defined, 20
reflexive, defined, 21
transitive, defined, 20
blocking coalition, defined, 54
Borda rule, 1, 25, 42–5, 126

choice by plurality voting, 25, 42, 46
Condorcet alternative, defined, 46
Condorcet condition, defined, 47
core of a simple game, defined, 35
core of an effectivity function, defined, 69, 159

effectivity function, defined, 111
additive, defined, 126
anonymous, defined, 117
convex, defined, 148
dual of, defined, 111
maximal, defined, 90
monotonic, defined, 113
monotonic cover of, defined, 130
monotonic with respect to the alternatives, defined, 112
monotonic with respect to the players, defined, 92
neutral, defined, 117
regular, defined, 91
stable, defined, 113
subadditive, defined, 114
subadditive cover of, defined, 132
superadditive, defined, 112
superadditive cover of, defined, 130

equilibrium point (e.p.), defined, 33, 158
exact, defined, 65
strong, defined, 68, 88

feasible elimination procedure (f.e.p.), defined, 99

game form (GF), defined, 87
α-effectivity function associated with, defined, 89
β-effectivity function associated with, defined, 89
Gibbard–Satterthwaite Theorem, 2–3, 11, 20, 32–4, 157–9

linear order, defined, 21

Nakamura's number of a simple game, 35–6, 48–9, 71–2

Pareto optimality, defined, 23, 155

rank-order method, 24–8
representation of a simple game, defined, 46
dynamic, defined, 79
dynamic in the limited sense, defined, 79
faithful, defined, 47
strong, defined, 71
strong and dynamic in the limited sense, defined, 79

simple game, defined, 34
capacity of, defined, 71
dictatorial, defined, 34
essential, defined, 53
proper, defined, 34
strong, defined, 34
symmetric, defined, 34
weak, defined, 34
weighted majority, defined, 59

168